Lady Mary Pierrepont Wortley Montagu, Adrian Ross

Lady Mary Wortley Montagu

Select Passages from her Letters

Lady Mary Pierrepont Wortley Montagu, Adrian Ross

Lady Mary Wortley Montagu
Select Passages from her Letters

ISBN/EAN: 9783744678421

Printed in Europe, USA, Canada, Australia, Japan

Cover: Foto ©Thomas Meinert / pixelio.de

More available books at **www.hansebooks.com**

LADY MARY

WORTLEY MONTAGU

SELECT PASSAGES FROM HER LETTERS

EDITED BY

A R T H U R R. R O P E S, M.A.

LATE FELLOW OF KING'S COLLEGE, CAMBRIDGE

With Nine Portraits
after SIR GODFREY KNELLER *and other Artists*

LONDON
SEELEY AND CO., LIMITED
ESSEX STREET, STRAND
1892

CONTENTS

LIST OF ILLUSTRATIONS

。 *The portraits of Lady Mary and her husband are engraved, by kind permission, from pictures in the possession of the Marquis of Bute and the Earl of Wharncliffe.*

LADY MARY WORTLEY MONTAGU

CHAPTER I

INTRODUCTORY SKETCH

"THE last pleasure that came in my way was Madame Sévigné's letters," wrote Lady Mary Wortley Montagu to her sister; "very pretty they are, but I assert, without the least vanity, that mine will be full as entertaining forty years hence." "In most of them," said Horace Walpole, fresh from reading a bundle of Lady Mary's letters, "the wit and style are superior to any letters I ever read but Madame Sévigné's." It is curious that the somewhat flattering opinion expressed by the writer of the letters herself should have been so nearly endorsed by one who was her

1

enemy by hereditary and personal feeling, and never alludes to her without a sneer; but Horace Walpole knew the craft of letter-writing, and "in spite of spite" could recognise the merit of another in his own favourite art.

These letters, then, as to whose merit author and author's enemy alike agree, need no apology for their presentment in the form of a selection. Neither they nor their writer, indeed, have been neglected. There have been plenty of editions of Lady Mary's works, and her name at once awakens a crowd of varied associations. She is remembered as the first English-woman who sent back accounts of the mysterious and magnificent East; as the friend and then the enemy of Pope; as the courageous introducer of inocula-tion; as the strong-minded, independent, eccentric traveller. Alike to friends and enemies, she has ever stood out as a strong, original figure—a personality among so many who are only names to us now, and were little more in their own time.

But though, for all who have the time and the taste, there is no pleasure greater than consulting the mass of the original letters, yet there are many who might be repelled by the bulk of the matter, by the super-fluity of contemporary gossip, much of which must be a tedious riddle to a modern reader, or even by the occasional bluntness of thought and coarseness of expression which Lady Mary shared with nearly all the writers of her time. For such readers, then, I have tried to select some of the more entertaining passages from the letters, stringing them together with a thread of explanation where necessary.

Lady Mary Wortley Montagu belonged to the great Whig aristocracy that ruled England for half the eighteenth century. Her father was Evelyn Pierrepont, the youngest of three brothers who successively became Earls of Kingston. Evelyn was so called from the maiden name of his mother, a cousin of the famous John Evelyn. He married Mary Fielding, daughter of that Earl of Denbigh from one of whose brothers Fielding the novelist was descended. Lady Mary was born in 1689, and her baptism was registered on May 20 of that year. She was the eldest child, the others being Frances (afterwards Countess of Mar), Evelyn (afterwards Lady Gower), and one son, William. In 1690 Evelyn Pierrepont became Earl of Kingston, and in 1692 his wife died. He did not marry again till 1714, when all his children were settled in life. He was busily engaged in public affairs, and met with his reward from the victorious Whigs, being made Marquis of Dorchester in 1706 (a title already granted by Charles I. to one of his family), and Duke of Kingston in 1715. His only son, William, died in 1713, leaving a son who succeeded to the dukedom in 1726, and whose after-life was made notorious by being linked with that of the famous Elizabeth Chudleigh, who was tried by the Peers for bigamy.

This early loss of her mother must have had considerable influence on Lady Mary's life. Her father, a public man and a man of pleasure, seems to have taken but little heed of his children's education. Lady Mary was left to grow up much at her own will, being given in charge to a pious old person who had been nurse to her mother, and who, if we may trust her pupil's later account, taught her little but to read and write, besides filling her head with superstitious stories, which found poor welcome there; for no one could be more destitute of illusions than Lady Mary. One pleasurable recollection she had of Lord Kingston's fondness, which I will leave her grand-daughter, Lady Louisa Stuart, to tell. "A trifling incident, which Lady Mary loved to recall, will prove how much she was the object of Lord Kingston's pride and fondness in her childhood. As a leader of the fashionable world, and a strenuous Whig in party, he of course belonged to the Kit-Kat Club. One day, at a meeting to choose toasts for the year, a whim seized him to nominate her, then not eight years old, a candidate; alleging that she was far prettier than any lady on their list. The other members demurred, because the rules of the club forbade them to elect a beauty whom they had never seen. 'Then you shall see her,' cried he; and in the gaiety of the moment sent orders home to have her finely dressed and brought to him at the tavern, where she was received with acclamations, her claim unanimously allowed, her health drunk by everyone present, and her name engraved in due form upon a drinking-glass. The company consisting of some of the most eminent men of England, she went from the lap of one poet, or patriot, or statesman, to the arms of

another, was feasted with sweetmeats, overwhelmed
with caresses, and, what perhaps already pleased her
better than either, heard her wit and beauty loudly
extolled on every side. Pleasure, she said, was too
poor a word to express her sensations; they amounted
to ecstasy: never again, throughout her whole future
life, did she pass so happy a day. Nor, indeed, could
she; for the love of admiration, which this scene was
calculated to excite or increase, could never again be
so fully gratified; there is always some allaying ingre-
dient in the cup, some drawback upon the triumphs of
grown people. Her father carried on the frolic, and,
we may conclude, confirmed the taste, by having her
picture painted for the club-room, that she might be
enrolled a regular toast."

Still, this single instance of fondness did not blind
Lady Mary's eyes in after-years to the neglect with
which she had been treated in childhood; and when
her father died, in 1726, we find her writing with
almost brutal directness to her sister, "*Au bout du
compte,* I don't know why filial piety should exceed
fatherly fondness. So much by way of consolation."

Lady Mary's precocity, however marked, did not (as
her first biographer erroneously stated) induce her
father to give her a course of classical study with her
brother; and her early education, as she herself said,
was "one of the worst in the world." But she had
the run of her father's library, and there browsed
in the pastures of French romance, Englished by
" persons of quality," the *Astrée* and the whole baggage

of the Scudérys and their school. As she grew up,
she extended the range of her reading; and it was on
the common ground of learning that she first met—by
her own account, when she was only fourteen—the
man who was to be her husband.

Edward Wortley Montagu, or Edward Wortley as
he was more often styled in the earlier part of his life,
was the son of the Hon. Sidney Wortley Montagu,
second son of Admiral Montagu, first Earl of Sandwich, well known in the Dutch wars of Charles II.
Sidney Montagu took the name of Wortley on marrying
the heiress of Sir Francis Wortley. One of Lady Mary
Pierrepont's closest friends in girlhood was Anne
Wortley, Edward's favourite sister; and whether
through her, or in some other way, the two were soon
acquainted. If, as Lady Mary stated, she was only
fourteen then, he must have been ten or eleven years
older than herself; but he was at once struck by her
intelligence and wit. Himself a scholar and a man of
literary tastes, the friend of Addison and Steele, he
directed her studies, and encouraged her to persevere
in teaching herself Latin; and some help she also
derived from the celebrated Bishop Burnet, to whom
she dedicated a translation (through the Latin) of the
"Enchiridion" of Epictetus. With Anne Wortley,
Lady Mary corresponded; and, as Anne's letters were
often written really by her brother—a fact of which the
recipient of them could hardly have been ignorant—
these letters formed a sort of indirect correspondence
between Edward Wortley and Lady Mary. After a

time hints of courtship appeared in the letters, and on Anne Wortley's death, in 1709, the correspondence was continued directly between Edward and his sister's friend. A number of her letters, and one of his, have been printed; they form a curious piece of love-making between two clear-headed, intellectual, un-romantic lovers, who yet could not refrain from loving each other. The bulk of the love-letters given might be said to consist in enumerations of the excellent reasons existing for putting an end to the attachment.

At last Edward Wortley formally asked the Marquis of Dorchester for the hand of his eldest daughter; but although in birth, fortune and tastes the two were well matched, the Marquis insisted on a settlement being made in favour of the children of the marriage. This Mr. Wortley flatly refused to do. He objected on principle to settling a large amount on a son who might turn out a fool or a villain; and in fact he had furnished the materials and the plan from which the essay in the *Tatler*, attacking settlements, was written : he had also, at all times, a strong sense of the value of money, and thought a dowry too dearly purchased if he must put a considerable part of his estate out of his own control. Thereupon the Marquis broke off the negotiation; but the lovers continued their corre-spondence, and, by the help of good - natured Sir Richard Steele and other friends, they sometimes met. At last Lord Dorchester brought matters to a crisis by ordering his daughter to accept the addresses of a certain " Mr. K.," as her letters call him, who had estates in Ireland, and liberal views as to settlements. Edward Wortley still refused to consent to a settlement and outbid his rival, and Lady Mary approved of his firmness; so the only way for her to escape the unwelcome suitor was to run away with the man of her choice. After some difficulties, the lovers eloped in 1712—probably August—and were married.

For some time, though never in financial straits, the two lived very quietly in the country, either in Yorkshire (but not at Wharncliffe Lodge, which had as many as it could hold already, and was described by Horace Walpole as " a wretched hovel "), at Hinchinbroke, Lord Sandwich's residence, or at Huntingdon, a town which the Wortley Montagu family long represented in Parliament. In 1713 their son Edward was born. By Lady Mary's letters he seems to have been very weakly at first, and caused her much anxiety. In 1714 the death of Queen Anne plunged the country into a frenzy of political excitement. What with the fears of a Jacobite rising, the hopes of favour with the new King, the sudden overthrow of the Tory Administration, there was enough to think of. Edward Wortley as a Whig, and a relation of Lord Halifax, was in the way of advancement, and his wife's letters to him at this time are full of a feverish eagerness to have him chosen for Parliament, so that he might be borne on to fortune on the crest of the party wave. It was not till 1715 that he was elected for Westminster; but he did not lack promotion, for he was made a Commissioner of the Treasury; and his wife, coming up with him to the

Court of George I., and becoming a brilliant figure among its ladies, had material for writing an amusing and rather caustic sketch of the chief actors in the rather unlovely comedy of the Hanoverian Court.

In 1716 Edward Wortley was named as Ambassador to Turkey and Consul-General of the Levant—a post always of high eminence, and now of especial importance, as England was trying to mediate a peace between the Porte and the Emperor Charles VI. Accordingly, Mr. Wortley, with his wife and child, travelled to Vienna, then—a hitch occurring in the negotiations — went to Hanover, where George I. was, and returned to Vienna, but after winter had set in. Previous British Ambassadors had either gone by sea, or down the Danube by boat from Vienna; and many friends urged Lady Mary to stay at Vienna rather than venture in the middle of winter through a desolate country and across the seat of war. However, the mission was urgent, and Lady Mary chose to accompany her husband. They arrived without mishap at Belgrade, then in Turkish hands, and thence went on by Nish and Sofia to Adrianople, where they stayed some time and then journeyed to Constantinople. Here, or near here, they stayed about a year; here, in 1718, their second child, Mary, afterwards Countess of Bute, was born; and here Lady Mary devoted herself to learning all she could of Oriental ways and languages. Among other researches, she inquired into the method of inoculation practised by the Turks. It is impossible for those who have grown up in an age of vaccination and sanitary improvement to realize the part played by the small-pox in the history of the eighteenth century, and the dread felt, especially among the highest society, lest the inevitable disease should take away life, or, what was even worse, destroy beauty. One of Lady Mary's Town Eclogues, describing the sorrows of the hapless and disfigured Flavia, was said to have reflected her own feelings while recovering from small-pox about 1715, though she escaped with the comparatively slight sacrifice of her eyelashes. She had her own children "engrafted," as she calls it, with satisfactory results. And besides all these varied interests, she found time to write many letters, corresponding with her two sisters, both now married, with Caroline, Princess of Wales, the poets Congreve and Pope, and several other friends. Pope, indeed, made her the object of one of those curious epistolary and merely literary courtships in which his soul delighted; and though she did not reply in kind to his hyperbolical adoration, neither she nor her husband was offended by them.

The Embassy, however, was a failure. The Emperor, for whom Prince Eugene had won victory after victory, was too exacting; the Turks, who had wrested the Morea from Venice, were too stubborn; and probably Edward Wortley himself was not cut out for a successful diplomatist. In one of the very few despatches of his preserved at the Record Office, he prides himself on telling the Turks " plain truths," a method not apt

to soothe wounded susceptibilities. In 1718, his friend
Addison, now Secretary of State, intimated to him his
recall, softening it by the prospect of a lucrative office ;
and embarking on the *Preston* man-of-war, he and his
family sailed to Genoa, touching at Tunis on the way.
Mr. Wortley's successors in the negotiation, abler or
more fortunate, succeeded in making the Peace of
Passarowitz. No monument of his own Embassy
remained but his wife's letters, and even these, as we
have them, do not represent her real correspondence.
Mr. Moy Thomas, her latest and best editor, in his
researches in the Wortley papers, came upon a list of
her letters written during part of the period of the
Embassy, with notes of their contents. The published
letters correspond only very imperfectly to this *précis*,
and only two are indexed as "copied at length." It
is, therefore, likely that such of the letters actually
written as had been copied were reproduced by Lady
Mary with some alteration, and that the rest were
reconstructed from the diary in which she was accustomed to note the events and thoughts of every
day, and from which she doubtless had drawn freely
for the original correspondence. Thus these letters
are not the real correspondence, but a more or less
"doctored" reconstruction of it ; and it is curious in
this connection to see how Horace Walpole, himself an
eminent letter-writer, passed over these letters with
faint praise or positive contempt, either as "not uninteresting," or as containing "no merit of any sort,"
while he gave high praise to the letters to Lady Mar,

which he saw as they were originally penned. The "Turkish Letters," though not published till after the death of the writer, were evidently prepared for publication, and seem to have been handed round in MS. among a few friends in 1724 or 1725. They bear prefaces of these dates by one " M. A.," said to be Mary Astell, a friend of Lady Mary's, and an early enthusiast for the rights of women.

On her return to England Lady Mary again mingled in society, and was one of the acknowledged beauties and wits of the time. She had many friends, and made not a few enemies. In that brilliant and frivolous society, where everyone dabbled in literature and could turn a couplet, every social event or scandal was greeted by a witticism, a satire, or a ballad. Of these, Lady Mary (whose poetical faculty, though hardly high, was above that of other ladies of the time) was responsible for some, and had many more attributed to her. Among her friends were, at first, Pope himself, and some of Pope's future enemies, Philip, Duke of Wharton, Pope's " Clodio," and John, Lord Hervey, known as the author of the " Memoirs of the Reign of George II.," and better known as " Lord Fanny " and " Sporus."

The friendship with Pope, always more or less of a literary make-believe, did not long survive Lady Mary's return. For a time, indeed, he continued his adoration ; partly at Pope's request, she sat to Kneller for a portrait, and some of the sittings took place at Pope's house at Twickenham—though the portrait, it is hardly necessary to state, was executed for Mr. Wortley and paid for by him. Pope, also, was the agent between the Wortleys and Sir Godfrey Kneller for the letting of a house of Kneller's to his friends; and he gave Lady Mary advice as to the South Sea stock-jobbing, in which she unluckily dabbled. But after a time the friendship cooled, and the correspondence died out. Although Lady Mary and her husband came to live at Twickenham, she apparently saw less and less of the poet, and she remarks, in a letter, that she never visited his famous grotto. What was the real cause of the final quarrel between them—a quarrel not creditable to Lady Mary, and very discreditable to Pope—it seems impossible to determine. Perhaps there was no one special cause for it. It seems hardly likely that (as Lady Louisa Stuart said) Pope hazarded a passionate, though doubtless strictly platonic, declaration to Lady Mary, and was answered only by a fit of laughter that reminded the sensitive poet too painfully of the contrast between his high-flown language and his deformed person. Such an incident might have occurred, if the friendship between the two had grown closer; but all the facts as known point to an opposite conclusion. And, indeed, it was only to be expected that such a friendship should have cooled. Pope had now gone over to the Tories, and the Wortleys were stanch and influential Whigs. Mr. Moy Thomas thinks that the final quarrel dates from 1724, when the manuscript volumes of Lady Mary's letters from the East began to be handed about among her friends. The last of these letters, nominally dashed off in haste in an inn at Dover on

her return, is an answer to Pope's celebrated epistle on
the Lovers Struck by Lightning, for which he had so
great a fondness as to send it in various forms to a
number of his friends. Lady Mary brings the poet
back to reality, reducing his high-flown epitaphs to
matter-of-fact doggerel, and his pastoral lovers to two
bumpkins whose death mattered little to any but
themselves. The date affixed to this answer by the
writer is *after* the day on which the newspapers assure
us she had returned to London ; so that we can hardly
be wrong in regarding her letter as written *après coup*.
If this were so, and Pope came to know of it, we need
seek no further for a cause of quarrel. The mere
suspicion of a far less wrong on the part of a far closer
friend was enough to make him write his famous
character of Atticus. And though he could afford to
despise the coarse and blundering attacks of his
Dunces, he would keenly feel this clever parody of
his loved pastoral.

Other rumours were current, then and afterwards, as
to the cause of the quarrel. Pope's own account of it
was that Lady Mary "had too much wit for him,"
which seems to point to an exercise of that wit at his
expense. But, in fact, some such quarrel was inevitable from the first. Pope, sooner or later, quarrelled
with most of his friends; his sensitive, suspicious and
spiteful nature was never long without a grievance, and
resented the merest shadow of a slight ; while Lady
Mary could seldom resist the temptation of ridiculing
the weaknesses of her friends, and yet displayed a

uriously innocent surprise when they resented her witticisms by any means in their power.

Even before the final breach with Pope, her social triumphs were often obscured by troubles due to her own imprudence or her misfortune; and in all of these Pope found pegs on which to hang his spiteful allusions. One of Lady Mary's greatest annoyances came from a certain French witling and poetaster, one M. Rémond, who had opened a correspondence of the usual hyperbolical sham love-making with her, and had persuaded her, against her will, to invest his available property for him. The money was ventured once successfully in the South Sea stock; a second time most of it went the way of so much more when the bubble broke. Rémond believed, or affected to believe, that Lady Mary still retained the money, and claimed the return of the whole, threatening to disclose the whole transaction to Mr. Wortley, and to print her letters. Lady Mary, knowing her husband's objection to speculation and his carefulness in money matters, dreaded his learning of her imprudence; she may also have naturally feared the wit and the scandal of which she would now be the object. How the matter ended, we know not; but probably Rémond told Mr. Wortley, and Lady Mary justified herself to her husband by producing Rémond's letters, for they seem to have passed under Mr. Wortley's eyes.

Other troubles Lady Mary had which were not due to her own faults. Her son Edward, as he grew up, was a constant source of anxiety. He ran away from

school to Oxford when thirteen; then next year ran
away again, and was discovered at Gibraltar, after a
series of adventures as a chimney-sweep and in other
capacities, such as those related in a dull and
scandalous so-called memoir of him published at
Dublin in 1779, and several times republished since.
It is curious to note that in the hand-bill offering
twenty pounds for his discovery, he is mentioned as
having the inoculation marks on his arm. This
practice Lady Mary had striven to introduce into
England, and with much success; though the opposition to the novelty, both from the prejudiced and
the medical profession, was great, and the introducer
of inoculation did not escape obloquy. It is remarkable that in hardly any of the letters written after her
return from the East does she refer to the subject.
Perhaps the reception of her labours had disgusted
her; though her friend Caroline, Princess of Wales,
afterwards Queen Caroline, stood by her.

Another domestic trouble also served as a theme
for Pope's attacks. Lady Mary had little happiness
in her family relations. Her father, who never quite
forgave her for disobeying him, died in 1726, and there
seem to have been troubles over his property with his
second wife. His only son had died in 1713. In 1727
Lady Mary's youngest sister, Lady Gower, died; and
not long after her other sister, Lady Mar, went out
of her mind. She seems to have been wretched with
her husband, the doubly treacherous " Bobbing John,"
now strongly suspected of betraying the Jacobites

whom he had led to defeat. Lady Mar was brought
over to England and placed in charge of her sister;
but she had some property, and on Mar's death his
unscrupulous brother, Lord Grange, tried to get hold of
his sister-in-law. He was helped in his endeavours by
Lady Hervey, jealous of her husband's friendship with
Lady Mary, and by Mrs. Murray, who had vowed
revenge on her for a scandalous ballad she was
supposed to have written. Failing, however, to secure
Lady Mar by legal means, Lord Grange had her
carried off; but she was brought back, and remained
in her sister's charge until her daughter, Lady Frances
Erskine, was old enough to take care of her, when, at
Edward Wortley's request, Lady Mary gave up her
charge a little while before leaving England. Grange
was loud in his complaints that Lady Mary ill-used
and starved her sister; and from him Pope seems to
have borrowed the charge, though Lady Mar herself
apparently knew nothing of such ill-usage.

Pope's first open attack on Lady Mary is often taken
to consist in two lines from the "Dunciad":

> "Whence hapless Monsieur much complains at Paris
> Of wrongs from Duchesses and Lady Marys."

This is held to allude to Rémond's story. However,
I think it doubtful whether Pope meant it so. The
context refers to the way in which worthless women
gulled simple foreigners by assuming titles of rank or
the names of noted beauties, and the reference, though
hardly friendly, still in strictness means no more than
that Lady Mary was a well-known beauty. But in

2

Pope's own notes of 1729 to the "Dunciad," the allusion
is direct and insulting. "This passage was thought
to allude to a famous lady, who cheated a French wit
out of £5,000 in the South Sea year;" and Pope goes
on to explain that he meant to satirize "all bragging
travellers," and all "cheats under the name of fine
ladies," heightening the insult by affecting to explain
it away. Worse than this followed. Pope suspected
Lady Mary of being concerned in some of the libels
showered on him in answer to the "Dunciad," especially
in "A Pop upon Pope," giving an account of a supposed whipping of the poet by some of those whom he
had attacked. In his "Imitation of the First Satire of
Horace's Second Book," a vile couplet on "Sappho"
was generally applied to Lady Mary; and henceforth,
under this or other names, she was constantly the
mark for malignant allusion. How far she was concerned in writing the "Verses addressed to the Imitator
of Horace," is doubtful. In a letter to Arbuthnot, she
declared that the lines were entirely the work of Lord
Hervey, whom Pope had satirized as "Lord Fanny."
Yet the verses are so much better than Lord Hervey's
avowed answer to Pope, that there must still be considerable doubt as to whether Lady Mary had not a
share in them. The piece first appeared as "By a
Lady." Pope evidently felt its coarse allusions to his
physical defects and "birth obscure," and was at great
pains to disprove the latter accusation in the epistle to
Dr. Arbuthnot prefixed to his "Satires." From that
time he never left the Wortley Montagus alone. The

frugality and care about money which Lady Mary shared with her husband, and which seems to have come at times near to stinginess, was satirized as the most sordid avarice under the names of Worldly (an obvious perversion of Wortley), Avidien, Gripus, etc. The carelessness of Lady Mary's dress is sometimes alluded to, and she is obliquely charged with profligacy under the title of Sappho. Her troubles with Rémond and Lady Mar are included in a double-barrelled allusion in the couplet,

> " And at a peer or peeress shall I fret,
> Who starves a sister, or denies a debt?"

as Horace Walpole carefully explains.

All these attacks may easily have disgusted Lady Mary with English society and England. The Court of George II., sordid without economy and dull without virtue, was hardly an attractive scene for a woman of intellect. Edward Wortley Montagu, while a sound Whig, was always hostile to the all-powerful Walpole, and, indeed, led some of the fierce attacks on him when his credit was waning. The marriage of Lady Mary's daughter to the Earl of Bute, Groom of the Stole to Frederick, Prince of Wales, and then to his son, and afterwards the favourite Minister of George III., must have tended still further to connect the mother with the Opposition, and may help to account for the indifference that she afterwards displayed to the great victories of the Seven Years' War. There was now nothing left to occupy her attention in England; her daughter was married, the care of her sister given up,

her son, after a youth of folly and vice, had ruined his
career by marrying in the Fleet a woman of low life (a
washerwoman, the scandalous memoir calls her), who
was too cunning to give him a pretext for divorce. He
usually resided abroad, too, so that there were no
duties to keep Lady Mary at home. Her husband and
she, though all their letters seem to prove that they
retained their respect and affection for each other,
seem to have found their tastes and ways incompatible;
and it is possible that Edward Wortley Montagu keenly
felt the unenviable notoriety which Pope had bestowed
on him merely because his wife and Pope had
quarrelled.

Lady Mary was fifty years old when, in 1739, she
determined to go abroad for a lengthened residence;
and she did not return to England till she came back,
in 1762, to die. It is these twenty-two or twenty-three
years that form the most interesting part of Lady Mary's
life to later times. Her letters from the East are too
laboured, too plainly " doctored " for the public; her
letters to Lady Mar are too full of petty gossip. The
later correspondence, mostly with her daughter, Lady
Bute, is both worthier in subjects and more natural in
tone.

In leaving for the Continent, Lady Mary apparently
expected her husband to follow her. He was detained,
however, by business, and she went on her way alone;
and gradually, whether by mutual understanding or by
the mere effect of time and habit, all thought of their
meeting again was given up. Mr. Wortley Montagu

often wrote to his wife in terms that imply that she still enjoyed his full confidence; he entrusted her with the task of seeing her son, trying to reclaim him, and furnishing him with the necessary funds: but though he left England twice on journeys, he never saw his wife again. Occasional glimpses of him and his son are to be caught from the letters of Horace Walpole, who, however, saw the whole family with unfriendly eyes. The elder Wortley Montagu he depicts as a morose miser, with no indulgence but his daily glass of tokay, hoarding "money and health" with such success that he died at the age of eighty-three worth half a million. The son, a weak and worthless fellow, had and misused every advantage. He sat for some years for the family seat of Huntingdon; was put in prison in Paris for a discreditable gambling affair; was chosen a member of the Royal Society on the strength of a curious iron wig; outlived both parents, and came into £2,000 a year; travelled in the East, and sent home an account of the Written Mountains of Sinai; adopted Armenian dress, married many wives, turned Roman Catholic, turned Mohammedan, and finally died, in 1776, at Padua.

In the summer of 1739, then, Lady Mary went abroad. Avoiding Paris, she journeyed through Dijon and Turin to Venice. Next summer she set out for Florence, where she met her friend Lady Pomfret, also Lady Walpole, wife of Sir Robert's eldest son. Horace Walpole met her there, and gives a picture of her which seems to have some truth, though a good deal of spite.

"Did I tell you," he writes to Conway, "Lady Mary
Wortley is here? She laughs at my Lady Walpole,
scolds my Lady Pomfret, and is laughed at by the
whole town. Her dress, her avarice, and her impudence must amuse anyone that never heard her
name. She wears a foul mob that does not cover
her greasy black locks, that hang loose, never combed
or curled; an old mazarine blue wrapper, that gapes
open and discovers a canvas petticoat. Her face
swelled violently on one side, partly covered with a
plaister, and partly with white paint, which for cheapness she has bought so coarse that you would not use
it to wash a chimney."

From Florence she went to Rome, visited Naples,
and returned through Rome, Leghorn, and Genoa to
Chambéry in Savoy. The outbreak of the War of the
Austrian Succession in Italy, and Sardinia's resolve to
take the side of Maria Theresa, made her fear a French
invasion, and she removed to Avignon, then, and until
the French Revolution, a Papal possession. After a
journey to Valence to see her son, she settled down at
Avignon for four years. The declaration of war between France and England, and still more the influx
of Jacobites into Avignon after the insurrection of
1745, made the place disagreeable to her. She determined to betake herself to the dominions of almost the
only civilized neutral state in Europe—Venice. Her
journey was not free from peril; she went by Genoa,
and outside that city met the retreating army of the
Infante Don Philip, whose troops, with their French

allies, had been beaten at Piacenza by the Austrians and Sardinians. Lady Mary pushed on through both armies, and reached Brescia in safety, but while staying with the mother of Count Palazzo, the Italian nobleman who had escorted her thither, she was seized by severe illness and had to remain in their house for some time. It seems possible, from a legal document in Italian, which Lord Wharncliffe says he saw among Lady Mary's papers, that either from officious friendship or desire for gain, this detention was continued longer than she desired; and though it was not for long, it gave rise to a scandalous story, eagerly gathered by Horace Walpole, of her having been detained by some Italian lover, determined to secure her wealth. The rumour seems to have been widely spread, and to have lasted long, for when Lady Mary came to Venice in 1756, I find the English Minister there, Mr. Murray, writing home: "She has been for some years past, and still continues, in the hands of a Brescian Count, who, it is said, plunders her of all her riches." There seems, however, no foundation in fact for this view of the incident.

In the summer of 1747 Lady Mary went to Lovere, a little place on the north shore of Lake Iseo, famed for its medicinal waters. Here she hired and then bought outright for a hundred pounds an old "shell of a palace," which she partly repaired and fitted up as a residence, and in which she led a retired life, amusing herself with a dairy, a poultry-yard, silkworms, bees, and the English novels of the day, forwarded to her by Lady

Bute. She wrote often to her husband and daughter, hearing from them sometimes details of the society she still remembered. In particular, she was interested in the works of Richardson and her cousin Henry Fielding.

She paid brief visits to places in the neighbourhood. At Gotolengo she stayed some time, but was recalled to the healing streams of Lovere by illness. In 1756 she moved to Padua, and between this city and Venice she spent the next few years. Her peace was troubled by the persecutions of Mr. Murray, the British Minister at Venice. I have not been able to discover from his despatches the reason for this quarrel; but his first notice of Lady Mary seems to show that he thought badly of her, and *her* first description of him is as " such a scandalous fellow, in every sense of that word, he is not to be trusted to change a sequin, despised by the Government for his smuggling, which was his original profession." So perhaps the quarrel was ready-made. Sir James Steuart, of Coltness, the economist, then an exile through his share in the '45, came to Venice with his wife, and both formed a warm friendship with Lady Mary, who exerted her influence with Lord Bute to get Sir James recalled. Murray, who seems from his despatches to have been nervously anxious not to compromise himself, refused to receive Sir James, and apparently thought Lady Mary a dangerous character for associating with the Steuarts.

In 1761 came the news of Mr. Wortley Montagu's death, and Lady Mary resolved, at her daughter's

request, to return to England to help in the settlement of his affairs. He had left his widow £1,200
a year, with reversion to her son, and £1,000 a year to
the son; the rest of his large fortune went to Lady
Bute. In a hard winter, and herself already smitten
with an incurable disease, Lady Mary journeyed to
England through Germany and Holland, France being
still at war with England. In January, 1762, she
arrived, and Horace Walpole gives a lively and spiteful account of his meeting with her. "But I will tell
you who is come too—Lady Mary Wortley. I went
last night to visit her; I give you my honour, and you,
who know me, would credit me without it, the following is a faithful description. I found her in a little
miserable bedchamber of a ready-furnished house, with
two tallow candles, and a bureau covered with pots and
pans. On her head, in full of all accounts, she had an
old black-laced hood, wrapped entirely round, so as to
conceal all hair or want of hair. No handkerchief, but
up to her chin a kind of horseman's coat, made of a
dark green (green I think it had been) brocade, with
coloured and silver flowers, and lined with furs; bodice
laced, a foul dimity petticoat sprig'd, velvet muffeteens
on her arms, gray stockings and slippers. Her face
less changed in twenty years than I could have imagined; I told her so, and she was not so tolerable
twenty years ago that she needed have taken it for
flattery, but she did, and literally gave me a box on the
ear. She is very lively, all her senses perfect, her language as imperfect as ever, her avarice greater. She

receives all the world, who go to homage her as Queen Mother, and crams them into this kennel."

Horace Walpole seems to have imagined that Lady Mary would try to make use of her position as mother-in-law of George III.'s favourite Minister, but he was mistaken; and though he apprehended all kinds of troubles from her interference with Lady Bute, he was compelled later on to admit that "she is much more discreet than I expected, and meddles with nothing." Indeed, knowing that she was dying, Lady Mary could hardly have brought herself to take much interest in affairs. It was soon known that she had cancer in the breast. "She behaves with great fortitude," writes Walpole, "and says she has lived long enough." She died in London, on August 21st, 1762, over seventy-three years of age. By her will, one or two remembrances were left to friends, legacies to servants, and the rest of her separate property, not much in amount, to her daughter. To her son, who seems to have caused her sorrow to the end, she left *one guinea ;* but, by her husband's will, her income went to him on her death.

Her letters had a curious fate, and their history is hardly less complicated than that of Pope's correspondence. She undoubtedly prepared for publication those written during the Embassy, and they had been in existence in manuscript ever since 1724, which is the date of Mrs. Mary Astell's first gushing preface. Yet they were known only to a few friends ; and Horace Walpole had not seen them, though he had been

allowed to read some of the letters to Lady Mar. On
her last journey to England, Lady Mary was delayed
at Rotterdam, and while there seems to have given
two volumes of manuscript, containing the "Turkish
Letters," to the Rev. Benjamin Sowden, an English
clergyman, at Rotterdam. The fact of the gift is
confirmed by an inscription on the first volume, in
Lady Mary's hand, dated December 11, 1761. Lady
Bute, hearing, after her mother's death, that some of
her letters were in the hands of a stranger, desired to
get them into her own hands. Horace Walpole hoped
that she would not succeed. " Though I do not
doubt," he writes, "but they" (the letters) "are an
olio of lies and scandal, I should like to see them.
She had parts, and had seen much." Eventually Mr.
Sowden gave up the volumes, whether freely, as his
friends said, or for £500, as Lady Louisa Stuart says,
or for a Crown living; and in 1763 these very letters
appeared in three volumes, with Mary Astell's two
prefaces and a note by the editor, who is said to have
been John Cleland, a man notorious as an editor and
fabricator of the correspondence of noted persons.
Naturally Sowden was charged with bad faith, though
not, it seems, justly; for Mr. Moy Thomas assures us
that the edition of 1763 agrees not with the Sowden
manuscript (which does not contain the prefaces), but
with another copy, given by Lady Mary to Mr. Moles-
worth. However, it is not impossible that the editor
was telling the truth when he informed his readers that
his selection was " transcribed from the original manu-

script of her ladyship at Venice." Another volume of
letters, attributed to Lady Mary, came out in 1767,
but these are probably fabrications of Cleland's own;
for though Lady Bute accepted them as genuine on
the strength of their style alone, yet their similarity to
the authentic letters does not seem beyond the reach
of a practised literary forger. No originals of the
letters of 1767 have ever come to hand; and it is
perhaps unfortunate that the lady known in letters as
Camille Selden, in her study of Lady Mary Wortley
Montagu, has been misled by Lord Wharncliffe's
uncritical acceptance into quoting as especially charac-
teristic some of these very letters.

The " Letters from the Levant," as they were
often called, were popular; and eventually the family
of Lady Mary resolved to give a further instalment
to the world, and employed the Rev. Mr. Dallaway
as editor. In 1803 appeared his volumes, containing
the bulk of the Letters now known to the public, but
altered and arranged in an arbitrary fashion, and
preceded by a memoir really remarkable for its absence
of accurate information. Even as Dallaway left them,
however, the Letters proved interesting, and several
editions were called for; the fifth, in 1805, contained
a number of additional letters. In 1837 Lord Wharncliffe edited Lady Mary Wortley Montagu's Letters
and Works, in three volumes, preceded by Dallaway's
memoir, and an interesting series of introductory
anecdotes, by Lady Louisa Stuart, grand-daughter
of Lady Mary. Finally, in 1861, appeared a new

edition of Lord Wharncliffe's selection, completely re-
edited by Mr. W. Moy Thomas from the Wortley
papers; and it is unlikely that any further editor will
find anything of importance to add to his careful and
thorough work. Besides her Letters and compositions
in prose and verse, Lady Mary left behind her a
voluminous Diary, the earlier part of which was read
by Lady Louisa Stuart, who gives some interesting
details about it. But this Diary—recording as it did
the events, rumours, and scandals of every day—was
thought too likely to make trouble if published; and
accordingly Lady Bute destroyed it shortly before her
own death, in 1794. How far the loss is a serious one
it is impossible to judge; but I should conjecture that
most probably the Diary, where it contained full
descriptions of events or places, was drawn upon for
the Letters, and that we have the cream of the journal
in the correspondence.

Lady Mary Wortley Montagu's character is depicted
too plainly in her Letters to stand in need of much
comment or explanation. No doubt the rumours and
traditions that have depicted her as a sort of modern
Sappho, a woman of extraordinary intellect and still
more extraordinary shamelessness, a strolling Semi-
ramis, are more striking and melodramatic than the
rather humdrum details told in the Letters; but it is
the misfortune of true history to be hardly ever completely romantic, and but seldom as scandalous as we
would fain think it. The aspersions on Lady Mary's
morality have no other visible foundation than the

malignity of Pope or the spiteful gossip of Horace
Walpole; and the latter was at least as ready to
believe ill reports of Lady Mary as the former to
invent or aggravate them.   The somewhat coarse
freedom of expression in some of her letters is merely
the tone of her time—a time when a fastidious invalid
like Pope wrote letters glowing with apparent passion
or deeply tainted with grossness, to ladies of unblemished fame, and was not even thought to have
failed in courtesy or respect.   The fact seems to have
been that Lady Mary, like many of the men of the
eighteenth century, had developed the intellectual and
practical side of her nature at the expense of the
emotions.   There is no proof that she was ever in love
with anyone but her husband ; and her affection for
him began in intellectual companionship, and consisted
to a considerable extent in respect, with a touch of
fear.   Her love-letters are full of business details,
plain speaking, and close reasoning.   Her lover gives
her up rather than violate his principles as to marriage
settlements, and she heartily approves him.   All this
is very sensible, but it is hardly the note of passion,
even allowing for the undemonstrative character of
the age.   Family affection was not strongly developed in Lady Mary : her father's death leaves little
impression on her.   He had neglected her; why should
she mourn for him ?   Her religion, again, was the
Whig Christianity of the day, the moderately
rationalistic, tolerant half-deism of the Georgian
Bishops : she never speaks but with contempt of past

mystics or present Methodists. Patriotism had little
hold on her — she was cosmopolitan ; and though
English defeats galled her a little, English victories
left her cold. All her failings—coarseness of phrase,
coldness of feeling, want of consideration in the use of
her wit, even the slovenliness of dress into which she
fell—are the faults of a nature too merely intellectual.
One may say that she was all her days a traveller,
regarding the world of life as she did the lands through
which she journeyed. The joys of existence were but
the chance of a fine day, or a good inn on the road ;
its griefs but the breaking of a wheel, the discomfort
of a hovel—all alike to be borne with quietly, because
they would be gone and almost forgotten to-morrow.
Friends, relations even, were but travelling-companions
--here to-day, gone to-morrow. A trashy novel was
just as good as a grave and instructive work ; the
former served to while away a tedious hour of the
long journey, and the latter could do no more.

Madame Camille Selden speaks of Lady Mary's life
as a failure, and blames her, or at least deplores her for
having neglected her womanly duties to please herself
in isolation and independence. Yet, what mission was
there for her to adopt, what duties to perform at home?
Her son had proved himself irreclaimably vicious, and
what she probably despised far more—irredeemably
weak ; her daughter was happily married. She was
long past the age of beauty and social success, and her
name was soiled by the attacks of the first poet of the
time. Her husband apparently could get on best

without her, as he and she alike seem to have realized
with the merciless good sense they had in common.
Doubtless, with her talents, her wealth, her position,
she might have been the leading spirit of some social
reform, some political change, some religious movement; but to engage in any of these enterprises she
must have changed her temperament, and ceased to be
the Lady Mary that we know—a change that might
conceivably have been very much for the worse.   Of
philanthropists, past and present, we have great plenty,
many of them fulfilling the cynical definition by "doing
good that evil may come"—but of letter-writers whose
letters bear reading, not many.   Lady Mary in her last
twenty years of lonely travel at least entertained
herself and her correspondents, and hurt no one in
particular: and if she did not found a church or
inaugurate a movement, she wrote some charming
letters, and taught the country-folk by Lake Iseo how
to make good butter and mince-pies, also cheese-cakes,
so that they would have set up her statue as that of a
public benefactress, but she declined the honour.   This
is something to have done, and not a little, as the
average of human achievement goes; even though her
arts of persuasion could not bend North Italian ortho-
doxy to approve of the "unnatural mixture" known as
" sillabub."

About the style of the letters of Lady Mary it is not
necessary to say much.   Her work speaks for itself.
We have it on the testimony of her relations that she
wrote with ease and fluency, never having occasion to

wait for words or exercise careful revision. About grammar and spelling she was no more careful than other writers of her time ; but her deviations from strict rule have still an ease and good breeding which lift them out of the category of vulgar blunders. The distinguished and elegant carelessness of past times was far removed from the ignoble lapses of modern cheap novelists and pushing journalists, who write " different *to* " and spell Sphinx with a *y*. Yet, while disdaining elaboration or pedantic accuracy of style, Lady Mary never forgot that she was *writing*, nor, apparently, that what she wrote might be seen by after generations. She seldom, if ever, talks on paper. There is little tenderness or playfulness in her style. Kind and affectionate as are her letters to her daughter, their prevailing note is good sense, clear reasoning. Seemingly incapable of very strong emotion, Lady Mary repressed with a truly English thoroughness what emotion she felt, and rather than yield to what she considered a weakness ("sentiments," she says, "are extreme silly "). affected a cold and stoical indifference which she did not always feel. In this, as in other respects, she was of her time—the first half of the eighteenth century. Not till after her death began the time of vague aspirations, of questioning discontent, of unrest and unsettlement, of theories and philosophies, of cosmopolitan and humanitarian ideas—the time which ended in the French Revolution. Lady Mary lived under the reign of Sense, not yet dethroned by Sensibility.

CHAPTER II

EARLY LIFE AND MARRIAGE

THE letters of Lady Mary Wortley Montagu are often
difficult to identify, nor is it always easy to tell to
whom or when they were sent. In her time the post-
office was far from safe, even in England; in other
countries, especially in time of wars and rumours of
wars, it was almost the exception for a letter to get
through. Hence comes a practice of leaving letters
unsigned, and alluding to persons by initials only,
which is at times troublesome to modern readers; and
even more vexatious is Lady Mary's habit of omitting
to date her letters—a defect which she seems to have
transmitted to her descendants and her first editors,
since neither Lord Wharncliffe nor Mr. Dallaway knew

the year of her birth. The earliest letters which we can date are to Mrs. Hewet, wife of the Surveyor-General to George I., and to Anne, sister of Edward Wortley. The letters to Mrs. Hewet are of comparatively slight interest. They turn mostly on the books which the two friends sent to each other--novels chiefly, and novels of the day, for which Lady Mary always had an unlimited appetite. Mrs. Manley's " New Atalantis " is the chief of them.

" I am very glad," Lady Mary writes, "you have the second part of the ' New Atalantis ': if you have read it, will you be so good as to send it to me? and in return, I promise to get you the key to it. I know I can. But do you know what has happened to the unfortunate authoress ? People are offended at the liberty she uses in her memoirs, and she is taken into custody. Miserable is the fate of writers : if they are agreeable, they are offensive ; and if dull, they starve. I lament the loss of the other parts which we should have had ; and have five hundred arguments at my fingers' ends to prove the ridiculousness of those creatures that think it worth while to take notice of what is only designed for diversion. After this, who will dare to give the history of Angella ? I was in hopes her faint essay would have provoked some better pen to give more elegant and secret memoirs ; but now she will serve as a scarecrow to frighten people from attempting anything but heavy panegyric ; and we shall be teazed with nothing but heroic poems, with names at length, and false characters, so daubed with flattery,

that they are the severest kind of lampoons, for they
both scandalize the writer and the subject, like that
vile paper the *Tatler*."

Yet again we find Lady Mary studying Italian,
going to the opera, seeing " Nicolini strangle a lion
with great gallantry" (as inimitably ridiculed in the
Spectator), in a highly realistic suit of tights, "which
convinced me that those prudes who would cry fie!
fie! at the word *naked*, have no scruples about the
thing."

The letters to Anne Wortley are, from the outset,
more serious. Beginning with the exaggerations of
girl-friendship, they soon pass into that veiled and
indirect love-making which was mentioned before.
Anne Wortley's first printed letter refers to "an humble
servant of yours, who is arguing so hotly about
marriage that I cannot go on with my letter."

The answer seems written in breathless haste.
Evidently the post was at its tricks again. "I shall
run mad—with what heart can people write, when
they believe their letters will never be received? I
have already writ you a very long scrawl, but it
seems it never came to your hands; I cannot bear to
be accused of coldness by one whom I shall love all my
life. This will, perhaps, miscarry as the last did; how
unfortunate am I if it does! You will think I forget
you, who are never out of my thoughts. You will
fancy me stupid enough to neglect your letters, when
they are the only pleasures of my solitude; in short,
you will call me ungrateful and insensible, when I

esteem you as I ought, in esteeming you above all the
world. If I am not quite so unhappy as I imagine,
and you do receive this, let me know it as soon as you
can ; for till then I shall be in terrible uneasiness ; and
let me beg you for the future, if you do not receive
letters very constantly from me, imagine the post-boy
killed, imagine the mail burnt, or some other strange
accident ; you can imagine nothing so impossible as
that I forget you, my dear Mrs. Wortley. I know no
pretence I have to your good opinion but my hearty
desiring it ; I wish I had that imagination you talk of,
to render me a fitter correspondent for you, who can
write so well on every thing. I am now so much
alone, I have leisure to pass whole days in reading,
but am not at all proper for so delicate an employment
as choosing you books. Your own fancy will better
direct you. My study at present is nothing but
dictionaries and grammars. I am trying whether it
be possible to learn without a master : I am not certain
(and dare hardly hope) I shall make any great progress;
but I find the study so diverting, I am not only easy,
but pleased with the solitude that indulges it. I forget
there is such a place as London, and wish for no
company but yours. You see, my dear, in making my
pleasures consist of these unfashionable diversions, I
am not of the number who cannot be easy out of the
mode. I believe more follies are committed out of
complaisance to the world, than in following our own
inclinations—Nature is seldom in the wrong, custom
always : it is with some regret I follow it in all the

impertinences of dress; the compliance is so trivial it comforts me; but I am amazed to see it consulted even in the most important occasions of our lives; and that people of good sense in other things can make their happiness consist in the opinions of others, and sacrifice everything in the desire of appearing in fashion. I call all people who fall in love with furniture, clothes, and equipage, of this number, and I look upon them as no less in the wrong than when they were five years old, and doted on shells, pebbles, and hobby-horses: I believe you will expect this letter to be dated from the other world, for sure I am you never heard an inhabitant of this talk so before. I suppose you expect, too, I should conclude with begging pardon for this extreme tedious and very nonsensical letter; quite contrary, I think you will be obliged to me for it. I could not better show my great concern for your reproaching me with neglect I knew myself innocent of, than proving myself mad in three pages."

The learned designs of Lady Mary met with a flattering rejoinder from Anne Wortley, or rather from her brother, who, it is needless to say, was the "Cambridge Doctor."

"Dear Lady Mary will pardon my vanity; I could not forbear reading to a Cambridge Doctor that was with me at Thoresby, a few of those lines that did not make me happy till this week: where you talk of turning over dictionaries and grammars, he stopped me, and said the reason why you had more wit than

any man, was that your mind had never been en-
cumbered with those tedious authors; that Cowley
never submitted to the rules of grammar, and therefore
excelled all of his own time in learning, as well as wit;
that without them, you would read with pleasure in
two or three months; but if you persisted in the use
of them, you would throw away your Latin after a
year or two, and the commonwealth would have
reason to mourn; whereas, if I could prevail with you,
it would be bound to thank me for a brighter ornament
than any it can boast of."

Gradually Lady Mary was drawn on further by
artful hints that she was in love with someone or
other, which she repudiated with playful scorn.

"After giving me imaginary wit and beauty, you
give me imaginary passions, and you tell me I'm in
love: if I am, 'tis a perfect sin of ignorance, for I don't
so much as know the man's name: I have been studying these three hours, and cannot guess who you mean.
I passed the days of Nottingham races, [at] Thoresby,
without seeing or even wishing to see one of the sex.
Now, if I am in love, I have very hard fortune to
conceal it so industriously from my own knowledge,
and yet discover it so much to other people. 'Tis
against all form to have such a passion as that, without
giving one sigh for the matter. Pray tell me the name
of him I love, that I may (according to the laudable
custom of lovers) sigh to the woods and groves here-
abouts, and teach it to the echo. You see, being I am
[*sic*] in love, I am willing to be so in order and rule:

have been turning over God knows how many books to look for precedents. Recommend an example to me; and, above all, let me know whether 'tis most proper to walk in the woods, increasing the winds with my sighs, or to sit by a purling stream, swelling the rivulet with my tears; maybe, both may do well in their turns."

Then Anne Wortley mentioned the suspected lover, with the result of eliciting an incautious avowal from her friend: "To be capable of preferring the despicable wretch you mention to Mr. Wortley, is as ridiculous, if not as criminal, as forsaking the Deity to worship a calf"—which was exactly the result for which Edward Wortley, under the mask of his sister, had been playing. Anne Wortley must have died towards the end of 1709, for in the spring of 1710 comes the first letter Lady Mary wrote directly to her lover.

"Perhaps you'll be surprised at this letter; I have had many debates with myself before I could resolve on it. I know it is not acting in form, but I do not look upon you as I do upon the rest of the world, and by what I do for *you*, you are not to judge my manner of acting with others. You are brother to a woman I tenderly loved; my protestations of friendship are not like other people's, I never speak but what I mean, and when I say I love, 'tis for ever. I had that real concern for Mrs. Wortley, I look with some regard on every one that is related to her. This and my long acquaintance with you may in some measure excuse what I am now doing. I am surprised at one of the *Tatlers* you send me; is it possible to have any sort

of esteem for a person one believes capable of having
such trifling inclinations? Mr. Bickerstaff* has very
wrong notions of our sex. I can say there are some of
us that despise charms of show, and all the pageantry
of greatness, perhaps with more ease than any of the
philosophers. In contemning the world, they seem to
take pains to contemn it ; we despise it, without taking
the pains to read lessons of morality to make us do it.
At least, I know I have always looked upon it with
contempt, without being at the expense of one serious
reflection to oblige me to it. I carry the matter yet
farther ; was I to choose of two thousand pounds a
year or twenty thousand, the first would be my choice.
There is something of an unavoidable *embarras* in
making what is called a great figure in the world ; [it]
takes off from the happiness of life ; I hate the noise
and hurry inseparable from great estates and titles,
and look upon both as blessings that ought only to be
given to fools, for 'tis only to them that they are
blessings. The pretty fellows you speak of, I own
entertain me sometimes : but is it impossible to be
diverted with what one despises ? I can laugh at a
puppet-show ; at the same time I know there is nothing
in it worth my attention or regard. General notions
are generally wrong. Ignorance and folly are thought
the best foundations for virtue, as if not knowing what
a good wife is was necessary to make one so. I confess
that can never be my way of reasoning ; as I always

---

* Isaac Bickerstaff was the fictitious personality of the *Tatler*,
written chiefly by Steele and Addison.

forgive an *injury* when I think it not done out of malice,
I can never think myself *obliged* by what is done without
design. Give me leave to say it (I know it sounds
vain), I know how to make a man of sense happy; but
then that man must resolve to contribute something
towards it himself. I have so much esteem for you, I
should be very sorry to hear you was unhappy; but for
the world I would not be the instrument of making
you so; which (of the humour you are) is hardly to be
avoided if I am your wife. You distrust me—I can
neither be easy, nor loved, where I am distrusted.
Nor do I believe your passion for me is what you
pretend it; at least, I am sure was I in love I could
not talk as you do. Few women would have spoke
so plainly as I have done ; but to dissemble is among
the things I never do. I take more pains to approve
my conduct to myself than to the world; and would
not have to accuse myself of a minute's deceit. I wish
I loved you enough to devote myself to be for ever
miserable, for the pleasure of a day or two's happiness.
I cannot resolve upon it. You must think otherwise of
me, or not at all."

However, the reasons against the marriage were of
little moment; we soon find Lady Mary discussing
future arrangements—of course in a purely hypothet-
ical way. "As to travelling, 'tis what I should do with
great pleasure, and could easily quit London upon your
account; but a retirement in the country is not so disagreeable to me, as I know a few months would make
it tiresome to you. Where people are tied for life, 'tis

heir mutual interest not to grow weary of one another. If I had all the personal charms that I want, a face is too slight a foundation for happiness. You would be soon tired with seeing every day the same thing. Where you saw nothing else, you would have leisure to remark all the defects; which would increase in proportion as the novelty lessened, which is always a great charm. I should have the displeasure of seeing a coldness, which, though I could not reasonably blame you for, being involuntary, yet it would render me uneasy; and the more because I know a love may be revived which absence, inconstancy, or even infidelity, has extinguished ; but there is no returning from a *dégoût* given by satiety." She closes by recommending him to ask her family to consent to the marriage.

Edward Wortley Montagu complied with the suggestion, and asked the Marquis of Dorchester for his daughter's hand ; but, as already mentioned, a disagreement arose over the settlement, and the lover started for the Continent. He seems to have put too much of his disappointment into the tone of his parting letter, to judge by Lady Mary's reply :

" Kindness, you say, would be your destruction. In my opinion, this is something contradictory to some other expressions. People talk of being in love just as widows do of affliction. Mr. Steele has observed, in one of his plays, the most passionate among them have always calmness enough to drive a hard bargain with the upholders.* I never knew a lover that would not

---

* *I. e.*, the undertakers.

willingly secure his interest as well as his mistress; or,
if one must be abandoned, had not the prudence (among
all his distractions) to consider, a woman was but a
woman, and money was a thing of more real merit than
the whole sex put together.   Your letter is to tell me,
you should think yourself undone if you married me;
but if I would be so tender as to confess I should break
my heart if you did not, then you'd consider whether
you would or no; but yet you hoped you should not.
I take this to be the right interpretation of—even your
kindness can't destroy me of a sudden—I hope I am
not in your power— I would give a good deal to be
satisfied, etc."

However, her natural resentment at the suspicion
of her lover did not last long, and on his return in the
autumn of 1710 the negotiations were to be resumed,
as we see from the following letter:

"I am going to comply with your request, and write
with all the plainness I am capable of.   I know what
may be said upon such a proceeding, but am sure you
will not say it.   Why should you always put the worst
construction upon my words?   Believe me what you
will, but do not believe I can be ungenerous or ungrateful.   I wish I could tell you what answer you will
receive from some people, or upon what terms.   If my
opinion could sway, nothing should displease you.   Nobody ever was so disinterested as I am.   I would not
have to reproach myself (I don't suppose you would)
that I had any way made you uneasy in your circumstances.   Let me beg you (which I do with the utmost

sincerity) only to consider yourself in this affair; and, since I am so unfortunate to have nothing in my own disposal, do not think I have any hand in making settlements. People in my way are sold like slaves; and I cannot tell what price my master will put on me. If you do agree, I shall endeavour to contribute, as much as lies in my power, to your happiness. I so heartily despise a great figure, I have no notion of spending money so foolishly; though one had a great deal to throw away. If this breaks off, I shall not complain of you: and as, whatever happens, I shall still preserve the opinion you have behaved yourself well. Let me entreat you, if I have committed any follies, to forgive them; and be so just to think I would not do an ill thing."

Yet neither humility nor resentment could cure Edward Wortley of his habit of finding fault, whether. as Mr. Moy Thomas thinks, it was an ungenerous device for drawing fresh avowals from Lady Mary, or —as I am inclined to conjecture—a necessity of his temperament. Sometimes we find her bidding him " adieu for ever," with what sincerity we may perhaps guess, on the ground of his inveterate suspicion. " I begin to be tired of my humility," she says : " I have carried my complaisances to you further than I ought. You make new scruples; you have a good deal of fancy; and your distrusts being all of your own making, are more immovable than if there was some real ground for them." And certainly the one love-letter of Mr. Wortley Montagu's printed in the corre-

spondence is of a provoking character. He complains
of having disobliged an influential friend to meet her,
and of her cutting short the interview, and plainly
declares that he thinks it wisest not to marry her.
" What need I add? I see what is best for me, I
condemn what I do, and yet I fear I must do it."
Truly a romantic lover! And yet we find him in the
same letter elaborately arranging half a dozen ways of
meeting Lady Mary by the help of Mrs. Steele. In
spite of their epistolary differences, the pair were
always coming together again. It is curious to read
Lady Mary's conception of wedded happiness :

" Happiness is the natural design of all the world; and
everything we see done, is meant in order to attain it.
My imagination places it in friendship. By friendship I
mean an entire communication of thoughts, wishes, interests, and pleasures, being undivided ; a mutual esteem,
which naturally carries with it a pleasing sweetness of
conversation, and terminates in the desire of making
one or another happy, without being forced to run into
visits, noise, and hurry, which serve rather to trouble
than compose the thoughts of any reasonable creature.
There are few capable of a friendship such as I have
described, and 'tis necessary for the generality of the
world to be taken up with trifles. Carry a fine lady
and a fine gentleman out of town, and they know no
more what to say. To take from them plays, operas,
and fashions, is taking away all their topics of discourse ; and they know not how to form their thoughts
on any other subjects. They know very well what it is

to be admired, but are perfectly ignorant of what it is to
be loved. I take you to have sense enough not to think
this scheme romantic : I rather choose to use the word
friendship than love; because, in the general sense
that word is spoke, it signifies a passion rather founded
on fancy than reason ; and when I say friendship, I
mean a mixture of tenderness and esteem, and which
a long acquaintance increases, not decays: how far I
deserve such a friendship, I can be no judge of myself.
I may want the good sense that is necessary to be
agreeable to a man of merit, but I know I want the
vanity to believe I have [it] ; and can promise you
shall never like me less upon knowing me better; and
that I shall never forget you have a better understanding than myself."

Events were now coming to a crisis, for in 1712 the
objectionable " Mr. K." with his offers of liberal settlements, appeared on the scene, and Lord Dorchester
ordered his daughter to accept him. The long letter
in which Lady Mary gives an account of her attempt
to shake her father's resolution is a striking picture
of the way in which ladies of high rank were disposed
of. The father, careless as he had been of his
daughter's education, would never hear of his not
having full power to bestow her hand ; and her plea to
be allowed to remain single at least was met by threats.

She writes to Edward Wortley Montagu :

" I wanted courage to resist at first the will of my
relations ; but as every day added to my fears, those, at
last, grew strong enough to make me venture the dis-

obliging them. A harsh word damps my spirits to
a degree of silencing all I have to say. I knew the
folly of my own temper, and took the method of writing
to the disposer of me. I said every thing in this letter
I thought proper to move him, and proffered, in atone-
ment for not marrying whom he would, never to marry
at all. He did not think fit to answer this letter, but
sent for me to him. He told me he was very much surprised that I did not depend on his judgment for my
future happiness; that he knew nothing I had to complain of, etc.; that he did not doubt I had some other
fancy in my head, which encouraged me to this disobedi-
ence; but he assured me, if I refused a settlement he had
provided for me, he gave me his word, whatever proposals were made him, he would never so much as enter
into a treaty with any other; that, if I founded any
hopes upon his death, I should find myself mistaken, he
never intended to leave me any thing but an annuity
of £400 per annum; that, though another would proceed in this manner after I had given so just a pretence
for it, yet he had [the] goodness to leave my destiny yet
in my own choice, and at the same time commanded
me to communicate my design to my relations, and ask
their advice. As hard as this may sound, it did not
shock my resolution; I was pleased to think, at any
price, I had it in my power to be free from a man
I hated. I told my intention to all my nearest relations. I was surprised at their blaming it, to the
greatest degree. I was told, they were sorry I would
ruin myself; but, if I was so unreasonable, they could

not blame my F. [father] whatever he inflicted on me.
I objected I did not love him. They made answer,
they found no necessity of loving; if I lived well with
him, that was all was required of me; and that if I
considered this town, I should find very few women in
love with their husbands, and yet a many happy. It
was in vain to dispute with such prudent people; they
looked upon me as a little romantic, and I found it impossible to persuade them that living in London at
liberty was not the height of happiness. However, they
could not change my thoughts, though I found I was to
expect no protection from them. When I was to give
my final answer to ——,* I told him that I preferred a
single life to any other; and, if he pleased to permit
me, I would take that resolution. He replied, he could
not hinder my resolutions, but I should not pretend
after that to please him; since pleasing him was only to
be done by obedience; that if I would disobey, I knew
the consequences; he would not fail to confine me,
where I might repent at leisure; that he had also consulted my relations, and found them all agreeing in his
sentiments. He spoke this in a manner hindered my
answering. I retired to my chamber, where I writ a
letter to let him know my aversion to the man proposed
was too great to be overcome, that I should be miserable
beyond all things could be imagined, but I was in his
hands, and he might dispose of me as he thought fit.
He was perfectly satisfied with this answer, and proceeded as if I had given a willing consent.—I forgot to

* This blank evidently refers to her father.

4

tell you, he named you, and said, if I thought that way, I was very much mistaken; that if he had no other engagements, yet he would never have agreed to your proposals, having no inclinations to see his grand-children beggars.

"I do not speak this to endeavour to alter your opinion, but to shew the improbability of his agreeing to it. I confess I am entirely of your mind. I reckon it among the absurdities of custom that a man must be obliged to settle his whole estate on an eldest son, beyond his power to recall, whatever he proves to be, and make himself unable to make happy a younger child that may deserve to be so. If I had an estate myself, I should not make such ridiculous settlements, and I cannot blame you for being in the right . . ."

Lady Mary's father took her submission as a consent to the marriage he proposed, and began to provide wedding clothes to the amount of £400. A plan for an elopement was concerted between the lovers—or rather several plans. A friendly lady would lend her house, and the lover was to call there with the license and a coach and six. This plan failed, and Lady Mary was sent with her brother to West Dean in Wiltshire; and, perhaps with his help, she eventually escaped and joined Edward Wortley Montagu, and they were married some time in August, 1712. Her first letter as a wife is dated from Walling Wells in Nottinghamshire, where she was staying with her friends the Whites, while her husband went to Durham on business.

"I don't know very well how to begin; I am

perfectly unacquainted with a proper matrimonial style. After all, I think 'tis best to write as if we were not married at all. I lament your absence, as if you was still my lover, and I am impatient to hear you are got safe to Durham, and that you have fixed a time for your return.

" I have not been very long in this family; and I fancy myself in that described in the *Spectator*. The good people here look upon their children with a fondness that more than recompenses their care of them. I don't perceive much distinction in regard to their merits; and when they speak sense or nonsense, it affects the parents with almost the same pleasure. My friendship for the mother, and kindness for Miss Biddy, make me endure the squalling of Miss Nanny and Miss Mary with abundance of patience: and my foretelling the future conquests of the eldest daughter, makes me very well with the family – I don't know whether you will presently find out that this seeming impertinent account is the tenderest expressions of my love to you; but it furnishes my imagination with agreeable pictures of our future life; and I flatter myself with the hopes of one day enjoying with you the same satisfactions; and that, after as many years together, I may see you retain the same fondness for me as I shall certainly mine for you, and the noise of a nursery may have more charms for us than the music of an opera."

But these high spirits soon passed away, when the answer to her letter did not come at the first oppor-

tunity. Her next note is full of complaints and fears,
the secret of which is perhaps found in her being
shortly after laid up with a swelled face, an ailment
which we find frequently recurring in her life, and for
which the dentistry of that time had no remedy.
Though the name of "neuralgia" was not invented, the
complaint probably existed. However, we soon find
Lady Mary at Hinchinbrook, ransacking the house for
books, failing to find any, but discovering in an old
trunk the letters of the first Earl of Sandwich, and " in
hopes that those from his lady will tend much to my
edification, being the most extraordinary lessons of
economy that ever I read in my life. . . . I walked
yesterday two hours on the terrace. These are the
most considerable events that have happened in your
absence; excepting that a good-natured robin red-
breast kept me company almost all the afternoon, with
so much good humour and humanity as gives me faith
for the piece of charity ascribed to these little creatures
in the 'Children in the Wood,' which I have hitherto
thought only a poetical ornament to that history."

In 1713 her first child was born, and her only brother
died, and her sister Frances was married in 1714 to
the Earl of Mar. There are frequent notices of the
health of young Edward Wortley. While she was staying at Middlethorpe, in Yorkshire, her husband being
then in London, came the surprising news of the death
of Queen Anne and the proclamation of George I. " I
went with my cousin to-day," she writes, "to see the
King proclaimed, which was done ; the archbishop

walking next the lord mayor, all the country gentry
following, with greater crowds of people than I believed
to be in York, vast acclamations, and the appearance
of a general satisfaction. The Pretender afterwards
dragged about the streets and burned. Ringing of
bells, bonfires, and illuminations, the mob crying,
' Liberty and Property!' and ' Long live King George!'
This morning all the principal men of any figure took
post for London, and we are alarmed with the fear of
attempts from Scotland, though all Protestants here
seem unanimous for the Hanover succession. The
poor young ladies at Castle Howard are as much
afraid as I am, being left all alone, without any hopes
of seeing their father again (though things should
prove well) this eight or nine months.* They have
sent to desire me very earnestly to come to them, and
bring my boy ; 'tis the same thing as pensioning in a
nunnery, for no mortal man ever enters the doors in
the absence of their father, who is gone post. During
this uncertainty, I think it will be a safe retreat ; for
Middlethorpe stands exposed to plunderers, if there be
any at all." There was much anxiety as to the prospects of a rising against the Hanoverian succession.
A fleet was said to be off Scotland; and Lady Mary's
brother-in-law, the Earl of Mar, was receiving suspicious letters. Soon, however, the first alarm passed
off; and Lady Mary's anxiety was chiefly directed

---

* The young ladies were the daughters of the Earl of Carlisle,
who had been chosen one of the Lords Justices till George I.'s
arrival.

towards securing for her husband a seat in the new
Parliament and a share in the honour and profit of the
great Whig victory. Her letters about this time read
like those of an election-agent. Could Lord Pelham
(afterwards the famous Duke of Newcastle) be persuaded, as he is "very silly, but very good-natured,"
that he was bound in honour to put Mr. Wortley
Montagu in for Aldburgh? Would his father insist
on standing for the family seat at Huntingdon? Then,
again, he is urged to stand for York, but does not
decide in time; perhaps he will have to buy a Cornish
borough. Is there a chance at Newark?—and so on,
a certain feverish impatience being manifest in the
tone of the letters. "'Tis surprising to me that you
are all this while in the midst of your friends without
being sure of a place, when so many insignificant
creatures come in without any opposition."

Lord Halifax had now made Edward Wortley the
offer of being a Commissioner of the Treasury, but the
latter was very doubtful whether he would accept the
post. His wife urged him strongly to do so. " I am
glad you think of serving your friends; I hope it will
put you in mind of serving yourself. I need not
enlarge upon the advantages of money; everything we
see, and everything we hear, puts us in remembrance
of it. If it was possible to restore liberty to your
country, or limit the encroachments of the pre—ve
[prerogative], by reducing yourself to a garret, I
should be pleased to share so glorious a poverty with
you; but as the world is, and will be, 'tis a sort of

duty to be rich, that it may be in one's power to do good ; riches being another word for power, towards the obtaining of which the first necessary qualification is impudence, and (as Demosthenes said of pronunciation in oratory) the second is impudence, and the third, still, impudence. No modest man ever did or ever will make his fortune. Your friend Lord H alifa]x, R. W alpolje, and all other remarkable instances of quick advancement, have been remarkably impudent. The Ministry is like a play at Court ; there's a little door to get in, and a great crowd without, shoving and thrusting who shall be foremost ; people who knock others with their elbows, disregard a little kick of the shins, and still thrust heartily forwards, are sure of a good place. Your modest man stands behind in the crowd, is shoved about by every body, his cloaths tore, almost squeezed to death, and sees a thousand get in before him, that don't make so good a figure as himself. I don't say it is impossible for an impudent man not to rise in the world ; but a moderate merit, with a large share of impudence, is more probable to be advanced than the greatest qualifications without it."

There is a tone of pique in her reference to the matter in the lively sketch of the Court of George I., written not long after. " I was then in Yorkshire : Mr. W. [Wortley] (who had, at that time, that sort of passion for me that would have made me invisible to all but himself, had it been in his power) had sent me thither. He stayed in town on the account of some business, and the Queen's death detained him there. Lord Halifax, his near relation, was put at the head of the Treasury; and, willing to have the rest of the commissioners such as he thought he could depend on, named him for one of them. It will be surprising to add that he hesitated to accept of it, at a time when his father was alive and his present income very small; but he had that opinion of his own merit as made him think any offer below that of Secretary of State not worth his acceptance, and had certainly refused it if he had not been persuaded to the contrary by a rich old uncle of mine, Lord Pierrepont, whose fondness for me gave him expectations of a large legacy." Possibly she was offended by her husband paying more attention to Lord Pierrepont's advice than to her own letters.

From whatever reason, the post was accepted; and Lady Mary came up to London, though not till the new Court had all arrived. Her lively pen gives an amusing character of George I. and his son in the sketch already quoted. Certainly she had no ideas of any divinity hedging a king. "The King's character may be comprised in very few words. In private life he would have been called an honest blockhead; and Fortune, that made him a king, added nothing to his happiness, only prejudiced his honesty, and shortened his days. No man was ever more free from ambition; he loved money, but loved to keep his own, without being rapacious of other men's. He would have grown rich by saving, but was incapable of laying schemes for getting; he was more properly dull than lazy,

and would have been so well contented to have remained in his little town of Hanover, that if the
ambition of those about him had not been greater than
his own, we should never have seen him in England;
and the natural honesty of his temper, joined with the
narrow notions of a low education, made him look
upon his acceptance of the crown as an act of usurpa-
tion, which was always uneasy to him. But he was
carried by the stream of the people about him, in that
as in every other action of his life. He could speak
no English, and was past the age of learning it. Our
customs and laws were all mysteries to him, which he
neither tried to understand nor was capable of understanding if he endeavoured it. He was passively
good-natured, and wished all mankind enjoyed quiet
if they would let him do so."

It is noteworthy that Lady Mary seems to have been
a favourite not only with George I., but—which was
unusual—with his son and his son's wife, Princess
Caroline, afterwards the stanch ally of Walpole.
Yet we do not find either of them spared any more
than George I. Perhaps the sketch was written
before the author was on intimate terms with Princess
Caroline; yet its language shows in a small compass
how Lady Mary contrived to make enemies. It
would be hard to write more contemptuously than
she does; still she had certainly no cause of enmity
towards the royal family, and their sole defect was
stupidity, for which she had a natural intolerance.

"I have not yet given the character of the Prince.

The fire of his temper appeared in every look and gesture; which, being unhappily under the direction of a small understanding, was every day throwing him upon some indiscretion. He was naturally sincere, and his pride told him that he was placed above constraint; not reflecting that a high rank carries along with it a necessity of a more decent and regular behaviour than is expected from those who are not set in so conspicuous a light. He was so far from being of that opinion, that he looked on all the men and women he saw as creatures he might kick or kiss for his diversion; and, whenever he met with any opposition in those designs, he thought his opposers impudent rebels to the will of God, who created them for his use, and judged of the merit of all people by their ready submission to his orders, or the relation they had to his person. And in this view he looked upon the Princess as the most meritorious of her sex; and she took care to keep him in that sentiment by all the arts she was mistress of. He had married her by inclination; his good-natured father had been so complaisant to let him choose a wife for himself. She was of the house of Anspach, and brought him no great addition either of money or alliance; but was at that time esteemed a German beauty, and had that genius which qualified her for the government of a fool, and made her despicable in the eyes of all men of sense; I mean a low cunning, which gave her an inclination to cheat all the people she conversed with, and often cheated herself in the first place, by showing her the wrong side of her interest, not having understanding enough to observe that falsehood in conversation, like red on the face, should be used very seldom and very sparingly, or they destroy that interest and beauty they are designed to heighten.

"Her first thought on her marriage was to secure to herself the sole and whole direction of her spouse ; and to that purpose [she] counterfeited the most extravagant fondness for his person ; yet, at the same time, so devoted to his pleasures (which she often told him were the rule of all her thoughts and actions), that whenever he thought proper to find them with other women, she even loved whoever was instrumental to his entertainment, and never resented anything but what appeared to her a want of respect for him ; and in this light she really could not help taking notice that the presents made to her on her wedding were not worthy of his bride, and at least she ought to have had all his mother's jewels. This was enough to make him lose all respect to his indulgent father. He downright abused his ministers, and talked impertinently to his old grandmother, the Princess Sophia ; which ended in such a coldness towards all his family as left him entirely under the government of his wife."

We owe to Lady Louisa Stuart, who alone, besides her mother, seems to have been allowed to look into Lady Mary's Diary, the account of a curious adventure at one of the little evening parties which George I. held with his German favourites :

" She [Lady Mary] had on one evening a par-

ticular engagement that made her wish to be dismissed unusually early; she explained her reasons
to the Duchess of Kendal, and the Duchess informed
the King, who, after a few complimentary remonstrances,
appeared to acquiesce. But when he saw her about to
take her leave, he began battling the point afresh, declaring it was unfair and perfidious to cheat him in
such a manner, and saying many other fine things, in
spite of which she at last contrived to escape. At the
foot of the great stairs she ran against Secretary Craggs
just coming in, who stopped her to inquire what was
the matter—were the company put off? She told him
why she went away, and how urgently the King had
pressed her to stay longer; possibly dwelling on that
head with some small complacency. Mr. Craggs made
no remark; but, when he had heard all, snatching her
up in his arms as a nurse carries a child, he ran at full
speed with her upstairs, deposited her within the ante-
chamber, kissed both her hands respectfully (still not
saying a word), and vanished. The pages seeing her
returned, they knew not how, hastily threw open the
inner doors, and, before she had recovered her breath,
she found herself again in the King's presence. ' *Ah!
la revoilà!*' cried he and the Duchess, extremely pleased,
and began thanking her for her obliging change of
mind. The motto on all palace-gates is ' Hush!' as
Lady Mary very well knew. She had not to learn that
mystery and caution ever spread their awful wings over
the precincts of a Court; where nobody knows what
dire mischief may ensue from one unlucky syllable

blabbed about anything, or about *nothing*, at a wrong
time. But she was bewildered, fluttered, and entirely
off her guard: so, beginning giddily with 'Oh Lord,
sir, I have been so frightened!' she told his majesty the
whole story exactly as she would have told it to anyone
else. He had not done exclaiming, nor his Germans
wondering, when again the door flew open, and the
attendants announced Mr. Secretary Craggs, who, but
that moment arrived, it should seem, entered with the
usual obeisance, and as composed an air as if nothing
had happened. '*Mais comment donc, Monsieur Craggs,*'
said the King, going up to him, '*est-ce que c'est l'usage de
ce pays de porter des belles dames comme un sac de froment?*'
'Is it the custom of this country to carry about fair
ladies like a sack of wheat?' The minister, struck
dumb by this unexpected attack, stood a minute or
two not knowing which way to look: then, recovering
his self-possession, answered with a low bow, 'There is
nothing I would not do for your majesty's satisfaction.'
This was coming off tolerably well; but he did not forgive the tell-tale culprit, in whose ear, watching his opportunity when the King turned from them, he muttered a
bitter reproach, with a round oath to enforce it; 'which
I durst not resent,' continued she, 'for I had drawn it
upon myself; and indeed I was heartily vexed at my
own imprudence.'"

But n the Hanoverian Court, which, if not decorous,
was certainly dull, Lady Mary was not long to remain.
She was destined to see and recount far more interesting scenes.

CHAPTER III

THE EMBASSY TO TURKEY

THE letters written by Lady Mary during the embassy to Constantinople are not perhaps the most interesting part of her correspondence; for they give rather too much useful information and too little of the personality of their writer; and there is reason for supposing them to be somewhat altered, or indeed re-written, for publication. Still, they probably represent the substance of the letters actually sent, since they were reconstructed from the Diary, which must

have related the same things in much the same way as
the letters written from day to day.

In the summer of 1716 Mr. Edward Wortley
Montagu set out with his wife, child and suite, for the
long journey to Constantinople. As at first intended,
he was to go to Vienna, and after having been placed in
possession of the views of the Emperor's Ministers, to
proceed to Turkey, and, if possible, arrange for the close
of the war then raging. As so many English travellers
have done since, Lady Mary went to Rotterdam, and
was charmed with the Dutch neatness and cleanliness.

"My arrival at Rotterdam presented me a new
scene of pleasure. All the streets are paved with broad
stones, and before the meanest artificer's doors seats of
various-coloured marbles, and so neatly kept, that, I
will assure you, I almost walked all over the town
yesterday, *incognita*, in my slippers, without receiving
one spot of dirt; and you may see the Dutch maids
washing the pavement of the streets with more application than ours do our bed-chambers. The town seems
so full of people, with such busy faces, all in motion,
that I can hardly fancy that it is not some celebrated
fair: but I see it is every day the same. 'Tis certain
no town can be more advantageously situated for commerce. Here are seven large canals, on which the
merchants' ships come up to the very doors of their
houses. The shops and warehouses are of a surprising
neatness and magnificence, filled with an incredible
quantity of fine merchandise, and so much cheaper
than what we see in England, I have much ado to

persuade myself I am still so near it.   Here is neither
dirt nor beggary to be seen.   One is not shocked with
those loathsome cripples, so common in London, nor
teazed with the importunities of idle fellows and wenches,
that choose to be nasty and lazy. The common servants
and little shopwomen here are more nicely clean than
most of our ladies ; and the great variety of neat dresses
(every woman dressing her head after her own fashion) is
an additional pleasure in seeing the town."

From Rotterdam she went by Nimeguen, which reminded her greatly of Nottingham, to Cologne, where
the profusion of relics aroused very mundane sentiments
in her.

" Having never before seen anything of that nature,
I could not enough admire the magnificence of the
altars, the rich images of the saints (all massy silver),
and the *enchassures* of the relics; though I could not
help murmuring, in my heart, at that profusion of
pearls, diamonds, and rubies, bestowed on the adorn-
ment of rotten teeth, dirty rags, etc. I own that I
had wickedness enough to covet St. Ursula's pearl
necklaces; though perhaps it was no wickedness at
all, an image not being certainly one's neighbour; but I
went yet farther, and wished even she herself converted
into dressing-plate, and a great St. Christopher I
imagined would have looked very well in a cistern."

Her Whig principles were evidently strengthened
by the contrast between the "free cities" of the
empire and the towns under princely rule. "I have
already passed a large part of Germany, have seen all

that is remarkable in Cologne, Frankfort, Wurtsburg, and this place [Nuremberg], and 'tis impossible not to observe the difference between the free towns and those under the government of absolute princes, as all the little sovereigns of Germany are. In the first, there appears an air of commerce and plenty. The streets are well built, and full of people neatly and plainly dressed. The shops loaded with merchandise, and the commonalty clean and cheerful. In the other, a sort of shabby finery, a number of dirty people of quality tawdered out; narrow, nasty streets out of repair, wretchedly thin of inhabitants, and above half of the common sort asking alms."

Lady Mary was compelled by a cold to stay some days at Ratisbon, where the Diet of the empire then sat. She seems to have been much amused by the ridiculous formalities of German diplomatic society.

"You know that all the nobility of this place are envoys from different states. Here are a great number of them, and they might pass their time agreeably enough, if they were less delicate on the point of ceremony. But, instead of joining in the design of making the town as pleasant to one another as they can, and improving their little societies, they amuse themselves no other way than with perpetual quarrels, which they take care to eternise, by leaving them to their successors; and an envoy to Ratisbon receives, regularly, half a dozen quarrels among the perquisites of his employment.

"You may be sure the ladies are not wanting, on

5

their side, in cherishing and improving these important *piques*, which divide the town almost into as many parties as there are families, and they choose rather to suffer the mortification of sitting almost alone on their assembly nights, than to recede one jot from their pretensions. I have not been here above a week, and yet I have heard from almost every one of them the whole history of their wrongs, and dreadful complaints of the injustice of their neighbours, in hopes to draw me to their party. But I think it very prudent to remain neuter, though, if I was to stay among them, there would be no possibility of continuing so, their quarrels running so high, they will not be civil to those that visit their adversaries. The foundation of these everlasting disputes turns entirely upon place, and the title of Excellency, which they all pretend to; and, what is very hard, will give it to nobody. For my part, I could not forbear advising them (for the public good) to give the title of Excellency to every body, which would include receiving it from every body; but the very mention of such a dishonourable peace was received with as much indignation as Mrs. Blackacre * did the notion of a reference; and I began to think myself ill-natured, to offer to take from them, in a town where there are so few diversions, so entertaining an amusement. I know that my peaceable disposition already gives me a very ill-figure, and that it is *publicly* whispered, as a piece of impertinent pride in me, that I have hitherto been saucily civil to everybody, as if I

* A litigious lady in Wycherley's comedy, "The Plain Dealer."

thought nobody good enough to quarrel with. I should
be obliged to change my behaviour if I did not intend
to pursue my journey in a few days."

From Ratisbon down the Danube to Vienna the
party travelled by boat; and what seems to have
struck Lady Mary most at Vienna was the custom of
occupying "flats" in the houses—a thing then unheard of in England.

"This town, which has the honour of being the
Emperor's residence, did not at all answer my ideas
of it, being much less than I expected to find it; the
streets are very close, and so narrow, one cannot
observe the fine fronts of the palaces, though many
of them very well deserve observation, being truly
magnificent, all built of fine white stone, and excessive
high, the town being so much too little for the number
of the people that desire to live in it, the builders seem
to have projected to repair that misfortune, by clapping
one town on the top of another, most of the houses
being of five, and some of them of six stories. You may
easily imagine, that the streets being so narrow, the
upper rooms are extremely dark; and, what is an
inconveniency much more intolerable, in my opinion,
there is no house that has so few as five or six families
in it. The apartments of the greatest ladies, and even
of the ministers of state, are divided but by a partition
from that of a tailor or a shoemaker; and I know nobody that has above two floors in any house, one for
their own use, and one higher for their servants. Those
that have houses of their own, let out the rest of them

5—2

to whoever will take them; thus the great stairs (which are all of stone) are as common and as dirty as the street. 'Tis true, when you have once travelled through them, nothing can be more surprisingly magnificent than the apartments. They are commonly a *suite* of eight or ten large rooms, all inlaid, the doors and windows richly carved and gilt, and the furniture such as is seldom seen in the palaces of sovereign princes in other countries—the hangings the finest tapestry of Brussels, prodigious large looking-glasses in silver frames, fine Japan tables, beds, chairs, canopies, and window curtains of the richest Genoa damask or velvet, almost covered with gold lace or embroidery. The whole made gay by pictures, and vast jars of Japan china, and almost in every room large lustres of rock crystal.

"I have already had the honour of being invited to dinner by several of the first people of quality; and I must do them the justice to say, the good taste and magnificence of their tables very well answers to that of their furniture. I have been more than once entertained with fifty dishes of meat, all served in silver, and well dressed; the dessert proportionable, served in the finest china. But the variety and richness of their wines is what appears the most surprising. The constant way is, to lay a list of their names upon the plates of the guests, along with the napkins; and I have counted several times to the number of eighteen different sorts, all exquisite in their kinds."

At Vienna she seems to have received a letter of

adoration from Pope, whose friendship for her was probably of very recent date. The poet protested that all his letters were " the most impartial representations of a free heart," a mere " thinking aloud." What affects to be the answer to this letter on Lady Mary's part passes over slightly the protestations of Pope, and goes on to give an account of the gaieties of Vienna—an account probably copied out of the Diary later on.

" I have so far wandered from the discipline of the Church of England to have been last Sunday at the opera, which was performed in the garden of the Favorita ; and I was so much pleased with it, I have not yet repented my seeing it. Nothing of that kind ever was more magnificent ; and I can easily believe what I am told, that the decorations and habits cost the Emperor thirty thousand pounds sterling. The stage was built over a very large canal, and, at the beginning of the second act, divided into two parts, discovering the water, on which there immediately came, from different parts, two fleets of little gilded vessels, that gave the representation of a naval fight. It is not easy to imagine the beauty of this scene, which I took particular notice of. But all the rest were perfectly fine in their kind. The story of the opera is the Enchantments of Alcina, which gives opportunity for a great variety of machines, and changes of the scene, which are performed with a surprising swiftness. The theatre is so large, that it is hard to carry the eye to the end of it ; and the habits in the utmost magnificence, to the number of one

hundred and eight. No house could hold such large
decorations; but the ladies all sitting in the open air,
exposes them to great inconveniences, for there is but
one canopy for the imperial family; and the first night
it was represented, a shower of rain happening, the
opera was broken off, and the company crowded away
in such confusion, I was almost squeezed to death."

As soon as her Court dress was ready, Lady Mary
went to call on the beautiful Elizabeth of Brunswick,
wife of the Emperor Charles VI.

" In order to that ceremony, I was squeezed up in a
gown, and adorned with a gorget and the other imple-
ments thereunto belonging : a dress very inconvenient,
but which certainly shows the neck and shape to great
advantage. I cannot forbear in this place giving you
some description of the fashions here, which are more
monstrous and contrary to all common sense and
reason than 'tis possible for you to imagine. They
build certain fabrics of gauze on their heads about a
yard high, consisting of three or four stories, fortified
with numberless yards of heavy ribbon. The foundation of this structure is a thing they call a *Bourle*, which
is exactly of the same shape and kind, but about four
times as big as those rolls our prudent milk-maids make
use of to fix their pails upon. This machine they
cover with their own hair, which they mix with a great
deal of false, it being a particular beauty to have their
heads too large to go into a moderate tub. Their hair
is prodigiously powdered, to conceal the mixture, and
set out with three or four rows of bodkins (wonderfully

large, that stick [out] two or three inches from their
hair), made of diamonds, pearls, red, green, and yellow
stones, that it certainly requires as much art and
experience to carry the load upright as to dance upon
May-day with the garland. Their whalebone petti-
coats outdo ours by several yards' circumference, and
cover some acres of ground.

"You may easily suppose how much this extraordinary dress sets off and improves the natural ugliness with which God Almighty has been pleased to
endow them all generally. Even the lovely Empress
herself is obliged to comply in some degree with these
absurd fashions, which they would not quit for all the
world. I had a private audience (according to ceremony) of half an hour, and then all the other ladies
were permitted to come [and] make their court. I was
perfectly charmed with the Empress: I cannot, however, tell you that her features are regular; her eyes
are not large, but have a lively look, full of sweetness;
her complexion the finest I ever saw; her nose and
forehead well made, but her mouth has ten thousand
charms that touch the soul. When she smiles, 'tis
with a beauty and sweetness that force adoration."

And so on, in a rather rapturous strain. Her comments on the course of love, true or otherwise, at
Vienna are, perhaps, more entertaining, though too
free in tone to quote at length. The passion for precedence seems to have been as great there as at
Ratisbon.

"Even their amours and their quarrels are carried

on with a surprising temper, and they are never lively
but upon points of ceremony. There, I own, they show
all their passions; and 'tis not long since two coaches,
meeting in a narrow street at night, the ladies in them
not being able to adjust the ceremonial of which should
go back, sat there with equal gallantry till two in the
morning, and were both so fully determined to die
upon the spot, rather than yield in a point of that importance, that the street would never have been cleared
till their deaths if the Emperor had not sent his guards
to part them; and even then they refused to stir, till
the expedient was found out of taking them both out in
chairs exactly at the same moment; after which it was
with some difficulty the *pas* was decided between the
two coachmen, no less tenacious of their rank than the
ladies."

The plan of Mr. Wortley Montagu's journey was
changed, and instead of going from Vienna to Leghorn
and thence by sea, he travelled to Hanover, to see
George I., and then returned to Vienna. The journey
through Prague to Dresden was not without its perils,
as the following extract shows:

"You may imagine how heartily I was tired with
twenty-four hours' post travelling, without sleep or
refreshment (for I can never sleep in a coach, however
fatigued). We passed by moonshine the frightful precipices that divide Bohemia from Saxony, at the bottom
of which runs the river Elbe; but I cannot say that I
had reason to fear drowning in it, being perfectly convinced that, in case of a tumble, it was utterly impos-

sible to come alive to the bottom. In many places the
road is so narrow that I could not discern an inch of
space between the wheels and the precipice. Yet I was
so good a wife not to wake Mr. W——, who was fast
asleep by my side, to make him share in my fears,
since the danger was unavoidable, till I perceived, by
the light of the moon, our postilions nodding on horseback, while the horses were on a full gallop, and I
thought it very convenient to call out to desire them to
look where they were going. My calling waked Mr.
W——, and he was much more surprised than myself
at the situation we were in, and assured me that he had
passed the Alps five times in different places without
ever having gone on a road so dangerous. I have been
told since it is common to find the bodies of travellers
in the Elbe; but, thank God, that was not our destiny;
and we came safe to Dresden, so much tired with fear
and fatigue it was not possible for me to compose myself to write."

One detail of this journey throws an interesting light
on the postal arrangements of the time. " I can assure
you the pacquet at Prague was tied behind my chaise,
and in that manner conveyed to Dresden. The secrets
of half the country were at my mercy, if I had had
any curiosity for them."

Hanover was crowded with the Court of George I.,
whose new greatness as King of England was over-
large for the Electoral capital. The German beauties
seem to have been somewhat monotonous.

" All the women have literally rosy cheeks, snowy

foreheads and bosoms, jet eye-brows, and scarlet lips, to which they generally add coal-black hair. These perfections never leave them till the hour of their deaths, and have a very fine effect by candle-light ; but I could wish they were handsome with a little more variety. They resemble one another as much as Mrs. Salmon's Court of Great Britain,* and are in as much danger of melting away by too near approaching the fire, which they for that reason carefully avoid, though it is now such excessive cold weather that I believe they suffer extremely by that piece of self-denial."

The German stoves particularly charmed Lady Mary, and she was resolved to introduce them into England on her return.

" I was particularly surprised at the vast number of orange trees, much larger than I have ever seen in England, though this climate is certainly colder. But I had more reason to wonder that night at the King's table. There was brought to him from a gentleman of this country, two large baskets full of ripe oranges and lemons of different sorts, many of which were quite new to me ; and, what I thought worth all the rest, two ripe ananas, which, to my taste, are a fruit perfectly delicious· You know they are naturally the growth of Brazil, and I could not imagine how they could come there but by enchantment. Upon enquiry, I learnt that they have brought their stoves to such perfection, they lengthen the summer as long as they please, giving to every plant the degree of heat it would receive from the sun in its

* The Madame Tussaud's of the period.

native soil. The effect is very near the same; I am surprised we do not practise in England so useful an invention.

"This reflection naturally leads me to consider our obstinacy in shaking with cold six months in the year, rather than make use of stoves, which are certainly one of the greatest conveniences of life; and so far from spoiling the form of a room, they add very much to the magnificence of it, when they are painted and gilt, as at Vienna, or at Dresden, where they are often in the shape of china jars, statues, or fine cabinets, so naturally represented, they are not to be distinguished."

From Hanover, instead of returning to England, as her friends hoped, Lady Mary accompanied her husband to Vienna. "Is Eurydice once more snatched to the shades?" mourned Pope. "If ever mortal had reason to hate the King it is I; for it is my particular misfortune to be almost the only innocent man whom he has made to suffer, both by his government at home and his negotiations abroad"—Pope being subject to disabilities as a Roman Catholic, and robbed of his friend by the mission to Constantinople. The Embassy reached Vienna at the end of 1716, and Mr. Wortley Montagu determined to lose no time, but proceed through Hungary. The Danube being frozen, the journey had to be made by land, and the great Prince Eugene of Savoy and all Lady Mary's other friends charged her earnestly not to set out till spring; but she was determined to go. The journey proved far less terrible than was anticipated, and the account of it is

therefore uninteresting, being a collection of historical
notes and descriptions too much savouring of a guide-
book. Hungary at that time was an unknown wilder-
ness to English people, and such details were new.
Some of the descriptions, however, may be still of
interest :

"The few people that inhabit Hungary live easily
enough ; they have no money, but the woods and
plains afford them provision in great abundance : they
were ordered to give us all things necessary, even what
horses we pleased to demand, *gratis;* but Mr. W——
[Wortley] would not oppress the poor country people
by making use of this order, and always paid them the
full worth of what we had from them. They were so
surprised at this unexpected generosity, which they are
very little used to, they always pressed upon us, at
parting, a dozen of fat pheasants, or something of that
sort, for a present. Their dress is very primitive, being
only a plain sheep's skin, without other dressing than
being dried in the sun, and a cap and boots of the same
stuff. You may imagine this lasts them for many winters;
and thus they have very little occasion for money."

After some delay at Peterwaradein, occupied in
arranging for the reception of the Embassy by the
Turks, the Ambassador and his train arrived at Belgrade, then held by the Turks, though next year it was
captured by Prince Eugene, after the greatest of his
victories. At Belgrade Lady Mary fell in with one of
those Europeanized modern Turks who have become
more common since.

" My only diversion is the conversation of our host, Achmet Beg, a title something like that of Count in Germany. His father was a great Pasha, and he has been educated in the most polite Eastern learning, being perfectly skilled in the Arabic and Persian languages, and is an extraordinary scribe, which they call *effendi*. This accomplishment makes way to the greatest preferments ; but he has had the good sense to prefer an easy, quiet, secure life, to all the dangerous honours of the Porte. He sups with us every night, and drinks wine very freely. You cannot imagine how much he is delighted with the liberty of conversing with me. He has explained to me many pieces of Arabian poetry, which, I observed, are in numbers not unlike ours, generally alternate verse, and of a very musical sound. Their expressions of love are very passionate and lively. I am so much pleased with them, I really believe I should learn to read Arabic if I was to stay here a few months. He has a very good library of their books of all kinds ; and, as he tells me, spends the greatest part of his life there. I pass for a great scholar with him, by relating to him some of the Persian tales, which I find are genuine.* At first he believed I understood Persian. I have frequent disputes with him concerning the difference of our customs, particularly the confinement of women. He assures me there is nothing at all in it ; only, says he, we have the advantage, that when our wives cheat us nobody knows it. He has wit, and is more polite than many Christian men of quality. I

* Translated by Petit de la Croix.

am very much entertained with him. He has had the
curiosity to make one of our servants set him an
alphabet of our letters, and can already write a good
Roman hand."

After awaiting orders some time at Belgrade, the
Embassy moved on by Nish, Sofia, and Philippopolis
to Adrianople, a country, as it seemed to Lady Mary,
"the finest in the world." "But this climate," so she
writes in a rather stiff letter to Princess Caroline, "as
happy as it seems, can never be preferred to England,
with all its snows and frosts, while we are blessed with
an easy government, under a King who makes his own
happiness consist in the liberty of his people, and
chooses rather to be looked upon as their father than
as their master." Perhaps Lady Mary expected this
letter to be opened in the post; for we may imagine
that this was hardly her private opinion of George I.,
still less the opinion of his daughter-in-law.

Somewhat curious is Lady Mary's first experience of
a Turkish bath, sent ostensibly to a lady unnamed:

"I won't trouble you with a relation of our tedious
journey; but I must not omit what I saw remarkable
at Sophia, one of the most beautiful towns in the
Turkish empire, and famous for its hot baths, that are
resorted to both for diversion and health. I stopped
here one day on purpose to see them. Designing to go
incognita, I hired a Turkish coach. These voitures are
not at all like ours, but much more convenient for the
country, the heat being so great that glasses would be
very troublesome. They are made a good deal in the

manner of the Dutch coaches, having wooden lattices
painted and gilded; the inside being painted with
baskets and nosegays of flowers, intermixed commonly
with little poetical mottoes. They are covered all over
with scarlet cloth, lined with silk, and very often richly
embroidered and fringed. This covering entirely hides
the persons in them, but may be thrown back at
pleasure, and the ladies peep through the lattices.
They hold four people very conveniently, seated on
cushions, but not raised.

"In one of these covered waggons, I went to the
bagnio about ten o'clock. It was already full of women.
It is built of stone, in the shape of a dome, with no
windows but in the roof, which gives light enough.
There were five of these domes joined together, the
outmost being less than the rest, and serving only as a
hall, where the portress stood at the door. Ladies of
quality generally give this woman the value of a crown
or ten shillings; and I did not forget that ceremony.
The next room is a very large one paved with marble,
and all round it, raised, two sofas of marble, one above
another. There were four fountains of cold water in
this room, falling first into marble basins, and then
running on the floor in little channels made for that
purpose, which carried the streams into the next room,
something less than this, with the same sort of marble
sofas, but so hot with steams of sulphur proceeding
from the baths joining to it, it was impossible to stay
there with one's clothes on. The two other domes were
the hot baths, one of which had cocks of cold water

turning into it, to temper it to what degree of warmth the bathers have a mind to.

"I was in my travelling habit, which is a riding dress, and certainly appeared very extraordinary to them. Yet there was not one of them who showed the least surprise or impertinent curiosity, but received me with all the obliging civility possible. I know no European Court where the ladies would have behaved themselves in so polite a manner to a stranger. I believe, in the whole, there were two hundred women, and yet none of those disdainful smiles, or satiric whispers, that never fail in our assemblies when anybody appears that is not exactly in the fashion. They repeated over and over to me, ' Uzelle, pék uzelle,' which is nothing but ' Charming, very charming.' The first sofas were covered with cushions and rich carpets, on which sat the ladies; and on the second, their slaves behind them. There were many amongst them as exactly proportioned as ever any goddess was drawn by the pencil of Guido or Titian — and most of their skins shiningly white, only adorned by their beautiful hair divided into many tresses, hanging on their shoulders, braided either with pearl or ribbon, perfectly representing the figures of the Graces.

"Some were in conversation, some working, others drinking coffee or sherbet, and many negligently lying on their cushions, while their slaves (generally pretty girls of seventeen or eighteen) were employed in braiding their hair in several pretty fancies. In short, it is the women's coffee-house, where all the news of the town is told, scandal invented, etc. They generally take this diversion once a-week, and stay there at least four or five hours, without getting cold by immediate coming out of the hot bath into the cold room, which was very surprising to me."

Lady Mary saw the Sultan. Achmet III., at Adrianople, where he was residing in the spring of 1717.

"I went yesterday with the French Embassadress* to see the Grand Signior† in his passage to the mosque. He was preceded by a numerous guard of janissaries, with vast white feathers on their heads, *spahis* and *bostangees* (these are foot and horse guard), and the royal gardeners, which are a very considerable body of men, dressed in different habits of fine lively colours, that, at a distance, they appeared like a parterre of tulips. After them the aga of the janissaries, in a robe of purple velvet, lined with silver tissue, his horse led by two slaves richly dressed. Next him the *kyzlár-aga* (your ladyship knows this is the chief guardian of the seraglio ladies) in a deep yellow cloth (which suited very well to his black face) lined with sables, and last his Sublimity himself, in green lined with the fur of a black Muscovite fox, which is supposed worth a thousand pounds sterling, mounted on a fine horse, with furniture embroidered with jewels. Six more horses richly furnished were led after him; and two of his principal courtiers bore, one his gold, and the other his silver coffee-pot, on a staff; another carried a silver stool on his head for him to sit on.

* Madame de Bonnac.　　　† Sultan Achmet III.

6

" It would be too tedious to tell your ladyship the
various dresses and turbans by which their rank is distinguished ; but they were all extremely rich and gay, to
the number of some thousands ; [so] that, perhaps,
there cannot be seen a more beautiful procession. The
Sultan appeared to us a handsome man of about forty,
with a very graceful air, but something severe in his
countenance, his eyes very full and black. He happened to stop under the window where we stood, and
(I suppose being told who we were) looked upon us very
attentively, [so] that we had full leisure to consider him,
and the French Embassadress agreed with me as to his
good mien : I see that lady very often ; she is young,
and her conversation would be a great relief to me, if I
could persuade her to live without those forms and
ceremonies that make life formal and tiresome. But
she is so delighted with her guards, her four-and-twenty
footmen, gentlemen ushers, etc., that she would rather
die than make me a visit without them : not to reckon a
coachful of attending damsels yclep'd maids of honour.
What vexes me is, that as long as she will visit with a
troublesome equipage, I am obliged to do the same :
however, our mutual interest makes us much together.

" I went with her the other day all round the town,
in an open gilt chariot, with our joint train of attendants, preceded by our guards, who might have sum-
moned the people to see what they had never seen, nor
ever would see again—two young Christian embassa-
dresses never yet having been in this country at the
same time, nor I believe ever will again. Your lady-

ship may easily imagine that we drew a vast crowd of
spectators, but all silent as death. If any of them had
taken the liberties of our mob upon any strange sight,
our janissaries had made no scruple of falling on them
with their scimitars, without danger for so doing, being
above law. Yet these people have some good qualities ; they are very zealous and faithful where they
serve, and look upon it as their business to fight for
you upon all occasions. Of this I had a very pleasant
instance in a village on this side Philippopolis, where we
were met by our domestic guard. I happened to
bespeak pigeons for my supper, upon which one of my
janissaries went immediately to the cadi (the chief civil
officer of the town), and ordered him to send in some
dozens. The poor man answered, that he had already
sent about, but could get none. My janissary, in the
height of his zeal for my service, immediately locked
him up prisoner in his room, telling him he deserved
death for his impudence, in offering to excuse his not
obeying my command ; but, out of respect to me, he
would not punish him but by my order, and accordingly, came very gravely to me, to ask what should be
done to him ; adding, by way of compliment, that if I
pleased he would bring me his head.—This may give
you some idea of the unlimited power of these fellows,
who are all sworn brothers, and bound to revenge the
injuries done to one another, whether at Cairo, Aleppo,
or any part of the world ; and this inviolable league
makes them so powerful, the greatest man at the Court
never speaks to them but in a flattering tone ; and in

Asia, any man that is rich is forced to enrol himself a janissary, to secure his estate."

At Adrianople she also adopted the Turkish dress, which she described to her sister at length, from slippers to aigrette.

Her classical recollections were awakened by the pastoral simplicity and Greek customs of the country.

" I am at this present writing in a house situated on the banks of the Hebrus, which runs under my chamber window. My garden is full of tall cypress-trees, upon the branches of which several couple of true turtles are saying soft things to one another from morning to night. How naturally do boughs and vows come into my head at this minute! and must not you confess, to my praise, that 'tis more than ordinary discretion that can resist the wicked suggestions of poetry, in a place where truth, for once, furnishes all the ideas of pastoral? The summer is already far advanced in this part of the world; and, for some miles round Adrianople, the whole ground is laid out in gardens, and the banks of the river set with rows of fruit-trees, under which all the most considerable Turks divert themselves every evening; not with walking, that is not one of their pleasures, but a set party of them choose out a green spot, where the shade is very thick, and there they spread a carpet, on which they sit drinking their coffee, and generally attended by some slave with a fine voice, or that plays on some instrument. Every twenty paces you may see one of these little companies listening to the dashing of the river ; and this taste is so universal, that the very gardeners are not without it. I have often seen them and their children sitting on the banks, and playing on a rural instrument, perfectly answering the description of the ancient *fistula*, being composed of unequal reeds with a simple but agreeable softness in the sound."

This extract is from a letter supposed to be written to Pope ; and as his translation of the " Iliad " was now appearing, his correspondent must, of course, refer to those Greek poets of whom her knowledge was but slight—as appears by her reference to Theocritus, in which she seems to forget that the pastoral life he de- scribed was that of Sicily.

" I no longer look upon Theocritus as a romantic writer ; he has only given a plain image of the way of life amongst the peasants of his country ; who, before oppression had reduced them to want, were, I suppose, all employed as the better sort of them are now. I don't doubt, had he been born a Briton, his *Idylliums* had been filled with descriptions of threshing and churning, both which are unknown here, the corn being all trod out by oxen ; and butter (I speak it with sorrow) unheard of.

" I read over your Homer here with an infinite pleasure, and find several little passages explained, that I did not before entirely comprehend the beauty of ; many of the customs, and much of the dress then in fashion, being yet retained, and I don't wonder to find more remains here of an age so distant, than is to be found in any other country, the Turks not taking that pains to introduce their own manners as has been generally practised by other nations, that imagine themselves more polite. It would be too tedious to you to point out all the passages that relate to the present customs. But I can assure you that the princesses and great ladies pass their time at their looms, embroidering veils and robes, surrounded by their maids, which are always very numerous, in the same manner as we find Andromache and Helen described. The description of the belt of Menelaus exactly resembles those that are now worn by the great men, fastened before with broad golden clasps, and embroidered round with rich work. The snowy veil that Helen throws over her face is still fashionable; and I never see (as I do very often) half a dozen of old pashas with their reverend beards, sitting basking in the sun, but I recollect good King Priam and his counsellors. Their manner of dancing is certainly the same that Diana is sung to have danced on the banks of the Eurotas. The great lady still leads the dance, and is followed by a troop of young girls, who imitate her steps, and, if she sings, make up the chorus. The tunes are extremely gay and lively, yet with something in them wonderfully soft. The steps are varied according to the pleasure of her that leads the dance, but always in exact time, and infinitely more agreeable than any of our dances, at least in my opinion. I sometimes make one in the train, but am not skilful enough to lead; these are Grecian dances, the Turkish being very different."

It is in a letter from Adrianople, dated like the rest,

April 1, 1717 (old style), Lady Mary gives an account
of the process of inoculation for the small-pox, which
she afterwards introduced into England. She calls the
practice "ingrafting."

"*A propos* of distempers, I am going to tell you a
thing that I am sure will make you wish yourself here.
The small-pox, so fatal, and so general amongst us, is
here entirely harmless by the invention of *ingrafting*,
which is the term they give it. There is a set of old
women who make it their business to perform the
operation every autumn, in the month of September,
when the great heat is abated. People send to one
another to know if any of their family has a mind to
have the small-pox : they make parties for this purpose,
and when they are met (commonly fifteen or sixteen
together), the old woman comes with a nut-shell full of
the matter of the best sort of small-pox, and asks what
veins you please to have opened. She immediately
rips open that you offer to her with a large needle
(which gives you no more pain than a common scratch),
and puts into the vein as much venom as can lie upon
the head of her needle, and after binds up the little
wound with a hollow bit of shell ; and in this manner
opens four or five veins. The Grecians have commonly the superstition of opening one in the middle of
the forehead, in each arm, and on the breast, to mark
the sign of the cross ; but this has a very ill effect, all
these wounds leaving little scars, and is not done by
those that are not superstitious, who choose to have
them in the legs, or that part of the arm that is con-

cealed.   The children or young patients play together
all the rest of the day, and are in perfect health to the
eighth.   Then the fever begins to seize them, and they
keep their beds two days, very seldom three.   They
have very rarely above twenty or thirty in their faces,
which never mark; and in eight days' time they are as
well as before their illness.   Where they are wounded,
there remain running sores during the distemper, which
I don't doubt is a great relief to it.   Every year thousands undergo this operation : and the French Embas-
sador says pleasantly, that they take the small-pox here
by way of diversion, as they take the waters in other
countries."

If Lady Louisa Stuart's account of the grudging
reception of inoculation by the medical profession is
correct, Lady Mary's letter was indeed prophetic.

" I am patriot enough to take pains to bring this
useful invention into fashion in England ; and I should
not fail to write to some of our doctors very particularly
about it, if I knew any one of them that I thought had
virtue enough to destroy such a considerable branch of
their revenue for the good of mankind.   But that distemper is too beneficial to them not to expose to all
their resentment the hardy wight that should undertake to put an end to it.   Perhaps, if I live to return,
I may, however, have courage to war with them."

While Mr. Wortley Montagu was negotiating with
the Grand Vizier, Azem, and telling the Turks " plain
truths," his wife paid visits to the great Turkish ladies,
not, indeed, being admitted to the harem of the Grand

Signior, though more or less scandalous rumours afterwards asserted that she had enjoyed that privilege.
But she visited the wife of the Grand Vizier and also
the fair Fatima, wife of the " Kiyáya," or deputy of the
Vizier.   With the latter lady she was quite enraptured.
" I was met at the door by two black eunuchs, who led
me through a long gallery between two ranks of
beautiful young girls, with their hair finely plaited,
almost hanging to their feet, all dressed in fine light
damasks, brocaded with silver.   I was sorry that
decency did not permit me to stop to consider them
nearer.   But that thought was lost upon my entrance
into a large room, or rather pavilion, built round with
gilded sashes, which were most of them thrown up,
and the trees planted near them gave an agreeable
shade, which hindered the sun from being troublesome.
The jessamines and honeysuckles that twisted round
their trunks, shedding a soft perfume, increased by a
white marble fountain playing sweet water in the lower
part of the room, which fell into three or four basins
with a pleasing sound.   The roof was painted with all
sort of flowers, falling out of gilded baskets, that seemed
tumbling down.   On a sofa, raised three steps, and
covered with fine Persian carpets, sat the Kiyáya's lady,
leaning on cushions of white satin, embroidered ; and
at her feet sat two young girls, the eldest about twelve
years old, lovely as angels, dressed perfectly rich, and
almost covered with jewels.   But they were hardly
seen near the fair Fatima (for that is her name), so
much her beauty effaced everything.   I have seen all

that has been called lovely either in England or
Germany, and must own that I never saw anything so
gloriously beautiful, nor can I recollect a face that
would have been taken notice of near hers. She stood
up to receive me, saluting me after their fashion,
putting her hand upon her heart with a sweetness full
of majesty, that no Court breeding could ever give.
She ordered cushions to be given to me, and took care
to place me in the corner, which is the place of honour.
I confess, though the Greek lady had before given me
a great opinion of her beauty, I was so struck with
admiration, that I could not for some time speak to
her, being wholly taken up in gazing. That surprising
harmony of features! that charming result of the
whole! that exact proportion of body! that lovely
bloom of complexion unsullied by art! the unutterable
enchantment of her smile! But her eyes!—large and
black, with all the soft languishment of the blue! every
turn of her face discovering some new charm."

The Sultan soon moved his camp from Adrianople,
in readiness for the campaign of 1717; but before
moving there was a procession of the tradesmen of
Adrianople, who were forced by custom to make a
present to the Sultan when he took the field in person.
The description purports to be written to the Abbé
Conti, an Italian man of letters, whose acquaintance
Lady Mary had made in England.

"I took the pains of rising at six in the morning to
see that ceremony, which did not, however, begin till
eight. The Grand Signior was at the seraglio window,

to see the procession, which passed through all the
principal streets.   It was preceded by an *effendi*
mounted on a camel, richly furnished, reading aloud
the Alcoran, finely bound, laid upon a cushion.   He
was surrounded by a parcel of boys, in white, singing
some verses of it, followed by a man dressed in green
boughs, representing a clean husbandman sowing seed.
After him several reapers, with garlands of ears of corn,
as Ceres is pictured, with scythes in their hands,
seeming to mow.   Then a little machine drawn by
oxen, in which was a windmill, and boys employed in
grinding corn, followed by another machine, drawn by
buffaloes, carrying an oven, and two more boys, one
employed in kneading the bread, and another in drawing it out of the oven.   These boys threw little cakes
on both sides among the crowd, and were followed by
the whole company of bakers, marching on foot, two
and two, in their best clothes, with cakes, loaves,
pasties, and pies of all sorts on their heads, and after
them two buffoons, or jack-puddings, with their faces
and clothes smeared with meal, who diverted the mob
with their antic gestures.   In the same manner followed
all the companies of trade in their empire ; the nobler
sort, such as jewellers, mercers, etc., finely mounted,
and many of the pageants that represented their trades
perfectly magnificent ; among which the furriers' made
one of the great figures, being a very large machine,
set round with the skins of ermines, foxes, etc., so well
stuffed, the animals seemed to be alive, followed by
music and dancers.   I believe they were, upon the

whole, at least twenty thousand men, all ready to follow his highness if he commanded them. The rear was closed by the volunteers, who came to beg the honour of dying in his service. This part of the show seemed to me so barbarous, I removed from the window upon the first appearance of it. They were all naked to the middle. Some had their arms pierced through with arrows, left sticking in them. Others had them sticking in their heads, the blood trickling down their faces, and some slashed their arms with sharp knives, making the blood spout out upon those that stood near ; and this is looked upon as an expression of their zeal for glory. I am told that some make use of it to advance their love ; and, when they are near the window where their mistress stands (all the women in town being veiled to see this spectacle), they stick another arrow for her sake, who gives some sign of approbation and encouragement to this gallantry. The whole show lasted near eight hours, to my great sorrow, who was heartily tired, though I was in the house of the widow of the Capitain-pasha (Admiral), who refreshed me with coffee, sweetmeats, sherbet, etc., with all possible civility."

When the camp moved from Adrianople, the Embassy went on to Constantinople, where Lady Mary was lodged in the ambassadorial palace at Pera. She was eager to investigate not only the manners and customs of the day, but all antiquities she could find, but without much help from local antiquaries.

" I have already made some progress in a collection

of Greek medals. Here are several professed antiquaries who are ready to serve any body that desires
them. But you cannot imagine how they stare in my
face when I inquire about them, as if nobody was permitted to seek after medals till they were grown a
piece of antiquity themselves. I have got some very
valuable of the Macedonian kings, particularly one of
Perseus, so lively, I fancy I can see all his ill qualities
in his face. I have a porphyry head, finely cut, of the
true Greek sculpture, but who it represents is to be
guessed at by the learned when I return. For you are
not to suppose these antiquaries, who are all Greeks,
know anything. Their trade is only to sell. They
have correspondents at Aleppo, Grand Cairo, in
Arabia and Palestine, who send them all they can
find, and very often great heaps that are only fit to
melt into pans and kettles. They get the best price
they can for any of them, without knowing those that
are valuable from those that are not. Those that
pretend to skill generally find out the image of some
saint in the medals of the Greek cities. One of them,
showing me the figure of a Pallas, with a victory in
her hand on a reverse, assured me it was the Virgin
holding a crucifix. The same man offered me the
head of a Socrates on a sardonyx, and, to enhance
the value, gave him the title of St. Augustin."

When the summer heats set in, Lady Mary retired
to the village of Belgrade, near Constantinople; as
she writes to Pope:

"The heats of Constantinople have driven me to

this place, which perfectly answers the description of the Elysian fields. I am in the middle of a wood, consisting chiefly of fruit-trees, watered by a vast number of fountains, famous for the excellency of their water, and divided into many shady walks upon short grass that seems to be artificial, but, I am assured, is the pure work of nature; within view of the Black Sea, from whence we perpetually enjoy the refreshment of cool breezes, that make us insensible of the heat of the summer. The village is only inhabited by the richest amongst the Christians, who meet every night at a fountain forty paces from my house to sing and dance, the beauty and dress of the women exactly resembling the ideas of the ancient nymphs as they are given us by the representations of the poets and painters. But what persuades me more fully of my decease is the situation of my own mind, the profound ignorance I am in of what passes among the living (which only comes to me by chance), and the great calmness with which I receive it. Yet I have still a hankering after my friends and acquaintance left in the world, according to the authority of that admirable author:

> " 'That spirits departed are wondrous kind
> To friends and relations left behind :
> Which nobody can deny '

—of which solemn truth I am a *dead* instance. I think Virgil is of the same opinion, that in human souls there will still be some remains of human passions:

> " '—— Curæ non ipsâ in morte relinquunt.'

And 'tis very necessary, to make a perfect Elysium, that there should be a river Lethe, which I am not so happy to find."

Some of Lady Mary's English correspondents were rather exacting in their commissions to her, and had a wide and vague idea of the resources of the East. Pope's request for a Circassian beauty with every possible accomplishment was not meant to be taken seriously; but some other friend seems to have asked for a Greek slave, which gave occasion for a dissertation on the position of the rayahs. The "balm of Mecca" was also much in demand for the complexion, though Lady Mary tried it on her own face with disastrous results.

In wandering about Constantinople in Turkish dress, in antiquarian research or Oriental study, the year 1717 passed away pleasantly. The terrors of an English winter were unknown at Pera.

"The climate is delightful in the extremest degree. I am now sitting, this present fourth of January, with the windows open, enjoying the warm shine of the sun, while you are freezing over a sad sea-coal fire, and my chamber set out with carnations, roses and jonquils fresh from my garden. I am also charmed with many points of the Turkish law, to our shame be it spoken, better designed and better executed than ours, particularly the punishment of convicted liars (triumphant criminals in our country, God knows): they are burnt in the forehead with a hot iron, being proved the authors of any notorious falsehood. How many white

foreheads should we see disfigured, how many fine
gentlemen would be forced to wear their wigs as low
as their eyebrows, were this law in practice with us !"

Early in 1718 was born Lady Mary's daughter
Mary, afterwards Countess of Bute. By this time
her husband must have been preparing to depart soon,
as he had received an intimation of his recall from
his friend Addison in the autumn of 1717. His delay
at Constantinople till his successor should arrive gave
Lady Mary the opportunity of renewing her acquaintance with the fair Fatima, and of calling on the
Sultana Hafitén, favourite of the late Sultan, whose
dress and diamonds defied valuation.

These visits gave her an opinion of the position of
Turkish women far different from that stated by most
travellers of the time :

" 'Tis very pleasant to observe how tenderly all the
voyage-writers lament the miserable confinement of the
Turkish ladies, who are perhaps freer than any ladies in
the universe, and are the only women in the world that
lead a life of uninterrupted pleasure exempt from cares;
their whole time being spent in visiting, bathing, or the
agreeable amusement of spending money, and inventing
new fashions. A husband would be thought mad that
exacted any degree of economy from his wife, whose
expenses are no way limited but by her own fancy. 'Tis
his business to get money, and hers to spend it : and
this noble prerogative extends itself to the very meanest
of the sex. Here is a fellow that carries embroidered
handkerchiefs upon his back to sell, as miserable a

figure as you may suppose such a mean dealer, yet I'll
assure you his wife scorns to wear anything less than
cloth of gold; has her ermine furs, and a very handsome set of jewels for her head. They go abroad when
and where they please. 'Tis true they have no public
places but the bagnios, and there can only be seen by
their own sex; however, that is a diversion they take
great pleasure in."

The seraglio, however, she did not enter, though
she gleaned what particulars she could from her
Turkish friends. "I have taken care," she writes to
her friend the Countess of Bristol, "to see as much
of the seraglio as is to be seen. It is on a point of
land running into the sea—a palace of prodigious
extent, but very irregular. The gardens [take in] a
large compass of ground, full of high cypress-trees,
which is all I know of them; the buildings all of white
stone, leaded on top, with gilded turrets and spires,
which look very magnificent; and, indeed, I believe
there is no Christian king's palace half so large."

Other palaces, however, of almost as great magnificence as the Sultan's, Lady Mary was admitted to see,
as the following description proves:

"Human grandeur being here yet more unstable
than anywhere else, 'tis common for the heirs of a
great three-tailed pasha not to be rich enough to keep
in repair the house he built; thus, in a few years, they
all fall to ruin. I was yesterday to see that of the late
Grand Vizier, who was killed at Peterwaradein. It was
built to receive his royal bride, daughter of the present

Sultan, but he did not live to see her there. I have a great mind to describe it to you; but I check that inclination, knowing very well that I cannot give you, with my best description, such an idea of it as I ought. It is situated on one of the most delightful parts of the canal, with a fine wood on the side of a hill behind it. The extent of it is prodigious; the guardian assured me there are eight hundred rooms in it; I will not answer for that number, since I did not count them; but 'tis certain the number is very large, and the whole adorned with a profusion of marble, gilding, and the most exquisite painting of fruit and flowers. The windows are all sashed with the finest crystalline glass brought from England; and all the expensive magnificence that you can suppose in a palace founded by a vain young luxurious man, with the wealth of a vast empire at his command. But no part of it pleased me better than the apartments destined for the bagnios. There are two built exactly in the same manner, answering to one another; the baths, fountains, and pavements, all of white marble, the roofs gilt, and the walls covered with Japan china; but adjoining to them, two rooms, the upper part of which is divided into a sofa; in the four corners falls of water from the very roof, from shell to shell of white marble, to the lower end of the room, where it falls into a large basin, surrounded with pipes, that throw up the water as high as the room. The walls are in the nature of lattices; and, on the outside of them, vines and woodbines planted, that form a sort of green tapestry, and give an agreeable obscurity to these delightful chambers.

" I should go on and let you into some of the other apartments (all worthy your curiosity) ; but, 'tis yet harder to describe a Turkish palace than any other, being built entirely irregular.   There is nothing can be properly called front or wings ; and though such a confusion is, I think, pleasing to the sight, yet it would be very unintelligible in a letter.   I shall only add, that the chamber destined for the Sultan, when he visits his daughter, is wainscoted with mother-of-pearl fastened with emeralds like nails.   There are others of mother-of-pearl and olive wood inlaid, and several of Japan china.   The galleries, which are numerous and very large, are adorned with jars of flowers, and porcelain dishes of fruit of all sorts, so well done in plaster, and coloured in so lively a manner, that it has an enchanting effect.   The garden is suitable to the house, where arbours, fountains, and walks, are thrown together in an agreeable confusion.   There is no ornament wanting, except that of statues.   Thus, you see, sir, these people are not so unpolished as we represent them. 'Tis true their magnificence is of a different taste from ours, and perhaps of a better.   I am almost of opinion they have a right notion of life ; while they consume it in music, gardens, wine, and delicate eating, we are tormenting our brains with some scheme of politics, or studying some science to which we can never attain, or, if we do, cannot persuade people to set that value upon it we do ourselves."

In such rambles round Constantinople the time passed till the *Preston* man-of-war came to take the

Ambassador away. On June 6/17, 1718, according
to the MS. book of letters—on July 4/11, according
to the more trustworthy announcement of Mr. Stanyan,
the new Ambassador—Lady Mary and her husband
and family sailed from Constantinople. They put in
at Sigæum, where Lady Mary copied the inscription
of the Sigæan tomb for her husband; "but the
Greek is too ancient for Mr. W.'s interpretation."

The long letter giving an account of the journey is
a sort of "Childe Harold" in prose, and full as wearisome. The vessel called at Tunis, and landed the
passengers at Genoa August 15/26. Thence the journey
followed the usual route, through Turin, and over the
Mont Cenis into France. Lady Mary called on the
wife of Victor Amadeus, the adventurous prince who
first grasped the royal title for Savoy. The Queen of
Sicily—as her style then ran—"entertained me with
a world of sweetness and affability, and seemed mistress of a great share of good sense. . . . I returned
her civility by giving her the title of majesty as often
as I could, which, perhaps, she will not have the
comfort of hearing many months longer." Alberoni's
plans for recovering the provinces taken from Spain
at Utrecht were having effect, and the Spanish forces
were now conquering Sicily; but the royal title was
not lost to the House of Savoy, though they had to
take poor Sardinia in exchange for rich Sicily. The
journey over Mont Cenis was not especially pleasant,
though a certain appreciation of Alpine scenery is
shown in the letter recounting it.

"The prodigious prospect of mountains covered with eternal snow, clouds hanging far below our feet, and the vast cascades tumbling down the rocks with a confused roaring, would have been solemnly entertaining to me if I had suffered less from the extreme cold that reigns here; but the misty rain which falls perpetually penetrated even the thick fur I was wrapped in; and I was half dead with cold before we got to the foot of the mountain, which was not till two hours after 'twas dark. This hill has a spacious plain on the top of it, and a fine lake there; but the descent is so steep and slippery, 'tis surprising to see these chairmen go so steadily as they do. Yet I was not half so much afraid of breaking my neck, as I was of falling sick; and the event has shewed that I placed my fears in the right place."

For the fatigue of travelling brought on a serious fever at Lyons; though, in spite of the doctors, Lady Mary pushed on as soon as possible to Paris.

"The air of Paris has already had a good effect on me; for I was never in better health, though I have been extremely ill all the road from Lyons to this place. You may judge how agreeable the journey has been to me; which did not need that addition to make me dislike it. I think nothing so terrible as objects of misery, except one had the God-like attribute of being capable to redress them; and all the country villages of France shew nothing else. While the post-horses are changed, the whole town comes out to beg, with such miserable starved faces, and thin tattered clothes, they need no other eloquence to persuade [one of] the wretchedness of their condition. This is all the French magnificence till you come to Fontainebleau. There you begin to think the kingdom rich when you are shewed one thousand five hundred rooms in the King's hunting-palace."

In Paris Lady Mary met her sister, the Countess of Mar, who now lived there for the most part with her exiled husband. Then in October, 1718, she crossed over to England, after a last peril in the packet.

" I arrived this morning at Dover, after being tossed a whole night in the packet-boat, in so violent a manner, that the master, considering the weakness of his vessel, thought it prudent to remove the mail, and gave us notice of the danger. We called a little fisher boat, which could hardly make up to us; while all the people on board us were crying to Heaven ; and 'tis hard to imagine one's self in a scene of greater horror than on such an occasion; and yet, shall I own it to you ? though I was not at all willing to be drowned, I could not forbear being entertained at the double distress of a fellow-passenger. She was an English lady that I had met at Calais, who desired me to let her go over with me in my cabin. She had bought a fine point head, which she was contriving to conceal from the custom-house officers. When the wind grew high, and our little vessel cracked, she fell very heartily to her prayers, and thought wholly of her soul. When it seemed to abate, she returned to the worldly care of her head-dress, and addressed herself to me: 'Dear madam, will you take care of this point? if it should be lost!——Ah, Lord, we shall all be lost!——Lord have mercy on my soul!---Pray, madam, take care of this head-dress.' This easy transition of her soul to her head-dress, and the alternate agonies that both gave her, made it hard to determine which she thought of greatest value. But, however, the scene was not so diverting but I was glad to get rid of it, and be thrown into the little boat, though with some hazard of breaking my neck. It brought me safe hither; and I cannot help looking with partial eyes on my native land. That partiality was certainly given us by nature, to prevent rambling, the effect of an ambitious thirst after knowledge, which we are not formed to enjoy. All we get by it is a fruitless desire of mixing the different pleasures and conveniences which are given to different parts of the world, and cannot meet in any one of them. After having read all that is to be found in the languages I am mistress of, and having decayed my sight by midnight studies, I envy the easy peace of mind of a ruddy milkmaid, who, undisturbed by doubt, hears the sermon with humility every Sunday, having not confused the sentiments of natural duty in her head by the vain enquiries of the schools, who may be more learned, yet, after all, must remain as ignorant. And, after having seen part of Asia and Africa, and almost made the tour of Europe, I think the honest English squire more happy, who verily believes the Greek wines

less delicious than March beer; that the African fruits
have not so fine a flavour as golden pippins; and the
becaficuas of Italy are not so well tasted as a rump
of beef; and that, in short, there is no perfect enjoyment of this life out of Old England. I pray God I
may think so for the rest of my life; and, since I must
be contented with our scanty allowance of daylight,
that I may forget the enlivening sun of Constantinople."

The letter to Pope, that closes the series of letters
during the Embassy, has already been mentioned; it
is dated from Dover, some weeks (according to the
newspapers) after Lady Mary was safe in London;
and on the whole it seems evident that it was not
really sent in answer to Pope's famous epistle on the
"Lovers struck by Lightning." The fun made of Pope's
artificial pastoral is clever, and must have been annoy-
ing to him, even with the concluding couplet of the
epitaph :

> " Now they are happy in their doom,
>   For Pope has wrote upon their tomb."

But in all probability it was years before Pope saw it.
Had it been otherwise, that final breach between him
and Lady Mary might, perhaps, have taken place at
once, instead of being led up to by some ten years of
waning friendship.

CHAPTER IV

LIFE IN ENGLAND

Gap in the Letters—Pope's Friendship—Kneller's Portrait —South Sea Stock – M. Rémond and his Money—Loss of the Money—Behaviour of Rémond - Letters to Lady Mar—The Herveys—Threats against Rémond — "Mrs. Murray's Affair" — Pope's Verses on his Garden—Abundance of Poets--Open Immorality of Society—The Schemers—Duke of Wharton—Quarrel with Mrs. Murray—Auction of Kneller's Pictures—Death of Lady Mary's Father — Family Disputes — Escapades of her Son—Mankind Fools and Knaves—Coronation of George II.--Letters to Arbuthnot on the Quarrel with Pope—Verses to the Imitator of Horace—Letters to Lady Pomfret Gossip—Lady Herbert's *Mésalliance*—Flattery of Lady Pomfret—Ladies storm the House of Lords.

AFTER Lady Mary's return to England, in 1718, there is a gap of some years in her published letters. No doubt, being in London for the most part and seeing the friends to whom she was accustomed to write, she had little need for correspondence. Her husband had his Parliamentary duties, and she had the training of her daughter, and her social engagements. Her son was sent to school, from which he took every opportunity of running away, as we shall see in later letters. In 1720, however, we begin to get glimpses of her, though rather through the letters of others than her own. We find her sitting to Sir Godfrey Kneller for her portrait, apparently at Pope's suggestion, and the poet writing to her in the old vein of adoration. " The picture dwells really at my heart, and I have made a perfect passion of preferring your present face to your past. I know and thoroughly esteem yourself of this year: I know no more of Lady Mary Pierrepont, than to admire at what I have heard of her, or be pleased with some fragments of hers as I am with Sappho's. But now—I can't say what I would say of you now. Only still give me cause to say you are good to me, and allow me as much of your person as Sir Godfrey can help me to. Upon conferring with him yesterday, I find he thinks it absolutely necessary to draw the face first, which he says can never be set right on the figure, if the drapery and posture be finished before. To give you as little trouble as possible, he proposes to draw your face with crayons, and finish it up at your own house in a morning; from whence he will transfer it to the canvas, so that you need not go to sit at his house. This, I must observe, is a manner in which they seldom draw any but crowned heads; and I observe it with secret pride and pleasure." But the picture in question was certainly ordered and paid for by Mr. Wortley Montagu. Pope also tried to find out a house at Twickenham for his friends.

The year 1720 was the year of the South Sea Company's rise and fall; and the universal gambling

mania that had seized on England did not leave Lady
Mary untouched. We find the younger Craggs, then
Secretary of State, promising to insert her name in
the next subscription for stock; we find the usually
prudent Pope writing that he has heard from the best
sources that the stock will rise. Lady Mary took the
advice, if not on her own account, at least with regard
to the money placed in her hands by M. Rémond, her
French adorer, who had been over to England, apparently, in 1720. In the letter to her sister, Lady Mar,
in which she gives an account of the transaction, she
varies from singular to plural in speaking of Rémond,
but seems to forget this device (intended probably to
deceive anyone who opened the letter in the post) as
she goes on.

"It came into my head, out of a high point of
generosity (for which I wished myself hanged), to do
this creature all the good I possibly could, since 'twas
impossible to make them happy their own way. I
advised him very strenuously to sell out of the subscription,* and in compliance to my advice he did so;
and in less than two days saw he had done very
prudently. After a piece of service of this nature, I
thought I could more decently press his departure,
which his follies made me think necessary for me.
He took leave of me with so many tears and grimaces
(which I can't imagine how he could counterfeit) as
really moved my compassion; and I had much ado to
keep to my first resolution of exacting his absence,

* For South Sea Stock.

which he swore would be his death. I told him that there was no other way in the world I would not be glad to serve him in, but that his extravagances made it utterly impossible for me to keep him company. He said that he would put into my hands the money I had won for him, and desired me to improve it, saying that if he had enough to buy a small estate, and retire from the world, 'twas all the happiness he hoped for in it.   I represented to him that if he had so little money as he said, 'twas ridiculous to hazard it all. He replied that 'twas too little to be of any value, and he would either have it double or quit. After many objections on my side and replies on his, I was so weak to be overcome by his entreaties, and flattered myself also that I was doing a very heroic action, in trying to make a man's fortune though I did not care for his addresses.   He left me with these imaginations, and my first care was to employ his money to the best advantage.   I laid it all out in stock, the general discourse and private intelligence then scattered about being of a great rise.   You may remember it was two or three days before the fourth subscription,* and you were with me when I paid away the money to Mr. Binfield.   I thought I had managed prodigious well in selling out the said stock the day after the shutting the books (for a small profit) to Cox and Cleeve, goldsmiths of very good reputation.   When the opening of the books came, my men went off, leaving the stock upon my hands, which was already sunk from near

* August, 1720.

nine hundred pounds to four hundred pounds. I
immediately writ him word of this misfortune, with
the sincere sorrow natural to have upon such an occasion, and asked his opinion as to the selling the stock
remaining in. He made me no answer to this part of
my letter, but a long eloquent oration of miseries of
another nature. I attributed this silence to his disinterested neglect of his money; but, however, resolved
to make no more steps in his business without direct
orders, after having been so unlucky. This occasioned
many letters to no purpose ; but the very post after
you left London, I received a letter from him, in which
he told me that he had discovered all my tricks ; that
he was convinced I had all his money remaining untouched; and he would have it again, or he would
print all my letters to him; which though, God knows,
very innocent in the main, yet may admit of ill con-
structions, besides the monstrousness of being exposed
in such a manner. I hear from other people that he
is liar enough to publish that I have borrowed the
money of him ; though I have a note under his hand,
by which he desires me to employ it in the funds, and
acquits me of being answerable for the losses that may
happen. At the same time I have attestations and
witnesses of the bargains I made, so that nothing can
be clearer than my integrity in this business ; but that
does not hinder me from being in the utmost terror for
the consequences (as you may easily guess) of his
villainy ; the very story of which appears so monstrous
to me, I can hardly believe myself while I write it ;

though I omit (not to tire you) a thousand aggravating circumstances."

The next letter of Lady Mary's is dated from Twickenham, where she now had a house. She is still in great anxiety about Rémond, offering to submit to any sort of investigation that may convince him of her honesty, if only her husband does not hear of the matter. The purchase seems to have been of five hundred pounds' stock, which, as the price was " near nine hundred," must have cost Rémond over four thousand pounds ; and his delay in giving orders to sell out probably prevented Lady Mary from disposing of the shares till they were down to three hundred pounds each ; for when Rémond afterwards offered to compromise for two thousand pounds, she declared that would be "sending him several hundreds out of her own pocket." Thus, if "hapless Monsieur" was not "cheated of five thousand pounds in the South Sea year," he certainly lost more than half that sum. He may therefore be excused for feeling some annoyance at the loss of his property, though his methods of procedure were hardly in accordance with his national gallantry. Lady Mary was thrown into a panic by finding that he had written to her husband. "I have actually, in my present possession, a formal letter directed to Mr. W., to acquaint him with the whole business. You may imagine the inevitable eternal misfortunes it would have thrown me into, had it been delivered by the person to whom it was entrusted." For a time there was a lull in the dispute, and Lady

Mary could find time to write a letter without reference to Rémond, whimsically complaining of the wearisome affection of her friend Mr. Hervey (afterwards better known as Lord Hervey) and his wife, the beautiful Molly Lepel. " They visited me twice or thrice a day, and were perpetually cooing in my rooms. I was complaisant a great while; but (as you know) my talent has never lain much that way; I grew at last so weary of those birds of paradise, I fled to Twickenham, as much to avoid their persecutions as for my own health, which is still in a declining way." But the " monster " again returned to the charge, and threatened to come over to England—a step which called for strong measures.

" I desire you would assure him that my first step shall be to acquaint my Lord Stair * with all his obligations to him, as soon as I hear he is in London; and if he dares to gives me further trouble, I shall take care to have him rewarded in a stronger manner than he expects; there is nothing more true than this; and I solemnly swear, that if all the credit or money that I have in the world can do it, either for friendship or hire, I shall not fail to have him used as he deserves; and since I know his journey can only be designed to expose me, I shall not value what noise is made. Perhaps you may prevent it; I leave you to judge of

---

* Lord Stair had been the English Ambassador at Paris, and seems to have employed Rémond. Possibly Rémond had played him false. In any case, Stair's influence in France was very great, and his enmity would be serious for Rémond.

the most proper method; 'tis certain no time should
be lost; fear is his predominant passion, and I believe
you may fright him from coming hither, where he will
certainly find a reception very disagreeable to him."

The threat seems to have been effectual in keeping
Rémond away; but he was still not to be appeased,
and threatened "to print I know not what stuff against
me. I am too well acquainted with the world (of
which poor Mrs. Murray's affair is a fatal instance),
not to know that the most groundless accusation is
always of ill consequence to a woman."

"Mrs. Murray's affair" happened on October 1, 1721,
which may serve to date the letter in which the reference occurs, for Lady Mary had not mended her habit
of leaving out the dates of her letters, in spite of Pope's
appeals. Mrs. Murray's footman, Arthur Grey, entered
her bedroom one night with a pistol, and declared his
passion for her; she called for help, he was seized,
and, after trial, transported. Such an occurrence, as
may readily be believed, gave rise to much scandal;
and it is curious that Lady Mary herself wrote a
poetical "Epistle from Arthur Grey in Newgate"—
which, though only complimentary to Mrs. Murray,
yet added to the publicity of the affair—and was more
than suspected of writing a ballad on the case, more
lively than proper.

After this there is an interval of some months
without a published letter. Probably the disclosure of
the Rémond affair to Mr. Wortley Montagu took place
in this interval; for it is never mentioned again by

Lady Mary. The Countess of Mar seems to have been a bad correspondent, or else, Mar being suspected by the Jacobites of betraying them, letters to him or his wife were intercepted. Still, however, Lady Mary continued to send the gossip of the day. It seems that Pope had already begun to cool in his friendship.

"I see sometimes Mr. Congreve, and very seldom Mr. Pope, who continues to embellish his house at Twickenham. He has made a subterranean grotto, which he has furnished with looking-glass, and they tell me it has a very good effect. I here send you some verses addressed to Mr. Gay, who wrote him a congratulatory letter on the finishing his house. I stifled them here, and I beg they may die the same death at Paris, and never go further than your closet :

> "'Ah, friend, 'tis true—this truth you lovers know—
> In vain my structures rise, my gardens grow,
> In vain fair Thames reflects the double scenes
> Of hanging mountains, and of sloping greens :
> Joy lives not here ; to happier seats it flies,
> And only dwells where W—— casts her eyes.

> "'What is the gay parterre, the chequer'd shade,
> The morning bower, the ev'ning colonnade,
> But soft recesses of uneasy minds,
> To sigh unheard in, to the passing winds ?
> So the struck deer in some sequestrate part
> Lies down to die, the arrow at his heart ;
> There, stretch'd unseen in coverts hid from day,
> Bleeds drop by drop, and pants his life away.'"

It seems a little singular, however, if W—— here stands for Wortley, that Pope should not have asked the deity to "cast her eyes" on his garden and grotto.

8

Perhaps, in his thrifty way, he made the verses do
duty for several ladies whose names had the proper
number of syllables.

Lady Mary discovered in 1723, after losing " at least
five-and-forty letters," that her sister did not get what
she wrote. The post was so unsafe, that she had to
find a private messenger for her budget of gossip and
scandal, including all the matches made or making in
high life.

" This is, I think, the whole state of love ; as to that
of wit, it splits itself into ten thousand branches ; poets
increase and multiply to that stupendous degree, you
see them at every turn, even in embroidered coats and
pink-coloured top-knots ; making verses is almost as
common as taking snuff, and God can tell what miserable stuff people carry about in their pockets, and offer
to all their acquaintances, and you know one cannot
refuse reading and taking a pinch.   This is a very
great grievance, and so particularly shocking to me,
that I think our wise lawgivers should take it into
consideration, and appoint a fast - day to beseech
Heaven to put a stop to this epidemical disease, as
they did last year for the plague with great success."

The general immorality of high society at the time
seems to have gone beyond Lady Mary's rather easy
tolerance, though she speaks of the scandals of the age
with the freedom of the age.

" The world improves in one virtue to a violent
degree, I mean plain-dealing. Hypocrisy being as the
Scripture declares, a damnable sin, I hope our publicans

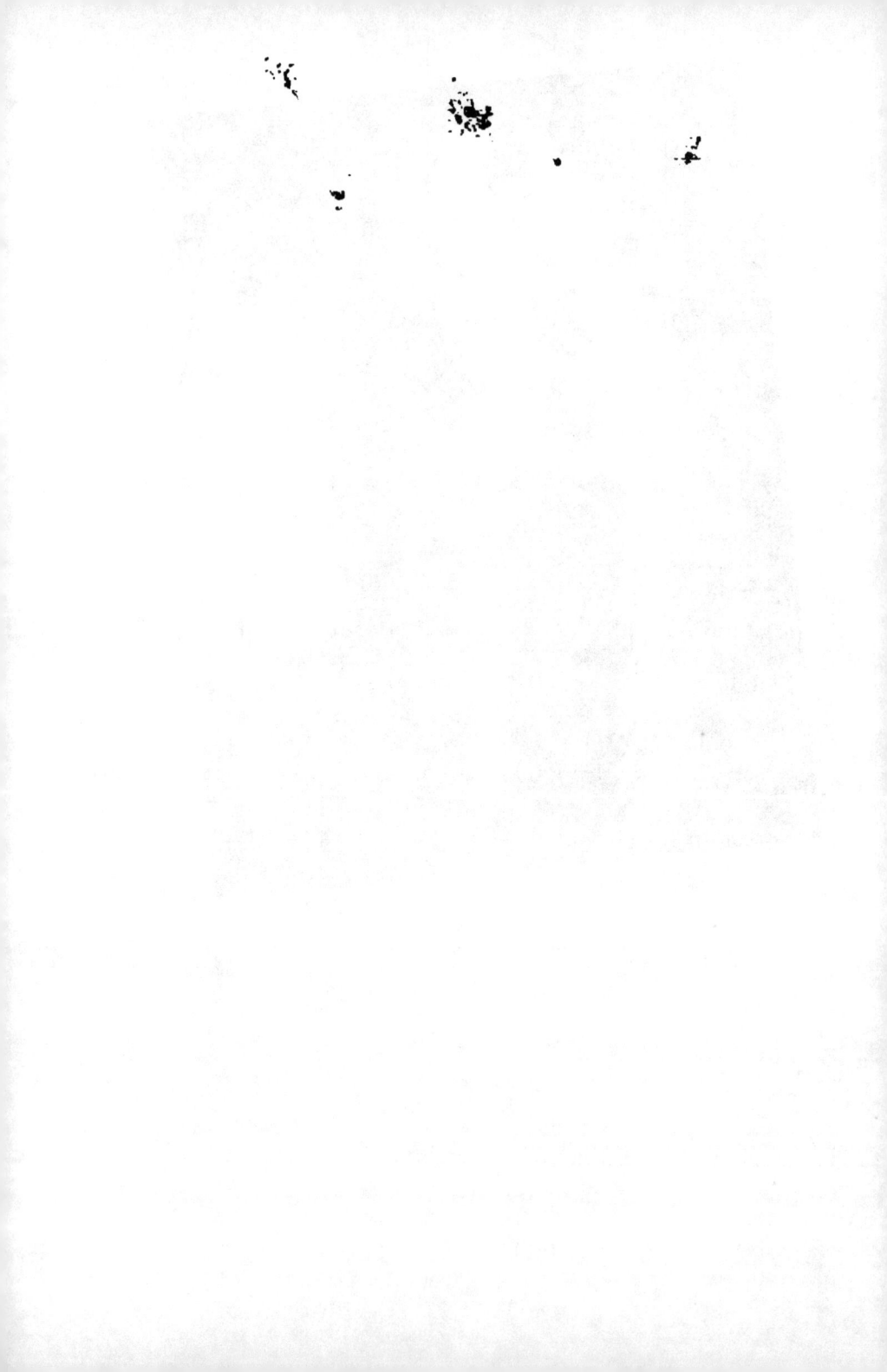

and sinners will be saved by the open profession of the contrary virtue. I was told by a very good author, who is deep in the secret, that at this very minute there is a bill cooking-up at a hunting-seat in Norfolk,* to have *not* taken out of the commandments and clapped into the creed, the ensuing session of Parliament. This bold attempt for the liberty of the subject is wholly projected by Mr. Walpole, who proposed it to the secret committee in his parlour. William Young seconded it, and answered for all his acquaintance voting right to a man : Dodington† very gravely objected, that the obstinacy of human nature was such, that he feared when they had positive commandments to do [so], perhaps people would not commit adultery and bear false witness against their neighbours with the readiness and cheerfulness they do at present. This objection seemed to sink deep into the minds of the greatest politicians at the board ; and I don't know whether the bill won't be dropped, though it is certain it might be carried with great ease, the world being entirely *revenue du* [*sic*] *bagatelle*, and honour, virtue, reputation, etc., which we used to hear of in our nursery, is as much laid aside and forgotten as crumpled riband."

In the same letter Lady Mary satirically affects to be ashamed of her own respectability : " You may imagine we married women look very silly ; we have

---

* Houghton, the house of Mr. —afterwards Sir Robert— Walpole.

† George Bubb Dodington, one of the most corrupt politicians of the time. The same objection to the same proposal was satirically made by Swift.

nothing to excuse ourselves, but that it was done a
great while ago, and we were very young when we did
it." In the follies of the time, her friend the Duke of
Wharton ("Clodio, the scorn and wonder of our
days") figured largely, as the following extract proves :

" In general, gallantry never was in so elevated a
figure as it is at present. Twenty very pretty fellows
(the Duke of Wharton being president and chief
director) have formed themselves into a committee of
gallantry. They call themselves *Schemers ;* and meet
regularly three times a week, to consult on gallant
schemes for the advantage and advancement of that
branch of happiness. . . . I consider the duty of a true
Englishwoman is to do what honour she can to her
native country; and that it would be a sin against the
pious love I bear the land of my nativity, to confine the
renown due to the Schemers within the small extent of
this little island, which ought to be spread wherever
men can sigh, or woman wish. 'Tis true they have
the envy and curses of the old and ugly of both sexes,
and a general persecution from all old women ; but
this is no more than all reformations must expect in
their beginning. . . ."

The very next letter published chronicles the Duke's
sudden, but too temporary, conversion ; and shortly
afterwards we learn that " Sophia [her nickname for
the Duke] and I have been quite reconciled, and are
now quite broke, and I believe not likely to piece up
again." Soon after he openly took the Jacobite side
and fled to the Continent.

All this whirl of fashionable life Lady Mary affected to look on with a philosophic indifference. "For my part, as it is my established opinion, that this globe of ours is no better than a Holland cheese, and the walkers about in it mutes, I possess my mind in patience, let what will happen; and should feel tolerably easy, though a great rat came and ate half of it up." But an old sin of hers seems to have found her out in 1725—the ballad which she seems practically to acknowledge having made on the affair of Arthur Grey :

"Among the rest a very odd whim has entered the little head of Mrs. Murray : do you know she won't visit me this winter? I, according to the usual integrity of my heart, and simplicity of my manners, with great *naïveté* desired to explain with her on the subject, and she answered that she was convinced that I had made the ballad upon her, and was resolved never to speak to me again. I answered (which was true), that I utterly defied her to have any one single proof of my making it, without being able to get anything from her, but repetitions that she knew it. I cannot suppose that any thing you have said should occasion this rupture, and the reputation of a quarrel is always so ridiculous on both sides, that you will oblige me in mentioning it to her, for 'tis now at that pretty pass, she won't curtsey to me whenever she meets me, which is superlatively silly (if she really knew it) after a suspension of resentment for two years together."

This quarrel caused yet further annoyance, as may be seen from an extract from a letter of 1726:

"Mrs. Murray is in open wars [*sic*] with me in such a manner as makes her very ridiculous without doing me much harm; my moderation having a very bright pretence of shewing itself. Firstly, she was pleased to attack me in very Billingsgate at a masquerade, where she was as visible as ever she was in her own clothes. I had the temper not only to keep silence myself, but enjoined it to the person with me; who would have been very glad to have shewn his great skill in sousing upon that occasion. She endeavoured to sweeten him by very exorbitant praises of his person, which might even have been mistaken for making love from a woman of less celebrated virtue; and concluded her oration with pious warnings to him, to avoid the conversation of one so unworthy his regard as myself, who to her certain knowledge loved another man. This last article, I own, piqued me more than all her preceding civilities. The gentleman she addressed herself to had a very slight acquaintance with me, and might possibly go away in the opinion that she had been confidante in some very notorious affair of mine. However, I made her no answer at the time, but you may imagine I laid up these things in my heart; and the first assembly I had the honour to meet her at, with a meek tone of voice, asked her how I had deserved so much abuse at her hands, which I assured her I would never return. She denied it in the spirit of lying; and in the spirit of folly owned it at length.

I contented myself with telling her she was very ill advised, and thus we parted. But two days ago, when Sir G. K.'s* pictures were to be sold, she went to my sister Gower, and very civily asked if she intended to bid for your picture ; assuring her that, if she did, she would not offer at purchasing it. You know crimp and quadrille incapacitate that poor soul from ever buying any thing ; but she told me this circumstance ; and I expected the same civility from Mrs. Murray, having no way provoked her to the contrary. But she not only came to the auction, but with all possible spite bid up the picture, though I told her that, if you pleased to have it, I would gladly part with it to you, though to no other person. This had no effect upon her, nor her malice any more on me than the loss of ten guineas extraordinary, which I paid upon her account. The picture is in my possession, and at your service if you please to have it. She went to the masquerade a few nights afterwards, and had the good sense to tell people there that she was very unhappy in not meeting me, being come there on purpose to abuse me. What profit or pleasure she has in these ways I cannot find out. This I know, that revenge has so few joys for me. I shall never lose so much time as to undertake it."

The death of her father, which happened in March, 1726, seems to have affected Lady Mary but little ; and there were unpleasant pecuniary disputes with his

---

* Sir Godfrey Kneller died in 1723, and some of his pictures, unclaimed by those who had ordered them, were sold at auction in 1726, and among them, apparently, Lady Mar's portrait.

second wife, who seems to have been alive to her own interests. The tone of the references to the subject is very cold: " I received yours, dear sister, this minute, and am very sorry both for your past illness and affliction; though, *au bout du compte*, I don't know why filial piety should exceed fatherly fondness. So much by way of consolation. As to the management at that time—I do verily believe, if my good aunt and sister had been less fools, and my dear mother-in-law less mercenary, things might have had a turn more to your advantage and mine too; when we meet, I will tell you many circumstances which would be tedious in a letter. I could not get my sister Gower to join to act with me, and mamma and I were in an actual scold when my poor father expired; she has shewn a hardness of heart upon this occasion that would appear incredible to any body not capable of it themselves."

The fortunes of her family Lady Mary regarded with the same indifference as the "wars and rumours of wars" distracting public attention from the time of the formation of the rival alliances of Vienna and Hanover, in 1725.

" All that I had to say to you was that my F. [father] really expressed a great deal of kindness to me at last, and even a desire of talking to me, which my Lady Duchess would not permit; nor my aunt and sister shew anything but a servile complaisance to her. This is the abstract of what you desire to know, and is now quite useless. 'Tis over and better to be forgot than remembered. The Duke of Kingston has hitherto had so ill an education, 'tis hard to make any judgment of him ; he has spirit, but I fear will never have his father's good sense. As young noblemen go, 'tis possible he may make a good figure amongst them. Wars and rumours of wars make all the conversation at present. The tumbling of the stocks, one way or other, influences most people's affairs. For my own part, I have no concern there or anywhere, but hearty prayers that what relates to myself may ever be exactly what it is now. Mutability ' of sublunary things is the only melancholy reflection I have to make on my own account. I am in perfect health, and hear it said I look better than ever I did in my life, which is one of those lies one is always glad to hear. However, in this dear minute, in this golden now, I am tenderly touched at your misfortune, and can never call myself quite happy till you are so."

Lady Mary's niece Frances, sister of the new Duke of Kingston. seems to have been a bone of contention in the family ; but Lady Mary herself had enough trouble with her own son not to care for more family worries.

" I have been *embourbée* in family affairs for this last fortnight. Lady F. [Frances] Pierrepont having four hundred pounds per annum for her maintenance, has awakened the consciences of half her relations to take care of her education ; and (excepting myself) they have all been squabbling about her ; and squabble to this day. My sister Gower carries her off to-morrow morning to Staffordshire. The lies, twaddles, and contrivances about this affair are innumerable. I

should pity the poor girl, if I saw she pitied herself. The
Duke of Kingston is in France, but is not to go to
your capital; so much for that branch of your family.
My blessed offspring has already made a great noise
in the world. That young rake, my son, took to his
heels t'other day and transported his person to Oxford;
being in his own opinion thoroughly qualified for the
University. After a good deal of search we found and
reduced him, much against his will, to the humble condition of a schoolboy. It happens very luckily that the
sobriety and discretion is of my daughter's side; I am
sorry the ugliness is so too, for my son grows extreme
handsome."

The second running away, however, in 1727, was a
more serious matter. " I am vexed to the blood," she
writes, " by my young rogue of a son; who has contrived at his age to make himself the talk of the whole
nation. He is gone knight-erranting, God knows
where; and hitherto 'tis impossible to find him." In
spite of an offered reward of £20, he did not turn up
for some months.

The Duchess of Kingston, indeed, did not long survive her husband, though so much younger. As Lady
Mary rather brutally put it : " The Duchess of Kingston
grunts on as usual, and I fear will put us in black
bombazine soon, which is a real grief to me." In June,
1727, died Lady Gower, from whom her sister seems to
have been somewhat estranged, in consequence of the
squabbles on the death of the Duke of Kingston. "We
are now but two in the world," wrote Lady Mary to

her remaining sister, Lady Mar, "and it ought to
endear us to one another." It was under the influence
of this loss, and probably still more under the vexation
of her son's running away, that Lady Mary wrote the
following letter :

" This is a vile world, dear sister, and I can easily
comprehend, that whether one is at Paris or London,
one is stifled with a certain mixture of fool and knave,
that most people are composed of. I would have
patience with a parcel of polite rogues, or your downright honest fools ; but father Adam shines through his
whole progeny. So much for our inside,—then our out-
ward is so liable to ugliness and distempers, that we
are perpetually plagued with feeling our own decays
and seeing those of other people. Yet, sixpennyworth
of common-sense, divided among a whole nation,
would make our lives roll away glibly enough ; but
then we make laws, and we follow customs. By the
first we cut off our own pleasures, and by the second
we are answerable for the faults and extravagances of
others. All these things, and five hundred more, convince me (as I have the most profound veneration for
the Author of Nature) that we are here in an actual
state of punishment : I am satisfied I have been one of
the condemned ever since I was born : and, in submission
to the Divine justice, I don't at all doubt but I deserved
it in some pre-existent state. I will still hope that I
am only in purgatory ; and that after whining and
grunting a certain number of years, I shall be translated to some more happy sphere, where virtue will be

natural, and custom reasonable; that is, in short, where common-sense will reign. I grow very devout, as you see, and place all my hopes in the next life, being totally persuaded of the nothingness of this. Don't you remember how miserable we were in the little parlour at Thoresby? We then thought marrying would put us at once into possession of all we wanted. Then came being with child, etc., and you see what comes of being with child. Though, after all, I am still of opinion that it is extremely silly to submit to ill-fortune. One should pluck up a spirit, and live upon cordials when one can have no other nourishment. These are my present endeavours, and I run about, though I have five thousand pins and needles running into my heart. I try to console myself with a small damsel, who is at present everything I like—but, alas! she is yet in a white frock. At fourteen, she may run away with the butler:—there's one of the blessed consequences of great disappointments; you are not only hurt by the thing present, but it cuts off all future hopes, and makes your future expectations melancholy. *Quelle vie ! ! !*"

Can this be the letter Horace Walpole refers to when he quotes from memory one of the letters to Lady Mar?—"We all partake of father Adam's folly and knavery, who first eat the apple like a sot and then turned informer like a scoundrel." The sentiment is the same.

The last of the letters to Lady Mar is a description of George II.'s coronation, in her usual critical vein :

" I cannot deny, but that I was very well diverted on the Coronation day. I saw the procession much at my ease, in a house which I filled with my own company, and then got into Westminster Hall without trouble, where it was very entertaining to observe the variety of airs that all meant the same thing. The business of every walker there was to conceal vanity and gain admiration. For these purposes some languished and others strutted ; but a visible satisfaction was diffused over every countenance, as soon as the coronet was clapped on the head. But she that drew the greatest number of eyes, was indisputably Lady Orkney.* She exposed behind, a mixture of fat and wrinkles ; and before, a very considerable protuberance which preceded her. Add to this, the inimitable roll of her eyes, and her gray hairs, which by good fortune stood directly upright, and 'tis impossible to imagine a more delightful spectacle. She had embellished all this with considerable magnificence, which made her look as big again as usual ; and I should have thought her one of the largest things of God's making if my Lady St. John had not displayed all her charms in honour of the day. The poor Duchess of Montrose crept along with a dozen of black snakes playing round her face ; and my Lady Portland† (who is fallen away since her dismission from Court) represented very finely an

* Lady Orkney must have been old, as she had been the favourite of William III.

† Lady Portland had been appointed by George I. to take charge of his grand-children against the wish of their father ; hence the latter, on succeeding to the throne, at once dismissed her.

Egyptian mummy embroidered over with hierogly-
phics. In general, I could not perceive but that the
old were as well pleased as the young; and I, who
dread growing wise more than anything in the world,
was overjoyed to find that one can never outlive one's
vanity."

Shortly after this letter was sent, Lady Mar went
out of her mind ; and in March, 1728, she was brought
to England, and remained in charge of her sister till
her daughter, Lady Frances Erskine, was old enough
to take over her care.

After Lady Mar became insane there is another
great gap in her sister's published correspondence.
From 1728 to 1738 there is hardly a letter of hers
printed ; the few that are, relate chiefly to the quarrel
with Pope, and are by no means favourable specimens
of the author's style. As already mentioned, Pope
suspected her of being concerned in some of the
answers to the "Dunciad," notably "A Pop upon Pope"
and "One Epistle to Mr. Alexander Pope," both of a
scurrilous character—the latter libelling Swift and
Esther Vanhomrigh, as well as Pope. The authorship
of this Lady Mary indignantly denied.

" I am told," she wrote to Arbuthnot, with whom she
remained on friendly terms, " Pope has had the surprising impudence to assert he can bring the lampoon
when he pleases to produce it, under my own hand ;
I desire he may be made to keep to this offer. If he is
so skilful in counterfeiting hands, I suppose he will not
confine that great talent to the gratifying his malice,

but take some occasion to increase his fortune by the same method, and may I hope (by such practices) to see him exalted according to his merit, which nobody will rejoice at more than myself. I beg of you, sir (as an act of justice), to endeavour to set the truth in an open light, and then I leave to your judgment the character of those who have attempted to hurt mine in so barbarous a manner. I can assure you (in particular) you named a lady to me (as abused in this libel) whose name I never heard before, as I never had any acquaintance with Dr. Swift, am an utter stranger to all his affairs and even his person, which I never saw to my knowledge, and am now convinced the whole is a contrivance of Pope's to blast the reputation of one who never injured him."

The savage attack on her as " Sappho," in Pope's "Imitations of Horace," drew forth a fresh remonstrance to Arbuthnot- -or, rather, a somewhat spiteful and ineffective rejoinder to Pope.

"Sir, -I have perused the last lampoon of your ingenious friend, and am not surprised you did not find me out under the name of Sappho, because there is nothing I ever heard in our characters or circumstances to make a parallel, but as the town (except you, who know better) generally suppose Pope means me, whenever he mentions that name, I cannot help taking notice of the horrible malice he bears against the lady signified by that name, which appears to be irritated by supposing her writer of the verses to the Imitator of Horace. Now I can assure him they were wrote (without my knowledge) by a gentleman of great merit, whom I very much esteem,* who he will never guess, and who, if he did know, he durst not attack; but I own the design was so well meant, and so excellently executed, that I cannot be sorry they were written. I wish you would advise poor Pope to turn to some more honest livelihood than libelling; I know he will allege in his excuse that he must write to eat, and he is now grown sensible that nobody will buy his verses except their curiosity is piqued to it, to see what is said of their acquaintance; but I think this method of gain so exceeding vile that it admits of no excuse at all."

Such tricks of fence were hardly calculated to parry the thrusts of Pope's satire. Nor were the verses of Lady Mary or her ally sharp enough weapons to make the conflict equal, though some lines of them have survived, and may be worth quoting here:

" In two large columns on thy motley page,
Where Roman wit is strip'd with English rage:
Where ribaldry to satire makes pretence,
And modern scandal rolls with ancient sense:
Whilst on one side we see how Horace thought,
And on the other how he never wrote;
Who can believe, who view the bad, the good,
That the dull copyist better understood
That spirit he pretends to imitate,
Than heretofore that Greek he did translate?
  Thine is just such an image of *his* pen,
As thou thyself art of the sons of men,
Where our own species in burlesque we trace,

* Lord Hervey.

A sign-post likeness of the human race,
That is at once resemblance and disgrace.
  Horace can laugh, is delicate, is clear,
You only coarsely rail, or darkly sneer ;
His style is elegant, his diction pure,
Whilst none thy crabbed numbers can endure ;
Hard as thy heart, and as thy birth obscure.
  If *he* has thorns, they all on roses grow ;
Thine all like thistles, and mean brambles show ;
With this exception, that, though rank the soil,
Weeds as they are, they seem produc'd by toil.
  Satire should, like a polish'd razor, keen,
Wound with a touch, that's scarcely felt or seen :
Thine is an oyster-knife, that hacks and hews ;
The rage, but not the talent to abuse ;

       *   *   *   *   *

Neither to folly, nor to vice confin'd,
The object of thy spleen is humankind :
It preys on all who yield, or who resist :
To thee 'tis provocation to exist."

When we again meet with a letter from Lady Mary, she is already contemplating a flight from England. Her friend Lady Pomfret had gone abroad after the death of her royal mistress Queen Caroline in 1737. Lady Mary corresponded with her for some time, and at last, in 1739, followed her abroad, eventually meeting her in Florence, as chronicled by Horace Walpole in a passage already quoted. The few letters written before Lady Mary's own departure give the gossip of the time in much the same way as those to Lady Mar :

" The Bath is the present scene of gallantry and magnificence, where many caresses are bestowed, not from admiration of the present, but from spite to the absent. The most remarkable circumstance I hear is a coolness in the Earl of Chesterfield, which occasions much speculation ; it must be disagreeable to play an under-part in a second-rate theatre. To me that have always been an humble spectator, it appears odd, to see so few desirous to quit the stage, though time and infirmities have disabled them from making a tolerable figure there. Our drama is at present carried on by such whimsical management, I am half inclined to think we shall shortly have no plays at all. I begin to be of opinion that the new Northern actress * has very good sense ; she hardly appears at all, and by that conduct almost wears out the disapprobation of the public. I believe you are already tired with this long dissertation on so trifling a subject ; I wish I could enliven my letter with some account of literature ; but wit and pleasure are no more, and people play the fool with great impunity ; being very sure there is not spirit enough left in the nation to set their follies in a ridiculous light. Pamphlets are the sole productions of our modern authors, and those profoundly stupid. To you that enjoy a purer air, and meet at least with vivacity whenever you meet company, this may appear extraordinary ; but recollect, dear madam, in what condition you left us ; and you will easily believe to what state we are fallen."

In another letter Lady Mary again complains of this universal preoccupation with politics :

" I hope, dear madam, you find at least some amuse-ment in your travels, and though I cannot wish you to forget those friends in England, who will never forget

---

° Madame Walmoden, mistress of George II.

you, yet I should be pleased to hear you were so far
entertained as to take off all anxiety from your mind.
I know you are capable of many pleasures that the herd
of mankind are insensible of; and wherever you go I
do not doubt you will find some people that will know
how to taste the happiness of your conversation. We
are as much blinded in England by politics and views
of interest as we are by mists and fogs, and 'tis necessary
to have a very uncommon constitution not to be tainted
with the distempers of our climate. I confess myself
very much infected with the epidemical dulness; yet,
as 'tis natural to excuse one's own faults as much as
possible, I am apt to flatter myself that my stupidity is
rather accidental than real; at least, I am sure that I
want no vivacity when I think of my Lady Pomfret,
and that it is with the warmest inclination as well
as the highest esteem that I am ever affectionately
yours."

One item of the gossip in the letters may be extracted
as showing Lady Mary's views on alliances between
the operatic stage and the aristocracy. Perhaps,
however, she was too severe on Mr. Beard, who seems
to have been "very respectable."

"Lady Harriet Herbert" (Lady Mary writes) "furnished the tea-tables here with fresh tattle for the last
fortnight. I was one of the first informed of her
adventure by Lady Gage, who was told that morning
by a priest, that she had desired him to marry her the
next day to Beard, who sings in the farces at Drury
Lane. He refused her that good office, and imme-

diately told Lady Gage, who (having been unfortunate
in her friends) was frighted at this affair and asked my
advice. I told her honestly, that since the lady was
capable of such amours, I did not doubt if this was
broke off she would bestow her person and fortune on
some hackney-coachman or chairman; and that I
really saw no method of saving *her* from ruin, and her
family from dishonour, but by poisoning her; and
offered to be at the expense of the arsenic, and even
to administer it with my own hands, if she would invite
her to drink tea with her that evening. But on her
not approving that method, she sent to Lady Monta-
cute, Mrs. Dunch, and all the relations within the
reach of messengers. They carried Lady Harriet to
Twickenham; though I told them it was a bad air for
girls. She is since returned to London, and some
people believe her to be married; others, that he is too
much intimidated by Mr. Waldegrave's * threats to
dare to go through the ceremony; but the secret is
now public, and in what manner it will conclude I
know not. Such examples are very detrimental to our
whole sex; and are apt to influence the other into a
belief that we are unfit to manage either liberty or
money."

In return for these instalments of gossip, Lady Pomfret returned descriptions of her travels, probably much
in the same vein as her published letters to Lady Hertford. Tedious as these epistles probably were, Lady
Mary either found or affected to find them welcome.

* A brother of Lady Herbert, who was the daughter of the Earl
of Waldegrave.

" I will say nothing of your complaints of your own dulness; I should say something very rough if I did; 'tis impossible to reconcile them to the sincerity that I am willing to flatter myself I find in the other parts of your letter. 'Tis impossible you should not be conscious that such letters as yours want not the trimmings of news, which are only necessary to the plain Spitalfields style, beginning with *hoping you are in good health,* and concluding *pray believe me to be,* etc., etc. You give me all the pleasure of an agreeable author : and I really wish you had leisure to give me all the length too, and that all your letters were to come to me in twelve tomes. You will stare at this impudent wish; but you know imagination has no bounds; and 'tis harder for me to be content with a moderate quantity of your writing, than it was for any South Sea director to resolve to get no more. This is a strange way of giving thanks; however, 'tis the clearest proof of my tasting my happiness in your correspondence, to beg so earnestly not only the continuance but the increase of it."

The last letter of any note to Lady Pomfret before Lady Mary's own journey abroad gives an amusing description of a raid made by certain noble ladies of the Opposition on the House of Lords. Politics were just now at fever-heat, as Sir Robert Walpole's power was tottering under ceaseless attacks from the so-called " Patriots "; and Mr. Wortley Montagu was zealous among the assailants.

" Here is no news to be sent you from this place, which has been for this fortnight and still continues overwhelmed with politics, and which are of so mysterious a nature, one ought to have some of the gifts of Lilly or Partridge * to be able to write about them ; and I leave all those dissertations to those distinguished mortals who are endowed with the talent of divination ; though I am at present the only one of my sex who seems to be of that opinion, the ladies having shown their zeal and appetite for knowledge in a most glorious manner. At the last warm debate in the House of Lords, it was unanimously resolved there should be no crowd of unnecessary auditors ; consequently the fair sex were excluded, and the gallery destined to the sole use of the House of Commons. Notwithstanding which determination, a tribe of dames resolved to show on this occasion that neither men nor laws could resist them. These heroines were Lady Huntingdon,† the Duchess of Queensberry, the Duchess of Ancaster, Lady Westmoreland, Lady Cobham, Lady Charlotte Edwin, Lady Archibald Hamilton and her daughter, Mrs. Scott, and Mrs. Pendarves, and Lady Frances Saunderson. I am thus particular in their names, since I look upon them to be the boldest assertors, and most resigned sufferers for liberty, I ever read of. They presented themselves at the door at nine o'clock in the morning, where Sir William Saunderson respectfully informed them the Chancellor

* Well-known astrologers and compilers of prophetic almanacs. It was on Partridge that Swift played his celebrated joke of announcing and describing his death.

† Foundress of the "Countess of Huntingdon's Connection."

had made an order against their admittance. The
Duchess of Queensberry, as head of the squadron,
pished at the ill-breeding of a mere lawyer, and desired
him to let them upstairs privately. After some modest
refusals, he swore by G— he would not let them in.
Her grace, with a noble warmth, answered, by G—
they would come in in spite of the Chancellor and the
whole House. This being reported, the Peers resolved
to starve them out; an order was made that the doors
should not be opened till they had raised their siege.
These Amazons now showed themselves qualified for
the duty even of foot soldiers; they stood there till
five in the afternoon, without sustenance, every now
and then playing volleys of thumps, kicks, and
raps against the door, with so much violence
that the speakers in the House were scarce heard.
When the Lords were not to be conquered by this,
the two Duchesses (very well apprised of the use of
stratagems in war) commanded a dead silence of half
an hour; and the Chancellor, who thought this a
certain proof of their absence (the Commons also being
very impatient to enter), gave order for the opening of
the door; upon which they all rushed in, pushed aside
their competitors, and placed themselves in the front
rows of the gallery. They stayed there till after eleven,
when the House rose; and during the debate gave
applause, and showed marks of dislike, not only by
smiles and winks (which have always been allowed in
these cases), but by noisy laughs and apparent con-
tempts; which is supposed the true reason why poor

Lord Hervey spoke miserably. I beg your pardon, dear madam, for this long relation ; but 'tis impossible to be short on so copious a subject ; and you must own this action very well worthy of record, and I think not to be paralleled in history, ancient or modern. I look so little in my own eyes (who was at that time ingloriously sitting over a tea-table), I hardly dare subscribe myself even,

" Yours."

A few months later Lady Mary was following in the steps of her friend, and had left England, only to return thither to die.

CHAPTER V

TRAVELS IN ITALY AND FRANCE

ON the 26th of July (o.s.), 1739, Lady Mary Wortley
Montagu arrived at Dover to embark for France. She
sent a note to her husband at every stage of the
journey, and received rather stiff but never unkindly
letters in reply; so that it is plain that there was no

quarrel between the two as a prelude to her departure. France was much changed from when Lady Mary had returned home in 1718. The long peace, only broken by the short and easy war of the Polish Succession, had effaced the misery of the last years of Louis XIV. Cardinal Fleury, the chief Minister of Louis XV., was as notoriously pacific as Walpole in England.

" France is so much improved, it is not to be known to be the same country we passed through twenty years ago. Everything I see speaks in praise of Cardinal Fleury; the roads are all mended, and the greatest part of them paved as well as the streets of Paris, planted on both sides like the roads in Holland; and such good care taken against robbers, that you may cross the country with your purse in your hand: but as to travelling *incognito*, I may as well walk *incognito* in the Pall-Mall. There is not any town in France where there is not English, Scotch, or Irish families established; and I have met with people that have seen me (though often such as I do not remember to have seen) in every town I have passed through; and I think the farther I go, the more acquaintance I meet."

And again, in the same letter:

" The French are more changed than their roads; instead of pale, yellow faces, wrapped up in blankets, as we saw them, the villages are all filled with fresh-coloured lusty peasants, in good cloth and clean linen. It is incredible the air of plenty and content that is over the whole country."

This letter was written at Dijon; and from there Lady Mary went on by Lyons to Turin, and determined to proceed to Venice for the carnival, in hopes of meeting Lady Pomfret, whose son, Lord Lempster, she had met at Lyons. Lord Carlisle, whose son was detained by serious illness, also came in her way; and friends or acquaintances were met at every turn. She writes to her husband on her arrival at Venice:

"I met nothing disagreeable in my journey but too much company. I find (contrary to the rest of the world) I did not think myself so considerable as I am; for I verily believe, if one of the pyramids of Egypt had travelled, it could not have been more followed; and if I had received all the visits that have been intended me, I should have stopped at least a year in every town I came through."

With Venice Lady Mary was charmed, and recommended it warmly to her friend Lady Pomfret, who had not yet arrived:

"I like this place extremely, and am of opinion you would do so too: as to cheapness, I think 'tis impossible to find any part of Europe where both the laws and customs are so contrived purposely to avoid expenses of all sorts; and here is a universal liberty that is certainly one of the greatest *agrémens* in life. We have foreign ambassadors from all parts of the world, who have all visited me. I have received visits from many of the noble Venetian ladies; and upon the whole I am very much at my ease here. If I was

writing to Lady Sophia,* I would tell her of the
comedies and operas which are every night, at very
low prices; but I believe even you will agree with me
that they are ordered to be as convenient as possible,
every mortal going in a mask, and consequently no
trouble in dressing, or forms of any kind.   I should be
very glad to see Rome, which was my first intention
(I mean next to seeing yourself); but am deterred
from it by reasons that are put into my head by all
sorts of people that speak to me of it.   There are
innumerable little dirty spies about all English; and I
have so often had the ill-fortune to have false witness
borne against me, I fear my star on this occasion."

And a few days later she returned to the charge on
the same topic:

"Upon my word, I have spoken my real thoughts in
relation to Venice; but I will be more particular in my
description, lest you should find the same reason of
complaint you have hitherto experienced.   It is impossible to give any rule for the agreeableness of conversation; but here is so great a variety, I think 'tis
impossible not to find some to suit every taste.   Here
are foreign ministers from all parts of the world, who,
as they have no Court to employ their hours, are overjoyed to enter into commerce with any stranger of
distinction.   As I am the only lady here at present, I
can assure you I am courted, as if I was the only one
in the world.   As to all the conveniences of life, they

* Lady Sophia Fermor, sister of Lord Pomfret, and a noted
beauty.   She afterwards married Lord Carteret.

are to be had at very easy rates; and for those that love public places, here are two playhouses and two operas constantly performed every night, at exceeding low prices. But you will have no reason to examine that article, no more than myself; all the ambassadors having boxes appointed them; and I have every one of their keys at my service, not only for my own person, but whoever I please to carry or send. I do not make much use of this privilege, to their great astonishment. It is the fashion for the greatest ladies to walk the streets, which are admirably paved; and a mask, price sixpence, with a little cloak, and the head of a domino, the genteel dress to carry you everywhere. The greatest equipage is a gondola, that holds eight persons, and is the price of an English chair. And it is so much the established fashion for everybody to live their own way, that nothing is more ridiculous than censuring the actions of another. This would be terrible in London, where we have little other diversion; but for me, who never found any pleasure in malice, I bless my destiny that has conducted me to a part where people are better employed than in talking of the affairs of their acquaintance. It is at present excessive cold (which is the only thing I have to find fault with); but in recompense we have a clear bright sun, and fogs and factions things unheard of in this climate."

Lady Pomfret, however, did not come, and apparently desired Lady Mary to come to her, to which the latter demurred, not knowing (she said) what her husband's wishes might be.

"You have put me to a very difficult choice; yet, when I consider we are both in Italy, and yet do not see one another, I am astonished at the capriciousness of my fortune. My affairs are so uncertain, I can answer for nothing that is future. I have taken some pains to put the inclination for travelling into Mr. Wortley's head, and was so much afraid he would change his mind, that I hastened before him in order (at least) to secure my journey. He proposed following me in six weeks, his business requiring his presence at Newcastle. Since that, the change of scene that has happened in England has made his friends persuade him to attend Parliament this session: so that what his inclinations, which must govern mine, will be next spring, I cannot absolutely foresee. For my own part, I like my own situation so well that it will be a displeasure to me to change it. To postpone such a conversation as yours a whole twelvemonth is a terrible appearance; on the other hand, I would not follow the example of the first of our sex, and sacrifice for a present pleasure a more lasting happiness. In short, I can determine nothing on the subject. When you are at Florence, we may debate it over again."

This decision to stay at Venice till summer seems to have caused some dispute with Lady Pomfret; but the winter and spring were too inclement for Lady Mary to venture over the Apennines, much as she professed to long for the Countess's conversation in the following letter :

'I am impatient to hear good sense pronounced in

my native tongue; having only heard my language out
of the mouths of boys and governors* for these five
months. Here are inundations of them broke in upon
us this carnival, and my apartment must be their
refuge; the greater part of them having kept an inviolable fidelity to the languages their nurses taught
them; their whole business abroad (as far as I can
perceive) being to buy new clothes, in which they
shine in some obscure coffee-house, where they are
sure of meeting only one another. . . . I find the spirit
of patriotism so strong in me every time I see them,
that I look on them as the greatest blockheads in
nature; and, to say truth, the compound of booby
and *petit maître* makes up a very odd sort of animal."

Thus, in spite of the importunities of Lady Pomfret
and her son Lord Lempster, who came to Venice, Lady
Mary resolved to remain, excusing herself as she best
could :

"To suspect me of want of desire to see you, is
accusing at once both my taste and my sincerity; and
you will allow that all the world are sensible upon these
subjects. But you have now given me an occasion to
thank you, in sending me the most agreeable young
man I have seen in my travels.† I wish it was in my
power to be of use to him; but what little services I
am able to do him, I shall not fail of performing with
great pleasure. I have already received a very considerable one from him in a conversation where you was the

---

* Private tutors travelling with their pupils.
† Lord Lempster, Lady Pomfret's son.

subject, and I had the satisfaction of hearing him talk
of you in a manner that agreed with my own way of
thinking. I wish I could tell you that I set out for
Florence next week; but the winter is yet so severe,
and by all report, even that of our friends, the roads so
bad, it is impossible to think of it. We are now in the
midst of carnival amusements, which are more than
usual, for the entertainment of the Electoral Prince
of Saxony, and I am obliged to live in a hurry very
inconsistent with philosophy, and extreme different
from the life I projected to lead. But 'tis long since
I have been of Prior's opinion, who, I think, somewhere
compares us to cards, who are but played with, do not
play. At least such has been my destiny from my youth
upwards; and neither Dr. Clarke nor Lady Sundon*
could ever convince me that I was a free agent; for
I have always been disposed of more by little accidents,
than either my own inclinations or interest."

The writer repeats the same excuse in a later letter
to Lady Pomfret:

" I send you this letter by so agreeable a companion,†
that I think it a very considerable present. He will tell
you that he has pressed me very much to set out for
Florence immediately, and I have the greatest inclination in the world to do it; but, as I have already said,
I am but too well convinced that all things are relative,
and mankind was not made to follow their own inclina-

* Dr. Samuel Clarke was in favour with Queen Caroline, who
studied philosophy with him and her confidante Lady Sundon.
† Lady Pomfret's son, Lord Lempster.

tions. I have pushed as fair for liberty as any one; I have most philosophically thrown off all the chains of custom and subjection; and also rooted out of my heart all seeds of ambition and avarice. In such a state, if freedom could be found, that lot would sure be mine; yet certain atoms of attraction and repulsion keep me still in suspense; and I cannot absolutely set the day of my departure, though I very sincerely wish for it, and have one reason more than usual: this town being at present infested with English, who torment me as much as the frogs and lice did the palace of Pharaoh, and are surprised that I will not suffer them to skip about my house from morning till night; me, that never opened my doors to such sort of animals in England. I wish I knew a corner of the world inaccessible to petits-maîtres and fine ladies. I verily believed when I left London I should choose my own company for the remainder of my days; which I find more difficult to do abroad than at home; and with humility I sighing own,

> " ' Some stronger power eludes the sickly will,
> Dashes my rising hope with certain ill,
> And makes me with reflective trouble see,
> That all is destin'd that I fancy'd free.' "

Venice was a scene of much gaiety, the Electoral Prince of Saxony (son of the Elector of Saxony, who was also King of Poland) having come there. He was a cripple, and was "carried about in a chair, though a beautiful person from the waist upwards: it is said his family design him for the Church." However, the

10

Prince afterwards succeeded his father as Elector in
1763, but died the same year. His "governor," Count
Wackerbarth, was an old friend of Lady Mary's, who
consequently saw a good deal of the Prince's party,
and came in for the festivities given in his honour,
which she could not well avoid. As she writes in
April, 1740, to Lady Pomfret:

"I have nothing to complain of here but too much
diversion, as it is called; and which literally diverts
me from amusements much more agreeable. I can
hardly believe it is me dressed up at balls, and stalking
about at assemblies; and should not be so much
surprised at suffering any of Ovid's transformations;
having more disposition, as I thought, to harden into
stone or timber, than to be enlivened into these
tumultuary entertainments, where I am amazed to
find myself seated by a sovereign prince, after travelling a thousand miles to establish myself in the bosom
of a republic, with a design to lose all memory of kings
and courts."

The shows arranged in honour of the Electoral
Prince culminated in a great regatta, which Lady
Mary witnessed from the windows of her friend the
Procurator Grimani, and of which she sent a full
description to her husband.

"You seem to mention the regatta in a manner as
if you would be pleased with a description of it. It
is a race of boats: they are accompanied by vessels
which they call Piotes, and Bichones, that are built
at the expense of the nobles and strangers that have

a mind to display their magnificence; they are a sort of machines adorned with all that sculpture and gilding can do to make a shining appearance. Several of them cost one thousand pounds sterling, and I believe none less than five hundred; they are rowed by gondoliers dressed in rich habits, suitable to what they represent. There was enough of them to look like a little fleet, and I own I never saw a finer sight. It would be too long to describe every one in particular : I shall only name the principal : the Signora Pisani Mocenigo's represented the Chariot of the Night, drawn by four sea-horses, and showing the rising of the moon, accompanied with stars, the statues on each side representing the hours to the number of twenty-four, rowed by gondoliers in rich liveries, which were changed three times, all of equal richness, and the decorations changed also to the dawn of Aurora and the mid-day sun, the statues being new dressed every time, the first in green, the second time red, and the last blue, all equally laced with silver, there being three races. Signor Soranzo's represented the kingdom of Poland, with all the provinces and rivers in that dominion, with a concert of the best instrumental music in rich Polish habits; the painting and gilding were exquisite in their kinds. Signor Contarini's piote showed the Liberal Arts ; Apollo was seated on the stern upon Mount Parnassus, Pegasus behind, and the Muses seated round him : opposite was a figure representing Painting, with Fame blowing her trumpet ; and on each side Sculpture and Music in their proper dresses. The Procurator Foscarini's was the Chariot of Flora guided by Cupids, and adorned with all sorts of flowers, rose-trees, etc. Signor Julio Contarini['s] represented the Triumphs of Valour; Victory was on the stern, and all the ornaments warlike trophies of every kind. Signor Correri's was the Adriatic Sea receiving into her arms the Hope of Saxony. Signor Alvisio Mocenigo's was the Garden of Hesperides; the whole fable was represented by different statues. Signor Querini had the Chariot of Venus drawn by doves, so well done, they seemed ready to fly upon the water; the Loves and Graces attended her. Signor Paul Doria had the Chariot of Diana, who appeared hunting in a large wood: the trees, hounds, stag, and nymphs, all done naturally: the gondoliers dressed like peasants attending the chase: and Endymion, lying under a large tree, gazing on the goddess. Signor Angelo Labbia represented Poland crowning of Saxony, waited on by the Virtues and subject Provinces. Signor Angelo Molino was Neptune waited on by the Rivers. Signor Vicenzo Morosini's piote showed the Triumphs of Peace: Discord being chained at her feet, and she surrounded with the Pleasures, etc."

At last, after numerous delays, Lady Mary succeeded in leaving Venice, though suffering herself, as she seems often to have done, from a swelled face, which she still had when she joined Lady Pomfret and Lady Walpole at Florence, and was visited by Horace Walpole.

The beauties of Florence and its artistic treasures she admired, but apparently left to Lady Pomfret to describe ; though the compiler of the volume of letters of 1767 duly supplied a long and dull description, which is written rather in the style of a bad imitation of Dr. Johnson than in Lady Mary's own livelier and less polysyllabic manner. After nearly two months at Florence she passed on to Rome, which was suffering under too great an emission of Papal paper-money. As she writes to her husband :

"Belloni, who is the greatest banker not only of Rome but all Italy, furnished me with fifty sequins, which he solemnly swore was all the money he had in the house. They go to market with paper, pay the lodgings with paper, and, in short, there is no specie to be seen, which raises the price of everything to the utmost extravagance, nobody knowing what to ask for their goods. It is said the present Pope* (who has a very good character) has declared he will endeavour a remedy, though it is very difficult to find one. He was bred a lawyer, and has passed the greatest part of his life in that profession ; and is so sensible of the misery of the State, that he is reported to have said, that he never thought himself in want till since his elevation. He has no relations which he takes any notice of. The country belonging to him, which I have passed, is almost uninhabited, and in a poverty beyond what I ever saw."

The chaise which she purchased to take her to Naples was no more firm than the credit of the Papal States, and collapsed promptly on the second day of

* Benedict XIV., but recently chosen.

the journey. However, it was cobbled together sufficiently to reach Naples, where Lady Mary thought of settling, preferring the manners of the Neapolitans to those of the Romans and Florentines, in spite of their worse reputation. She writes to her husband :

"I like the climate extremely, which is now so soft, I am actually sitting without any want of a fire. I do not find the people so savage as they were represented to me. I have received visits from several of the principal ladies; and I think I could meet with as much company here as I desire; but here is one article both disagreeable and incommodious, which is the grandeur of the equipages. Two coaches, two running footmen, four other footmen, a gentleman usher, and two pages, are as necessary here as the attendance of a single servant is at London. All the Spanish customs are observed very rigorously. I could content myself with all of them except this : but I see plainly, from my own observation as well as intelligence, that it is not to be dispensed with, which I am heartily vexed at.

"The affairs of Europe are now so uncertain, it appears reasonable to me to wait a little, before I fix my residence, that I may not find myself in the theatre of war, which is threatened on all sides."

However, the Spanish formality kept up by the Spanish Bourbon prince on the throne (Charles, afterwards Charles III. of Spain) repelled her; and the death of the Emperor Charles VI. in October, 1740, had thrown European politics into such confusion, owing to the impending struggle for the inheritance

of the Austrian domains, that it was hard to say where
or when war might break out. Meanwhile, to gratify
her own taste and that of her husband for classical
antiquities, she tried to see the ruins of Herculaneum.

"The town lately discovered is at Portici, about
three miles from this place. Since the first discovery,
no care has been taken, and the ground fallen in, [so]
that the present passage to it is, as I am told by everybody, extreme dangerous, and for some time nobody
ventures into it. I had been assured by some English
gentlemen, that were let down into it the last year,
that the whole account given in the newspapers is
literally true. Probably great curiosities might be
found there; but there has been no expense made,
either by propping the ground, or clearing a way into
it; and as the earth falls in daily, it will possibly be
soon stopped up, as it was before."

She wrote again a fortnight later to her husband :

"I did not write to you last post, hoping to have
been able to have given you an account in this of
everything I had observed at Portici, but I have not
yet obtained the King's license, which must be had
before I can be admitted to see the pictures, and fragments of statues which have been found there, and has
been hitherto delayed on various pretences, it being at
present a very singular favour. They say that some
English carried a painter with them the last year to
copy the pictures, which renders it more difficult at
present to get leave to see them. I have taken all
possible pains to get information of this subterranean

building, and am told 'tis the remains of the ancient
city of Hercolana, and by what I can collect, there was
a theatre entire, with all the scenes and ancient decorations : they have broke it to pieces by digging irre-
gularly.   I hope in a few days to get permission to go,
and will then give you the exactest description I am
capable of."

The permission, however, was refused—a circumstance which by no means raised Lady Mary's opinion
of the King of the Two Sicilies.

" I returned hither last night," she wrote from Rome,
in January, 1741, " after six weeks' stay at Naples ;
great part of that time was vainly taken up in endeavouring to satisfy your curiosity and my own, in relation to the late-discovered town of Hercolana.   I
wasted eight days, in hopes of permission to see the
pictures and other rarities taken from thence, which is
preserved in the King's palace at Portici ; but I found
it was to no purpose, his majesty keeping the key in
his own cabinet, which he would not part with, though
the Prince de Zathia (who is one of his favourites), I
believe, very sincerely tried his interest to obtain it for
me.   He is son to the Spanish Ambassador I knew at
Venice, and both he and his lady loaded me with
civilities at Naples.   The Court in general is more
barbarous than any of the ancient Goths.   One proof
of it, among many others, was melting down a beautiful
copper statue of a vestal found in this new ruin, to
make medallions for the late solemn christening.   The
whole Court follow the Spanish customs and politics.

I could say a good deal on this subject if I thought my letter would come safe to your hands; the apprehension it may not, hinders my answering another inquiry you make, concerning a family here, of which, indeed, I can say little, avoiding all commerce with those that frequent it."

The " family " referred to was, of course, that of the Pretender James, or the Chevalier, as he was called by those who wished to be neutral. He was now residing at Rome with his two sons, Charles Edward and Henry. As a good Whig, Lady Mary carefully avoided them, though she saw the two young Stuarts once at a ball.

"I never saw the Chevalier during my whole stay at Rome. I saw his two sons* at a public ball in masque; they were very richly adorned with jewels. The eldest seems thoughtless enough, and is really not unlike Mr. Lyttelton in his shape and air. The youngest is very well made, dances finely, and has an ingenuous countenance ; he is but fourteen years of age. The family live very splendidly, yet pay everybody, and (wherever they get it) are certainly in no want of money."

At Rome she spent the rest of the winter, and seems to have had a sort of " salon " for the English then at Rome, to keep them out of the way of mischief, moral or political. She wrote about it long afterwards to her daughter, Lady Bute.

* Charles Edward, the Young Pretender, and Henry, afterwards Cardinal of York.

" The winter I passed at Rome there was an unusual concourse of English, many of them with great estates, and their own masters : as they had no admittance to the Roman ladies, nor understood the language, they had no way of passing their evenings but in my apartment, where I had always a full drawing-room.   Their governors encouraged their assiduities as much as they could, finding I gave them lessons of economy and good conduct ; and my authority was so great, it was a common threat amongst them, I'll tell Lady Mary what you say.   I was judge of all their disputes, and my decisions always submitted to.   While I stayed, there was neither gaming, drinking, quarrelling, nor keeping. The Abbé Grant (a very honest, good-natured North Briton, who has resided several years at Rome) was so amazed at this uncommon regularity, he would have made me believe I was bound in conscience to pass my life there, for the good of my countrymen.   I can assure you my vanity was not at all raised by this influence over them, knowing very well that had Lady Charlotte de Roussi* been in my place, it would have been the same thing.   There is that general emulation in mankind, I am fully persuaded if a dozen young fellows bred a bear amongst them, and saw no other creature, they would every day fall out for the bear's favours, and be extremely flattered by any mark of distinction shown by that ugly animal."

But this stay at Rome can have lasted only some five

---

* A French Protestant lady, governess to George II.'s children, and apparently rather a dull person.

or six weeks; for at the end of February, 1741, Lady
Mary had gone to Leghorn to meet her baggage, which
had come by sea from England. From here, after
some uncertainty, she went to Genoa and Turin. The
change in Italian manners since she had passed through
Genoa with her husband in 1718, much impressed her,
as she wrote to Mr. Wortley Montagu.

" The manners of Italy are so much altered since we
were here last, the alteration is scarce credible. They
say it has been by the last war. The French, being
masters, introduced all their customs, which were
eagerly embraced by the ladies, and I believe will
never be laid aside; yet the different governments
make different manners in every state. You know,
though the republic is not rich, here are many private
families vastly so, and live at a great superfluous expense: all the people of the first quality keep coaches
as fine as the Speaker's, and some of them two or three,
though the streets are too narrow to use them in the
town; but they take the air in them, and their chairs
carry them to the gates. The liveries are all plain:
gold or silver being forbidden to be worn within the
walls, the habits are all obliged to be black, but they
wear exceeding fine lace and linen; and in their country-
houses, which are generally in the faubourg, they dress
very rich, and have extreme fine jewels. Here is nothing
cheap but houses. A palace fit for a prince may be
hired for fifty pounds per annum: I mean unfurnished.
All games of chance are strictly prohibited, and it seems
to me the only law they do not try to evade: they play at

quadrille, piquet, etc., but not high. Here are no regular public assemblies. I have been visited by all of the first rank, and invited to several fine dinners, particularly to the wedding of one of the house of Spinola, where there were ninety-six sat down to table, and I think the entertainment one of the finest I ever saw. There was the night following a ball and supper for the same company, with the same profusion. They tell me that all their great marriages are kept in the same public manner. Nobody keeps more than two horses, all their journeys being post; the expense of them, including the coachman, is (I am told) fifty pounds per annum. A chair is very near as much; I give eighteen francs a week for mine. The senators can converse with no strangers during the time of their magistracy, which lasts two years. The number of servants is regulated, and almost every lady has the same, which is two footmen, a gentleman-usher, and a page, who follows her chair."

From Turin Lady Mary had an opportunity of sending by a friend to her husband, and hence ventured to touch on the politics of the time. England was now engaged in a war with Spain over commercial and colonial disputes; and France was expected to join with Spain in virtue of the Bourbon Family Compact of 1733. The Queen of Spain, Elizabeth Farnese, second wife of Philip V., having placed her eldest son Charles on the throne of Naples, was about to take advantage of the disputed state of the Austrian succession to seize Milan for her second son Philip. Lady Mary seems to suggest that by threatening to excite a revolt in Naples, which the Spaniards had only held since 1735, the English Government could bring Spain to terms—forgetting, apparently, that Naples was nominally at peace with England. This means was afterwards employed to prevent the Neapolitan army from joining the Spaniards.

" The English politics are the general jest of all the nations I have passed through ; and even those who profit by our follies cannot help laughing at our notorious blunders : though they are all persuaded that the Minister* does not act from weakness but corruption, and that the Spanish gold influences his measures. I had a long discourse with Count Mahony on this subject, who said, very freely, that half the ships sent to the coast of Naples, that have lain idle in our ports last summer, would have frightened the Queen of Spain into a submission to whatever terms we thought proper to impose. The people, who are loaded with taxes, hate the Spanish Government, of which I had daily proofs, hearing them curse the English for bringing their King to them,† whenever they saw any of our nation : but I am not much surprised at the ignorance of our Ministers, after seeing what creatures they employ to send them intelligence. Except Mr. Villette, at this

* Sir Robert Walpole, then near his fall from power.

† The English had not brought Charles to Naples, but had brought him to Tuscany, in consequence of the Treaty of Seville, 1729 ; and this establishment of the Spaniards in Italy helped them to conquer Naples later on.

Court,* there is not one that has common sense: I say
this without prejudice, all of them having been as civil
and serviceable to me as they could."

Sardinia was making preparations for the impending
struggle for Milan.   Her position holding the Alps,
between France and the Austrian possession of Milan,
made her courted by both sides.

From Turin Lady Mary went on to Geneva, where
the people were more to her taste than the prices.   In
spite of the Republican simplicity, living was as dear
as in London, all provisions being brought in from outside.   This and the " sharpness of the air " soon drove
her to Chambéry, in Savoy, where everything was as
cheap as it was dear at Geneva.

" Here is the most profound peace and unbounded
plenty that is to be found in any corner of the universe;
but not one rag of money.   For my part, I think it
amounts to the same thing, whether one is obliged to
give several pence for bread, or can have a great deal
of bread for a penny, since the Savoyard nobility here
keep as good tables, without money, as those in London,
who spend in a week what would be here a considerable
yearly revenue.   Wine, which is equal to the best Bur-
gundy, is sold for a penny a quart, and I have a cook
for very small wages, that is capable of rivalling Chloé.†
Here are no equipages but chairs, the hire of which is

* Mr. Villette was English Minister at the Sardinian Court.
He was afterwards of great service in keeping Sardinia on the
Austrian side.

† Monsieur Chloé was a celebrated French cook in the service
of the Duke of Newcastle.

about a crown a week, and all other matters proportionable. I can assure you I make the figure of the
Duchess of Marlborough, by carrying gold in my purse;
there being no visible coin but copper. Yet we are all
people that can produce pedigrees to serve for the Order
of Malta. Many of us have travelled, and 'tis the
fashion to love reading. We eat together perpetually,
and have assemblies every night for conversation. To
say truth, the houses are all built after the manner of the
old English towns; nobody having had money to build
for two hundred years past. Consequently the walls
are thick, the roofs low, etc., the streets narrow, and
miserably paved."

At Chambéry Lady Mary spent the winter; but in
the spring of 1742, fearing the outbreak of war and a
French invasion of Savoy, she moved to Lyons. Here
she received a letter from her husband, asking her to
arrange an interview with their son, Edward Wortley
Montagu, who had been rusticating in Holland and had
come back to England for three months. He (it
seems) was very anxious to get free from his Fleet
wife, making and breaking countless promises of reformation, and wanting to go into the army. To this
interview Lady Mary consented, and arranged for her
son, under an assumed name, to meet her at Valence.
She writes to her husband:

"On recollection (however inconvenient it may be
to me on many accounts), I am not sorry to converse
with my son. I shall at least have the satisfaction of
making a clear judgment of his behaviour and temper,

which I shall deliver to you in the most sincere and un-
prejudiced manner. You need not apprehend that I
shall speak to him in passion. I do not know that I
ever did in my life. I am not apt to be over-heated in
discourse, and am so far prepared, even for the worst
on his side, that I think nothing he can say can alter the
resolution I have taken of treating him with calmness.
Both nature and interest (were I inclined to follow
blindly the dictates of either) would determine me to
wish him your heir rather than a stranger; but I think
myself obliged both by honour, conscience, and my
regard for you, no way to deceive you; and I confess,
hitherto I see nothing but falsehood and weakness
through his whole conduct."

Before arranging the meeting, however, Lady Mary,
desirous of avoiding any possible theatre of war, and
unwilling to remain in France when a war with England was imminent, established herself in Avignon, then,
and until the Revolution, a papal possession, though
surrounded by French territory. She wrote to the
Countess of Pomfret on arriving there:

" I have changed my situation, fearing to find myself
blocked up in a besieged town; and not knowing where
else to avoid the terrors of war, I have put myself under
the protection of the Holy See. Your ladyship being
well acquainted with this place, I need not send you a
description of it; but I think you did not stay in it long
enough to know many of the people. I find them very
polite and obliging to strangers. We have assemblies
every night, which conclude with a great supper; and

comedies which are tolerably well acted. In short, I
think one may while away an idle life with great tranquillity; which has long since been the utmost of my
ambition."

From Avignon Lady Mary went to Orange, where
she had directed her son to meet her. Mr. Wortley
Montagu had heard a rumour that his son had been
"made an enthusiast in Holland," the eighteenth-
century equivalent of joining the Salvation Army
to-day. Lady Mary's account was reassuring on that
topic, if on no other:

"I am just returned from passing two days with our
son, of whom I will give you the most exact account I
am capable of. He is so much altered in his person, I
should scarcely have known him. He has entirely lost
his beauty, and looks at least seven years older than he
is; and the wildness that he always had in his eyes is
so much increased it is downright shocking, and I am
afraid will end fatally. He is grown fat, but is still
genteel, and has an air of politeness that is agreeable.
He speaks French like a Frenchman, and has got all
the fashionable expressions of that language, and a
volubility of words which he always had, and which
I do not wonder should pass for wit with inconsiderate
people. His behaviour is perfectly civil, and I found
him very submissive; but in the main, no way really
improved in his understanding, which is exceedingly
weak; and I am convinced he will always be led by the
person he converses with either right or wrong, not
being capable of forming any fixed judgment of his

own. As to his enthusiasm, if he had it, I suppose he has already lost it; since I could perceive no turn of it in all his conversation. But with his head I believe it is possible to make him a monk one day and a Turk* three days after. He has a flattering, insinuating manner, which naturally prejudices strangers in his favour. He began to talk to me in the usual silly cant I have so often heard from him, which I shortened by telling him I desired not to be troubled with it; that professions were of no use where actions were expected; and that the only thing could give me hopes of a good conduct was regularity and truth."

The topic of their son often turns up in the letters between Lady Mary and her husband; but no satisfactory or lasting reformation was to be looked for from him. From these and occasional allusions in Horace Walpole's letters we get glimpses of him, flitting between London and Paris, blazing out in splendid dresses on a scanty allowance, put in prison at Paris over a discreditable gambling quarrel with a Jew of several names, running away with "the famous Miss Ashe," and adding her "to the number of his wives." Perhaps the idea that he was hardly sane is the truest as well as most charitable way of accounting for his adventures. His mother was glad to turn from his affairs to more grateful topics.

"You may, perhaps, hear of a trifle which makes a great noise in this part of the world, which is, that I

---

* It was believed that he did turn Mohammedan after the death of his parents.

am building; but the whole expense which I have contracted for is but twenty-six pounds sterling. You know
the situation of this town is on the meeting of the Rhône
and Durance. On one side of it, within the walls, was
formerly a fortress built on a very high rock; they say
it was destroyed by lightning: one of the towers was
left part standing, the walls being a yard in thickness:
this was made use of some time for a public mill, but
the height making it inconvenient for the carriage of
meal, it has stood useless many years. Last summer,
in the hot evenings, I walked often thither, where I
always found a fresh breeze, and the most beautiful
land-prospect I ever saw (except Wharncliffe*); being
a view of the windings of two great rivers, and over-
looking the whole country, with part of Languedoc and
Provence. I was so much charmed with it, that I said
in company, that, if that old mill was mine, I would
turn it into a belvidere; my words were repeated, and
the two consuls waited on me soon after, with a dona-
tion from the town of the mill and the land about it:
I have added a dome to it, and made it a little rotunda
for the 'foresaid sum. I have also amused myself with
patching up an inscription, which I have communicated
to the Archbishop, who is much delighted with it; but
it is not placed, and perhaps never shall be."

The inscription in question was an adaptation of
Cowley's "Epitaphium Vivi Auctoris," the gender
being changed to feminine to suit Lady Mary. As
this change spoilt the scansion of some of the lines

* Wharncliffe was the country seat of Mr. Wortley Montagu.

11—2

Mr. Wortley Montagu was less delighted with the piece than the Archbishop; and his wife probably gave up the idea of placing it on her "belvidere." She gave her husband many particulars of the town and neighbourhood of Avignon; and having to send a man-servant back to England, she took the opportunity of writing a piece of information about the descent which the French were then planning on England in the interests of the Pretender—war having been declared in March, 1744, after fighting had been going on for some time.

"I take this opportunity of informing you in what manner I came acquainted with the secret I hinted at in my letter of the 5th of February. The society of Freemasons at Nismes presented the Duke of Richelieu,* Governor of Languedoc, with a magnificent entertainment; it is but one day's post from hence, and the Duchess of Crillon, with some other ladies of this town, resolved to be at it, and almost by force carried me with them, which I am tempted to believe an act of Providence, considering my great reluctance, and the service it proved to be to unhappy innocent people. The greatest part of the town of Nismes are secret Protestants, which are still severely punished according to the edicts of Lewis XIV. whenever they are detected in any public worship. A few days before we came, they had assembled; their minister and about a dozen of his congregation were seized and imprisoned.

* Well known for his dissipations, and afterwards better known by his capture of Minorca in 1756, and his making the Convention of Kloster Zeven in 1757.

I knew nothing of this; but I had not been in the town two hours, when I was visited by two of the most considerable of the Huguenots, who came to beg of me, with tears, to speak in their favour to the Duke of Richelieu, saying none of the Catholics would do it, and the Protestants durst not, and that God had sent me for their protection. The Duke of Richelieu was too well-bred to refuse to listen to a lady, and I was of a rank and nation to have liberty to say what I pleased; they moved my compassion so much, I resolved to use my endeavours to serve them, though I had little hope of succeeding. I would not therefore dress myself for the supper, but went in a domino to the ball, a masque giving opportunity of talking in a freer manner than I could have done without it. I was at no trouble in engaging his conversation: the ladies having told him I was there, he immediately advanced towards me; and I found, from a different motive, he had a great desire to be acquainted with me, having heard a great deal of me. After abundance of compliments of that sort, I made my request for the liberty of the poor Protestants; he with great freedom told me he was so little a bigot, he pitied them as much as I did, but his orders from Court were to send them to the galleys. However, to show how much he desired my good opinion, he was returning. and would solicit their freedom (which he has since obtained). This obligation occasioned me to continue the conversation, and he asked me what party the Pretender had in England; I answered, as I thought, a very small one. ' We are

told otherwise at Paris,' said he ; ' however, a bustle at
this time may serve to facilitate our other projects,
and we intend to attempt a descent ; * at least it will
cause the troops to be recalled, and perhaps Admiral
Mathews will be obliged to leave the passage open for
Don Philip.'† You may imagine how much I wished
to give you immediate notice of this ; but as all letters
are opened at Paris, it would have been to no purpose
to write it by the post, and have only gained me a
powerful enemy in the Court of France,‡ he being so
much a favourite of the King's, he is supposed to stand
candidate for the Ministry.   In my letter to Sir
R[obert] W[alpole] from Venice, I offered my service,
and desired to know in what manner I could send
intelligence, if anything happened to my knowledge
that could be of use to England.   I believe he imagined
that I wanted some gratification, and only sent me
cold thanks."

The relics of Roman municipal life here and in other
towns of the South of France must have interested Mr.
Wortley Montagu, who retained his taste for classical
antiquities.

" This town is considerably larger than either Aix
or Montpelier, and has more inhabitants of quality than

* Marshal Saxe was to command the army, and the transports
were gathered at Dunkirk, but were shattered by a storm.   The
Young Pretender's enterprise next year was made almost without
French aid.

† Admiral Mathews commanded the English fleet in the
Mediterranean, and was occupied in preventing the Spanish forces
from coming over by sea to Italy.

‡ The Duc de Richelieu.

of any other sort, having no trade, from the exactions of the French, though better situated for it than any inland town I know. What is most singular is the government, which retains a sort of imitation of the old Roman : here are two consuls chosen every year, the first of whom from the chief noblesse ; and there is as much struggling for that dignity in the Hôtel de Ville as in the Senate. The vice-legate cannot violate their privileges, but as all governors naturally wish to increase their authority, there are perpetual factions of the same kind as those between prerogative and liberty of the subject. We have a new Vice-legate, arrived a few days since, nephew to Cardinal Acquaviva, young, rich, and handsome, and sets out in a greater figure than has ever been known here. The magistrate next to him in place is called the Viguier,* who is chosen every year by the Hôtel de Ville, and represents the person of the Pope in all criminal causes, but his authority [is] so often clipped by the vice-legates, there remains nothing of it at present but the honour of precedence, during his office, and a box at the play-house gratis, with the *surintendance* of all public diversions. When Don Philip passed here, he began the ball with his lady, which is the custom of all the princes that pass.

"The beginning of Avignon was probably a colony from Marseilles, there having been a temple of Diana on that very spot where I have my little pavilion. If there was any painter capable of drawing it, I would

* Viguier is derived from *vicarius*, a vicar or deputy.

send you a view of the landscape, which is one of the most beautiful I ever saw."

At Avignon Lady Mary stayed altogether over four years, but her correspondence during that time is rather scanty. As all letters had to pass through France, and war was going on between England and France during most of the time—though not formally declared till 1744—we may imagine that she wrote but few letters, and that not many of these arrived at their destination. Some English gossip she gathered from her friend, the Countess of Oxford. She heard of the death of her old friend and enemy, Pope, in 1744, and was curious to know what had become of his house at Twickenham; no animosity, however, is betrayed in the reference to him. Nor was much emotion aroused by hearing of the destruction of the house where much of her girlhood had been spent—Thoresby, which was burnt down in April, 1745.

The French victories in the Netherlands—notably the battle of Fontenoy—made Avignon a less pleasant place of sojourn. " I pass my time very disagreeably at present among the French," Lady Mary writes; "their late successes have given them an air of triumph that is very difficult for an English heart to suffer; I think less of politics than most people, yet cannot be entirely insensible of the misfortunes of my country."

She had long been desirous of leaving Avignon; but Italy was disturbed by the war between Austrians and Sardinians on one side, and French and Spaniards on the other, and in 1745 the latter had been completely successful. Thus it was dangerous to travel to Italy, and France would be even worse than Avignon, especially as the French *droit d'aubaine* gave to the King the goods of foreigners dying in his dominions, a circumstance which will explain the meaning, though not the grammar, of the following extract :

" I am very impatient to leave this town, which has been highly disagreeable to me ever since the beginning of this war, but the impossibility of returning into Italy, and the law in France which gives to the King all the effects any person deceased dies possessed of, and I own that I am very desirous my jewels and some little necessary plate that I have bought, should be safely delivered into your hands, hoping you will be so good to dispose of them to my daughter. The Duke of Richelieu flattered me for some time that he would obtain for me a permission to dispose of my goods, but he has not yet done it, and you know the uncertainty of Court promises."

Avignon became still more intolerable when in 1746 the failure of the Jacobite insurrection brought a swarm of Jacobite refugees into the city. Lady Mary, who was notoriously Whig in views, and who was constantly endeavouring to send letters to her friends in England, probably got the reputation of a spy. She resolved to take the first possible opportunity of escape, and the following letter to her husband gives a graphic account of her perilous journey :

" Brescia. Aug. 23, N.S. [1746].

" You will be surprised at the date of this letter, but Avignon has been long disagreeable to me on many

us, we got into the town, but, when we came there, it
was impossible to find any lodging, all the inns being
filled with wounded Spaniards. The Count went to
the Governor, and asked a chamber for a Venetian
lady, which he granted very readily; but there was
nothing in it but the bare walls, and in less than a
quarter of an hour after the whole house was empty
both of furniture and people, the Governor flying into
the citadel, and carrying with him all his goods and
family. We were forced to pass the night without
beds or supper. About daybreak the victorious
Germans entered the town. The Count went to wait
on the generals, to whom, I believe, he had a com-
mission. He told them my name, and there was no
sort of honour or civility they did not pay me. They
immediately ordered me a guard of hussars (which
was very necessary in the present disorder), and sent
me refreshments of all kinds. Next day I was visited
by the Prince of Badin Dourlach, the Prince Loües-
tein,* and all the principal officers, with whom I
passed for a heroine, showing no uneasiness, though
the cannon of the citadel (where was a Spanish
garrison) played very briskly. I was forced to stay
there two days for want of post-horses, the postmaster
being fled, with all his servants, and the Spaniards
having seized all the horses they could find. At length
I set out from thence the 19th instant, with a strong
escort of hussars, meeting with no further accident on

* Baden Durlach and Löwestein are meant, unless the last is a
mistake for Prince Lichtenstein, the Austrian Commander-in-chief.

the road, except at the little town of Vogherra, where they refused post-horses, till the hussars drew their sabres. The 20th I arrived safe here. It is a very pretty place, where I intend to repose myself at least during the remainder of the summer. This journey has been very expensive; but I am very glad I have made it. I am now in a neutral country, under the protection of Venice. The Doge is our old friend Grimani, and I do not doubt meeting with all sort of civility."

Thus happily was Lady Mary arrived in one of the few neutral countries of the time; and in the hospitable land of the Venetian republic she was to remain for fifteen years.

CHAPTER·VI

RESIDENCE AT LOVERE

HARDLY had Lady Mary reached Brescia when the
health she had boasted of in the last lines of her letter
to her husband broke down, either from fatigue or
some other cause. She was seized with a fever, which
kept her in bed for two months. But fortunately
Count Palazzo's mother had insisted on taking her
in, and nursed her, as she herself said, as if she had
been a sister. Lady Mary expresses herself in the

most grateful way concerning the kindness of the
Countess. What happened afterwards to embroil the
guest with her hosts it is impossible to conjecture.
The Italian paper seen by Lord Wharncliffe, and
drawn up for Lady Mary, seemed to refer to some
forcible detention by an Italian Count and his mother,
who could hardly be other than Count Palazzo and his
parent. Did the Count presume upon his services to
Lady Mary, and did his mother take his side? Did
the family try to make a profit out of their presumably
wealthy guest? or did they simply try to prolong their
direction of her affairs later than was necessary? In
any case, some quarrel there seems to have been, for
there is apparently no further mention of the Palazzo
family in the correspondence, though one would naturally expect them to remain Lady Mary's most valued
friends while she was in the neighbourhood of Brescia.
However, by March, 1747, she was restored to fair
health, and living in a house of her own near Brescia
But the ague from which she had suffered returned on
her, and her doctors recommended her to try Lovere,
a place at the northern extremity of Lake Iseo, valued
for its medicinal springs. Her first impressions of the
place are recorded in a letter to her daughter, Lady
Bute :

"DEAR CHILD,—I am now in a place the most
beautifully romantic I ever saw in my life : it is the
Tunbridge of this part of the world, to which I was
sent by the doctor's order, my ague often returning,
notwithstanding the loads of bark I have taken. To

say truth, I have no reason to repent my journey,
though I was very unwilling to undertake it, it being
forty miles, half by land and half by water; the land
so stony I was almost shook to pieces, and I had the ill
luck to be surprised with a storm on the lake, that if I
had not been near a little port (where I passed a night
in a very poor inn), the vessel must have been lost. A
fair wind brought me hither next morning early. I
found a very good lodging, a great deal of good company, and a village in many respects resembling Tunbridge Wells, not only in the quality of the waters,
which is the same, but in the manner of the buildings,
most of the houses being separate at little distances,
and all built on the sides of hills, which indeed are far
different from those of Tunbridge, being six times as
high : they are really vast rocks of different figures,
covered with green moss, or short grass, diversified by
tufts of trees, little woods, and here and there vineyards, but no other cultivation, except gardens like
those on Richmond Hill. The whole lake, which is
twenty-five miles long, and three broad, is all surrounded with these impassable mountains, the sides of
which, towards the bottom, are so thick set with
villages (and in most of them gentlemen's seats), that I
do not believe there is anywhere above a mile distance
from one another, which adds very much to the beauty
of the prospect.

" We have an opera here, which is performed three
times in the week. I was at it last night, and should
have been surprised at the neatness of the scenes,

goodness of the voices, and justness of the actors, if I had not remembered I was in Italy. Several gentlemen jumped into the orchestra, and joined in the concert, which I suppose is one of the freedoms of the place, for I never saw it in any great town. I was yet more amazed (while the actors were dressing for the farce that concluded the entertainment) to see one of the principal among them, and as errant a *petit maitre* as if he had passed all his life at Paris, mount the stage, and present us with a cantata of his own performing. He had the pleasure of being almost deafened with applause. The ball began afterwards, but I was not witness of it, having accustomed myself to such early hours that I was half asleep before the opera finished ; it begins at ten o'clock, so that it was one before I could get to bed, though I had supper before I went, which is the custom."

From the time of her establishing herself at Lovere, Lady Mary's letters were chiefly written to her daughter. She still continued to correspond with her husband ; but a certain constraint is always to be observed in her letters to him, whereas to her daughter she pours out her thoughts with an affectionate garrulity. She soon settled down into the quiet Italian country life ; and, liberal as are the ideas Horace Walpole seems to have entertained on her dissipations, she apparently contented herself with whist at penny points. As she wrote to Lady Bute in December, 1747 :

" I find I amuse myself here in the same manner as if at London, according to your account of it ; that is,

I play at whist every night with some old priests that
I have taught it to, and are my only companions.   To
say truth, the decay of my sight will no longer suffer
me to read by candlelight, and the evenings are now
long and dark, that I am forced to stay at home.   I
believe you'll be persuaded my gaming makes nobody
uneasy, when I tell you that we play only a penny per
corner.   'Tis now a year that I have lived wholly in the
country, and have no design of quitting it.   I am
entirely given up to rural amusements, and have forgot
there are any such things as wits or fine ladies in the
world."

But the free and easy hospitality in vogue among the
nobility of Venetian Lombardy was rather too much
for Lady Mary's philosophy—shall we say for her
frugality?

" The way of living in this province being," she
writes, " what I believe it is now in the sociable part
of Scotland, and was in England a hundred years ago.
I had a visit in the beginning of these holidays of thirty
horse of ladies and gentlemen, with their servants (by the
way, the ladies all ride like the late Duchess of Cleve-
land).   They came with the kind intent of staying
with me at least a fortnight, though I had never seen
any of them before; but they were all neighbours
within ten miles round.   I could not avoid entertaining
them at supper, and by good luck had a large quantity
of game in the house, which, with the help of my
poultry, furnished out a plentiful table.   I sent for the
fiddles, and they were so obliging as to dance all night,

and even dine with me next day, though none of them had been in bed ; and were much disappointed I did not press them to stay, it being the fashion to go in troops to one another's houses, hunting and dancing together a month in each castle. I have not yet returned any of their visits, nor do not intend it for some time, to avoid this expensive hospitality. The trouble of it is not very great, they not expecting any ceremony. I left the room about one o'clock, and they continued their ball in the saloon above stairs, without being at all offended at my departure. But the greatest diversion I had was to see a lady of my own age comfortably dancing with her own husband, some years older ; and I can assert that she jumps and gallops with the best of them."

This kind of friendly irruption seems to have been common in carnival time, though the next instance was not so expensive.

" Some ladies in the neighbourhood favoured me last week with a visit in masquerade. They were all dressed in white like vestal virgins, with garlands in their hands. They came at night with violins and flambeaux, but did not stay more than one dance ; pursuing their way to another castle some miles from hence."

But Lady Mary retained a lively interest in English doings, particularly in those of her children. Her son at this time was secretary to his relation, Lord Sandwich, English Plenipotentiary at the Congress of Aix-la-Chapelle ; but her pleasure at the good report given by Lord Sandwich was dashed by the fear that it might be dictated by interested motives. Lord and Lady Bute had also been more in public, the former having developed a taste for private theatricals, by which he gratified both himself and his master, Frederick, Prince of Wales. It appears that Lord Bute and his friends acted Young's " Revenge," one of the plays the poet wrote before he became a royal chaplain. Young was a friend of Lady Mary's, and had submitted some of his plays to her for criticisms and suggestions. She contrasted the dramatic diversions of the Court with her own experience of carnival gaieties at Lovere.

"I give you thanks, dear child, for your entertaining account of your present diversions. I find the public calamities have no influence on the pleasures of the town. I remember very well the play of the ' Revenge,' having been once acquainted with a party that intended to represent it (not one of which is now alive). I wish you had told me who acted the principal parts. I suppose Lord Bute was Alonzo, by the magnificence of his dress. I think they have mended their choice in the ' Orphan ': I saw it played at Westminster School, where Lord Erskine was Monimia, and then one of the most beautiful figures that could be seen. I have had here (in low life) some amusements of the same sort. I believe I wrote you word I intended to go to the opera at Brescia; but the weather being cold, and the roads bad, prevented my journey; and the people of this village (which is the largest I know: the curate tells me he has two thousand communicants) presented me a petition for leave to erect a theatre in my saloon.

This house has stood empty many years before I took it, and they were accustomed to turn the stables into a playhouse every carnival: it is now occupied by my horses, and they had no other place proper for a stage. I easily complied with their request, and was surprised at the beauty of their scenes, which, though painted by a country painter, are better coloured, and the perspective better managed, than in any of the second-rate theatres in London. I liked it so well, it is not yet pulled down. The performance was yet more surprising, the actors being all peasants; but the Italians have so natural a genius for comedy, they acted as well as if they had been brought up to nothing else, particularly the Arlequin, who far surpassed any of our English, though only the tailor of the village, and I am assured never saw a play in any other place. It is a pity they have not better poets, the pieces being not at all superior to our drolls. The music, habits, and illumination were at the expense of the parish, and the whole entertainment, which lasted the three last days of the carnival, cost me only a barrel of wine, which I gave the actors, and is not so dear as small beer in London. At present, as the old song says,

> " 'All my whole care
> Is my farming affair,
> To make my corn grow, and my apple-trees bear.'

My improvements give me great pleasure, and so much profit, that if I could live a hundred years longer, I should certainly provide for all my grandchildren: but,

alas! as the Italians say, *h'o sonato vingt & quatro ora :*
and it is not long I must expect to write myself your
most affectionate mother."

In later letters Lady Mary described to her daughter
her establishment at Lovere, where she had not only
rented an old château or "castle," as she calls it, but
took a garden and farm-house near the river Oglio for
the summer heats. Soon after the date of this letter
she bought the "castle" outright for a small sum, and
fitted it up partly as a residence. The description of
her "dairy-house" and garden is entertaining :

"I have been these six weeks, and still am, at my
dairy-house, which joins to my garden. I believe I
have already told you it is a long mile from the castle,
which is situate in the midst of a very large village,
once a considerable town, part of the walls still remaining, and has not vacant ground enough about it
to make a garden, which is my greatest amusement,
it being now troublesome to walk, or even go in the
chaise till the evening. I have fitted up in this farm-
house a room for myself—that is to say, strewed the
floor with rushes, covered the chimney with moss and
branches, and adorned the room with basins of
earthenware (which is made here to great perfection)
filled with flowers, and put in some straw chairs, and
a couch bed, which is my whole furniture. This spot
of ground is so beautiful, I am afraid you will scarce
credit the description, which, however, I can assure
you, shall be very literal, without any embellishment

* So in the original. Lady Mary's Italian was not very accurate.

from imagination. It is on a bank, forming a kind
of peninsula, raised from the river Oglio fifty feet, to
which you may descend by easy stairs cut in the turf,
and either take the air on the river, which is as large
as the Thames at Richmond, or by walking [in] an
avenue two hundred yards on the side of it, you find
a wood of a hundred acres, which was all ready cut
into walks and ridings when I took it. I have only
added fifteen bowers in different views, with seats of
turf. They were easily made, here being a large
quantity of underwood, and a great number of wild
vines, which twist to the top of the highest trees, and
from which they make a very good sort of wine they
call *brusco*. I am now writing to you in one of these
arbours, which is so thickly shaded, the sun is not
troublesome, even at noon. Another is on the side of
the river, where I have made a camp kitchen, that I
may take the fish, dress, and eat it immediately, and
at the same time see the barks, which ascend or
descend every day to or from Mantua, Guastalla, or
Pont de Vie, all considerable towns. This little wood
is carpeted, in their succeeding seasons, with violets
and strawberries, inhabited by a nation of nightingales,
and filled with game of all kinds, excepting deer and
wild boar, the first being unknown here, and not being
large enough for the other.

" My garden was a plain vineyard when it came into
my hands not two years ago, and it is, with a small
expense, turned into a garden that (apart from the
advantage of the climate) I like better than that of

Kensington. The Italian vineyards are not planted like those in France, but in clumps, fastened to trees planted in equal ranks (commonly fruit-trees), and continued in festoons from one to another, which I have turned into covered galleries of shade, that I can walk in the heat without being incommoded by it. I have made a dining-room of verdure, capable of holding a table of twenty covers; the whole ground is three hundred and seventeen feet in length, and two hundred in breadth. You see it is far from large; but so prettily disposed (though I say it), that I never saw a more agreeable rustic garden, abounding with all sort of fruit, and produces a variety of wines. I would send you a piece [*sic*] if I did not fear the customs would make you pay too dear for it. I believe my description gives you but an imperfect idea of my garden. Perhaps I shall succeed better in describing my manner of life, which is as regular as that of any monastery. I generally rise at six, and as soon as I have breakfasted, put myself at the head of my weeder [*sic*] women and work with them till nine. I then inspect my dairy, and take a turn among my poultry, which is a very large inquiry. I have, at present, two hundred chickens, besides turkeys, geese, ducks, and peacocks. All things have hitherto prospered under my care; my bees and silkworms are doubled, and I am told that, without accidents, my capital will be so in two years' time. At eleven o'clock I retire to my books: I dare not indulge myself in that pleasure above an hour. At twelve I constantly dine, and sleep after dinner till about three. I then send for some of my old priests, and either play at piquet or whist, till 'tis cool enough to go out. One evening I walk in my wood, where I often sup, take the air on horseback the next, and go on the water the third. The fishery of this part of the river belongs to me; and my fisherman's little boat (where I have a green lutestring awning) serves me for a barge. He and his son are my rowers without any expense, he being very well paid by the profit of the fish, which I give him on condition of having every day one dish for my table. Here is plenty of every sort of fresh-water fish (excepting salmon); but we have a large trout so like it, that I, that have almost forgot the taste, do not distinguish it."

And in the very next letter to her daughter, Lady Mary returns to the subject of her garden:

"I am really as fond of my garden as a young author of his first play when it has been well received by the town, and can no more forbear teasing my acquaintance for their approbation: though I gave you a long account of it in my last, I must tell you I have made two little terraces, raised twelve steps each, at the end of my great walk; they are just finished, and a great addition to the beauty of my garden. I enclose to you a rough draft of it, drawn (or more properly scrawled) by my own hand, without the assistance of rule or compasses, as you will easily perceive. I have mixed in my espaliers as many rose and jessamine trees as I can cram in; and in the squares designed for the use of the kitchen, have avoided putting anything disagreeable either to sight or smell, having another garden below for cabbage, onions, garlic, etc. All the walks are garnished with beds of flowers, beside the parterres, which are for a more distinguished sort. I have neither brick nor stone walls: all my fence is a high hedge, mingled with trees; but fruit [is] so plenty in this country, nobody thinks it worth stealing. Gardening is certainly the next amusement to reading; and as my sight will now permit me little of that, I am glad to form a taste that can give me so much employment, and be the plaything of my age, now my pen and needle are almost useless to me."

The greatest personages in this part of Italy seem to have conformed to the fashion of making impromptu visits, as we see by the following letter:

" I was surprised not many days ago by a very extraordinary visit: it was from the Duchess of Guastalla, who you know is a Princess of the house d'Armstadt,* and reported to be near marriage with the King of Sardinia. I confess it was an honour I could easily have spared, she coming attended with the greatest part of her Court; her grand-master, who is brother to Cardinal Valenti, the first lady of her bed-chamber, four pages, and a long et cetera of inferior servants, besides her guards. She entered with an easy French air, and told me, since I would

* This Princess of the house of Hesse-Darmstadt was the Duchess Dowager of Guastalla, the Duke being dead. The Duchy of Guastalla was added to Parma and Piacenza, given to Don Philip by the Treaty of Aix-la-Chapelle in 1748.

not oblige her by coming to her Court, she was resolved
to come to me, and eat a salad of my raising, having
heard much fame of my gardening. You may imagine
I gave her as good a supper as I could. She was (or
seemed to be) extremely pleased with an English sack-
posset of my ordering. I owned to her freely that my
house was much at her service, but it was impossible
for me to find beds for all her suite. She said she
intended to return when the moon rose, which was an
hour after midnight. In the mean time I sent for the
violins to entertain her attendants, who were very well
pleased to dance, while she and her grand-master and
I played at piquet. She pressed me extremely to return
with her to her jointure-house, where she now resides
(all the furniture of Guastalla being sold). I excused
myself on not daring to venture in the cold night
fifteen miles, but promised I would not fail to pay her
my acknowledgments for the great honour her highness had done me, in a very short time, and we parted
very good friends. She said she intended this spring
to retire into her native country. I did not take the
liberty of mentioning to her the report of her being in
treaty with the King of Sardinia, though it has been
in the newspaper of Mantua; but I found an opportunity of hinting it to Signor Gonzagna, her grand-
master, who told me the Duchess would not have been
pleased to talk of it, since, perhaps, there was nothing
in it more than a friendship that had long been between
them, and since her widowhood the King sends her an
express every day."

In the spring of 1749 Lady Mary moved to Gotolengo, a place near Brescia, of about the same size as
Lovere. Here she found a seemingly Roman monument.

"A very fair inscription, in large characters, on a
large stone found in the pavement of the old church,
and makes now a part of the wall of the new one, which
is now building. The people here, who are as ignorant
as their oxen, and live like them on the product of their
land, without any curiosity for the history of it, would
infer from thence that this town is of Roman foundation, though the walls, which are yet the greatest part
standing (only the towers and battlements demolished),
are very plainly Gothic, and not one brick to be found anywhere of Roman fabric, which is very easily distinguished.
I can easily believe their tradition, that the old church,
which was pulled down two years ago, being ready to
drop, was a pagan temple, and do not doubt it was a considerable town, founded by the Goths when they overran
Italy. The fortifications were strong for that age : the
ditch still remaining without the walls being very broad
and deep, in which ran the little river that is now before
my house, and the moat turned into gardens for the use
of the town, the name of which being Gotolengo, is a
confirmation of my conjecture. The castle, which certainly stood on the spot where my house now does,
being on an eminence in the midst of the town, was
probably destroyed by fire. When I ordered the court
to be levelled, which was grown uneven by long neglect,
there was found such quantities of burnt bricks, that

plainly showed the remains of a considerable fire; but whether by the enemy, or accidental, I could get no information. They have no records, or parish books, beyond the time of their coming under the Venetian dominion, which is not much above three hundred years ago, at which time they were, as they now are, a large village, being two miles in circuit, and contains [*sic*] at present (as the curate told me) two thousand communicants. The ladies of this neighbourhood that had given themselves the trouble and expense of going to see Don Philip's entry into Parma, are returned, according to the French saying, *avec un pied de nez*. As they had none of them ever seen a court before, they had figured to themselves prodigious scenes of gallantry and magnificence."

The mildness of the winter created fears of epidemics :

"We have hitherto had no winter, to the great sorrow of the people here, who are in fear of wanting ice in the summer, which is as necessary as bread. They also attribute a malignant fever, which has carried off great numbers in the neighbouring towns, to the uncommon warmth of the air. It has not infected this village, which they say has ever been free from any contagious distemper. It is very remarkable that when the disease amongst the cattle raged with great violence all round, not one died or sickened here. The method of treating the physician in this country, I think, should be the same everywhere : they make it his interest that the whole parish should be in good health, giving him a stated pension, which is collected by a tax on every house, on condition he neither demands nor receives any fees, nor even refuses a visit either to rich or poor. This last article would be very hard, if we had as many vapourish ladies as in England ; but those imaginary ills are entirely unknown here. When I recollect the vast fortunes raised by doctors amongst us, and the eager pursuit after every new piece of quackery that is introduced, I cannot help thinking that there is a fund of credulity in mankind that must be employed somewhere, and the money formerly given to monks for the health of the soul, is now thrown to doctors for health of the body, and generally with as little real prospect of success."

This last reflection is a repetition of what Lady Mary had written to her husband before, on hearing of the popularity of tar-water in England.

" We have no longer faith in miracles and relics, and therefore with the same fury run after recipes and physicians. The same money which three hundred years ago was given for the health of the soul is now given for the health of the body, and by the same sort of people—women and half-witted men. In the countries where they have shrines and images, quacks are despised, and monks and confessors find their account in managing the fear and hope which rule the actions of the multitude."

Perhaps the spread of incredulity in matters of religion has assimilated other countries to England in this respect. Italy no longer believes its priests without questioning, and hence can find faith to spare for a vendor of "blue electricity" and the like, though it is but fair to his native country to state that his clients seem to be largely English, of the classes mentioned by Lady Mary.

The manners and customs of North Italy were to her a constant source of entertainment, and she is constantly comparing them with those of England—as, for instance, even in a matter of gossip about the interesting topic of gambling :

"Your new-fashioned game of brag was the genteel amusement when I was a girl; crimp succeeded to that, and basset and hazard employed the town when I left it to go to Constantinople. At my return, I found them all at commerce, which gave place to quadrille, and that to whist; but the rage of play has been ever the same, and will ever be so among the idle of both sexes. It is the same in every great town, and I think more particularly all over France. Here is a young man of quality, one mile from hence, just of age (which is nineteen through all the Venetian state), who lost last carnival, at Brescia, ten thousand pounds, being all the money his guardians had laid up in his minority; and, as his estate is entailed, he cannot raise one farthing on it, and is now a sort of prisoner in his castle, where he lives upon rapine--I mean running in debt to poor people, who perhaps he will never be able to pay. I am afraid you are tired with this insignificant letter; we old women love tattling; you must forgive the infirmities of your most affectionate mother."

Lovere was not wanting in aristocratic inhabitants :

"There is a numerous gentry of great names and little fortunes; six of those families inhabit this town. You may fancy this forms a sort of society; but far from it, as there is not one of them that does not think (for some reason or other) they are far superior to all the rest : there is such a settled aversion amongst them, they avoid one another with the utmost care, and hardly ever meet, except by chance at the castle (as they call my house), where their regard for me obliges them to behave civilly, but it is with an affected coldness that is downright disagreeable, and hinders me from seeing any of them often."

One of the longest letters gives an amusing but rather too free-spoken account of a domestic difficulty in one of these families, in which Lady Mary's intervention prevented the use of the stiletto—she having been called in to reconcile an injured husband and an erring wife, by the remarkable discretion of a servant, which discretion, as she goes on to say, is no wonder in Italy, though unusual in England—for " any servant that presumes to talk of his master will most certainly be incapable of talking at all in a short time, their lives being entirely in the power of their superiors : I do not mean by law, but by custom, which has full as much force. If one of them was killed, it would either never be inquired into at all, or very slightly passed over; yet it seldom happens, and I know no instance of it, which I think is owing to the great submission of domestics, who are sensible of their dependence, and the national temper not being hasty, and never inflamed by wine, drunkenness being a vice abandoned to the vulgar, and spoke of with greater detestation than murder, which is mentioned with as little concern as a drinking-bout in England, and is almost as frequent. It was extreme shocking to me at my first coming, and still gives me a sort of horror, though custom has in some degree familiarised it to my imagination. Robbery would be pursued with great vivacity, and punished with the utmost rigour, therefore is very rare, though stealing is in daily practice; but as all the peasants are suffered the use of fire-arms, the slightest provocation is sufficient to shoot, and they see one of their own species lie dead before them with as little remorse as a hare or a partridge, and when revenge spurs them on, with much more pleasure."

The care of her health generally brought Lady Mary back to Lovere after any absence, as she found the waters there beneficial; and most of her letters are written from there. In the autumn of 1750 she paid a visit to a former palace of the Duke of Tuscany, at Salo, on Lake Garda, and gives a detailed account of it to her daughter:

" I have been persuaded to go to a palace near Salo, situate on the vast lake of Gardia [*sic*], and do not repent my pains since my arrival, though I have passed a very bad road to it. It is, indeed, take it altogether, the finest place I ever saw : the King of France has nothing so fine, nor can have in his situation. It is large enough to entertain all his Court, and much larger than the royal palace of Naples, or any of those of Germany

or England. It was built by the great Cosmo, Duke
of Florence, where he passed many months, for several
years, on the account of his health, the air being
esteemed one of the best in Italy. All the offices and
conveniences are suitably magnificent: but that is
nothing in regard to the beauties without doors. It is
seated in that part of the lake which forms an amphitheatre, at the foot of a mountain near three miles high,
covered with a wood of orange, lemon, citron, and
pomegranate trees, which is all cut into walks, and
divided into terraces, that you may go into a several
garden from every floor in the house, diversified with
fountains, cascades, and statues, and joined by easy
marble staircases, which lead from one to another.
There are many covered walks, where you are secure
from the sun in the hottest part of the day, by the
shade of the orange-trees, which are so loaded with
fruit, you can hardly have any notion of their beauty
without seeing them: they are as large as lime-trees
in England. You will think I say a great deal: I will
assure you I say far short of what I see, and you must
turn to the fairy tales to give any idea of the real
charms of this enchanting palace, for so it may justly
be called. The variety of the prospects, the natural
beauties, and the improvements by art, where no cost
has been spared to perfect it, render it the most
complete habitation I know in Europe. While the
poor present master of it (to whose ancestor the Grand-
Duke presented it, having built it on his land), having
spent a noble estate by gaming and other extravagance,

would be glad to let it for a trifle, and is not rich enough to live in it. Most of the fine furniture is sold ; there remains only a few of the many good pictures that adorned it, and such goods as were not easily to be transported, or for which he found no chapman. I have said nothing to you of the magnificent bath, embellished with statues, or the fish-ponds, the chief of which is in the midst of the garden to which I go from my apartment on the first floor. It is circled by a marble baluster, and supplied by water from a cascade that proceeds from the mouth of a whale, on which Neptune is mounted, surrounded with reeds : on each side of him are Tritons, which, from their shells, pour out streams that augment the pond. Higher on the hill are three colossal statues of Venus, Hercules, and Apollo. The water is so clear, you see the numerous fish that inhabit it, and it is a great pleasure to me to throw them bread, which they come to the surface to eat with great greediness."

But although by this time Lady Mary was somewhat tired of Lovere, she was compelled again and again to return there. On one of these returns she writes : " I find much more company than ever. I have done by these waters as I formerly did by those at Islington : you may remember when I first carried you there, we scarce saw any but ourselves, and in a short time we could hardly find room for the crowd."*

The inhabitants of Lovere seem to have been alive

* Islington Spa had revived about 1732. Perhaps Lady Mary had induced her royal and noble friends to follow her there.

to the advantages of having the celebrated English lady in their midst, and omitted no means to retain her there—she was to them, in a smaller way, what Lord Brougham afterwards was to Cannes. Besides this, she had introduced certain useful arts in vogue in England, though possibly rather to employ herself than to benefit those for whom she professed an utter indifference.

"The people I see here make no more impression on my mind than the figures in the tapestry: while they are directly before my eyes, I know one is clothed in blue, and another in red: but out of sight, they are so entirely out of memory, I hardly remember whether they are tall or short. I sometimes call myself to account for this insensibility, which has something of ingratitude in it, this little town thinking themselves highly honoured and obliged by my residence: they intended me an extraordinary mark of it, having determined to set up my statue in the most conspicuous place: the marble was bespoke, and the sculptor bargained with, before I knew anything of the matter; and it would have been erected without my knowledge, if it had not been necessary for him to see me to take the resemblance. I thanked him very much for his intention; but utterly refused complying with it, fearing it would be reported (at least in England) that I had set up my own statue. They were so obstinate in the design, I was forced to tell them my religion would not permit it. I seriously believe it would have been worshipped, when I was forgotten, under the name of some

saint or other, since I was to have been represented
with a book in my hand, which would have passed for
a proof of canonisation. This compliment was certainly
founded on reasons not unlike those that first framed
goddesses, I mean being useful to them, in which I am
second to Ceres. If it be true she taught the art of
sowing wheat, it is sure I have learned them to make
bread, in which they continued in the same ignorance
Misson* complains of (as you may see in his letter from
Padua). I have introduced French rolls, custards,
minced pies, and plum pudding, which they are very
fond of. 'Tis impossible to bring them to conform to
sillabub, which is so unnatural a mixture in their eyes,
they are even shocked to see me eat it : but I expect
immortality from the science of butter-making, in which
they are become so skilful from my instructions, I can
assure you here is as good as in any part of Great
Britain."

In 1751 Mr. Wortley Montagu came as far as Vienna,
and seems to have made a further trip into Hungary—
perhaps to provision himself with his favourite tokay.
He did not attempt to join his wife ; and, indeed, the
journey over the Tyrolese or Carinthian mountains,
with the roads of those times, was one that a man
of seventy-three might well shrink from, though well
able to endure the easy route along the Danube. He
wrote, however, to Lady Mary, apparently giving an
account of some marvellous instances of longevity in

---

* Misson was a French traveller, who published his account of
Italy in 1691.

Hungary, which she capped with an account of the famous old woman of Lovere:

"I have often read and been told, that the air of Hungary is better, and the inhabitants in general longer lived, than in any other part of Europe. You have given me a very surprising instance of it, far surpassing in age the old woman of Lovere, though, in some circumstances, I think her story as extraordinary. She died but ten years ago; and it is well remembered by the inhabitants of that place, the most creditable of whom have all assured me of the truth of the following facts :— She kept the greatest inn there till past fifty: her husband then dying, and she being rich, she left off that trade ; and having a large house, with a great deal of furniture, she let lodgings, which her daughters (two maids past seventy) still continue. I lodged with them the first year of my going to those waters. She lived to one hundred with good health ; but in the last five years of it fell into the decays common to that period—dimness of sight, loss of teeth, and baldness ; but in her hundredth year, her sight was totally restored, she had a new set of teeth, and a fresh head of brown hair. . . . She lived in this renewed vigour ten years, and had then her picture drawn, which has a vivacity in the eyes and complexion that would become five-and-twenty, though, by the falls in the face, one may discern it was drawn for a very old person. She died merely of an accident, which would have killed any other—tumbling down a very bad stone staircase which goes into the cellar; she broke her head in such a

manner, she lived but two days. The physician and
surgeon who attended her told me her age no way con-
tributed to her death. I inquired whether there was
any singularity in her diet, but heard of none, excepting
that her breakfast was every morning a large quantity
of bread sopped in cold water. The common food of
the peasants in this country is the Turkish wheat you
mention,* which they dress in various manners, but use
little milk, it being chiefly reserved for cheese, or the
tables of the gentry. I have not observed, either among
the poor or rich, that in general they live longer than
in England. This woman of Lovere is always spoken
of as a prodigy; and [I] am surprised she is neither
called saint nor witch, being [sic] very prodigal of those
titles."

This letter of her husband's, which she answered in
the epistle just quoted, must have been the "entertaining letter out of Germany" to which she alludes in
writing to her daughter. Lady Bute, it appears, had
formed notions of Italian life from Misson and other
obsolete books of travel, and also from the gossip of
English travellers returning from abroad; and her
mother cautioned her against accepting these reports
as trustworthy :

" I find you have many wrong notions of Italy, which
I do not wonder at. You can take your ideas of it only
from books or travellers; the first are generally anti-
quated or confined to trite observations, and the other

* Maize, or Indian corn, still the staple food of the peasants in
North Italy.

yet more superficial; they return no more instructed than they might have been at home by the help of a map. The boys only remember where they met with the best wine or the prettiest women; and the governors (I speak of the most learned amongst them) have only remarked situations and distances, or, at most, statues and edifices, as every girl that can read a French novel, and boy that can construe a scene in Terence, fancies they have attained to the French and Latin languages, when, God knows, it requires the study of a whole life to acquire a perfect knowledge of either of them : so, after a tour (as they call it) of three years round Europe, people think themselves qualified to give exact accounts of the customs, policies, and interests of the dominions they have gone through post ; when a very long stay, a diligent inquiry, and a nice observation, are requisite even to a moderate degree of knowing a foreign country, especially here, where they are naturally very reserved. France, indeed, is more easily seen through: the French always talking of themselves, and the government being the same, there is little difference from one province to another; but, in Italy, the different laws make different customs and manners, which are in many things very particular here, from the singularity of the government. Some I do not care to touch upon, and some are still in use here, though obsolete in almost all other places, as the estates of all the great families being unalienable, as they were formerly in England. This would make them very potent, if it was

not balanced by another law, that divides whatever
land the father dies possessed of among all the sons,
the eldest having no advantage but the finest house
and best furniture. This occasions numerous branches
and few large fortunes, with a train of consequences
you may imagine. But I cannot let pass in silence the
prodigious alteration, since Misson's writing, in regard
to our sex. This reformation (or, if you please, depra-
vation) began so lately as the year 1732, when the
French overrun this part of Italy; but it has been
carried on with such fervour and success, that the
Italian go far beyond their patterns, the Parisian ladies,
in the extent of their liberty. I am not so much surprised at the women's conduct, as I am amazed at the
change in the men's sentiments. Jealousy, which was
once a point of honour among them, is exploded to that
degree, it is the most infamous and ridiculous of all
characters; and you cannot more affront a gentleman
than to suppose him capable of it. Divorces are also
introduced, and frequent enough; they have long been
in fashion in Genoa; several of the finest and greatest
ladies there having two husbands alive."

Into the particulars of the humours of Italian divorce
we need not follow Lady Mary.

CHAPTER VII

LETTERS ON ENGLISH NOVELS

Lady Mary's Taste for Novels— Her Defence of Novel-reading—
All Ages must have Playthings—Fielding's Works —*Joseph
Andrews*—An Italian Fanny—Bad Influence of Fielding's
Novels—His Happy Temperament—Smollett's Works—*The
Parish Girl—Pompey the Little*—Lady Mary's Nervousness—
Her Diet—Criticism the only Subject to write about—The
Rambler a Misnomer—Lord Orrery and Swift—Swift like
Caligula—Pope and Swift—Lord Bolingbroke's Political Doctrines
—His Diffuseness— Madame de Sévigné's "Tittle-tattle"—
Bolingbroke's Defects—The Character of Atticus—Richardson's
Novels —*Pamela — Clarissa Harlowe* —Lady Mary touched by
his Pathos—*Sir Charles Grandison*—Richardson's Ignorance of
Italy and of High Life — Levelling Tendencies of English Life
reflected in English Novels.

DURING her stay at Lovere and in the neighbourhood,
Lady Mary Wortley Montagu by no means forgot her
taste for reading. She does not seem to have cared
much for French literature—or, possibly, she had no
friends in France who could send her new books ; and
the outbreak of war in 1756 must have still further
increased the difficulty of obtaining French works.
Italian literature was to her only represented at the

time by a few antiquarians, or *virtuosi*, like her friends
Cardinal Querini and the Marquis Maffei; and she was
thrown back on English books. Of these she seems to
have preferred the more diverting class of fiction, and
the boxes of books, for whose safe arrival she was often
so anxious, were of much the same character as Mudie
sows broadcast through the land.

She often defends her taste for fiction against her
own past notions of "self-improvement" and the
objections of her daughter. Lady Mary had the
courage of her frivolity, and openly avowed her return
to the tastes of her youth.

"I thank God," she writes, "my taste still continues
for the gay part of reading. Wiser people may think
it trifling, but it serves to sweeten life to me, and is at
worst better than the generality of conversation." And
again, in another letter: "To say truth, I am as fond
of baubles as ever, and am so far from being ashamed
of it, it is a taste I endeavour to keep up with all the
art I am mistress of. I should have despised them at
twenty, for the same reason that I would not eat tarts
or cheesecakes at twelve years old, as being too childish
for one capable of more solid pleasures. I now know
(and, alas! have long known) all things in the world
are almost equally trifling, and our most secret projects have scarce more foundation than those edifices
that your little ones raise in cards." And Lady Bute's
allusions to the "trash" her mother read drew down a
humorous rejoinder, with a sly allusion to Lord Bute's
Court ambitions:

"Daughter! daughter! don't call names; you are always abusing my pleasures, which is what no mortal will bear. Trash, lumber, sad stuff, are the titles you give to my favourite amusement. If I called a white staff a stick of wood, a gold key gilded brass, and the ensigns of illustrious orders coloured strings, this may be philosophically true, but would be very ill received. We have all our playthings: happy are they that can be contented with those they can obtain: those hours are spent in the wisest manner, that can easiest shade the ills of life, and are least productive of ill consequences. I think my time better employed in reading the adventures of imaginary people, than the Duchess of Marlborough's, who passed the latter years of her life in paddling with her will, and contriving schemes of plaguing some, and extracting praise from others, to no purpose; eternally disappointed, and eternally fretting. The active scenes are over at my age. I indulge, with all the art I can, my taste for reading. If I would confine it to valuable books, they are almost as rare as valuable men. I must be content with what I can find. As I approach a second childhood, I endeavour to enter into the pleasures of it. Your youngest son is, perhaps, at this very moment riding on a poker with great delight, not at all regretting that it is not a gold one, and much less wishing it an Arabian horse, which he would not know how to manage. I am reading an idle tale, not expecting wit or truth in it, and am very glad it is not metaphysics to puzzle my judgment, or history to mislead my opinion. He fortifies his health

by exercise ; I calm my cares by oblivion. The methods may appear low to busy people ; but, if he improves his strength, and I forget my infirmities, we attain very desirable ends."

The first box of any importance seems to have arrived at the end of September, 1749. It contained Fielding's works, and Lady Mary gives an amusing testimony to the interest her cousin's novels had for her :

" MY DEAR CHILD,—I have at length received the box, with the books enclosed, for which I give you many thanks, as they amused me very much. I gave a very ridiculous proof of it, fitter indeed for my grand-daughter than myself. I returned from a party on horseback ; and after having rode twenty miles, part of it by moonshine, it was ten at night when I found the box arrived. I could not deny myself the pleasure of opening it ; and, falling upon Fielding's works, was fool enough to sit up all night reading. I think Joseph Andrews better than his Foundling.* I believe I was the more struck with it, having at present a Fanny in my own house,† not only by the name, which happens to be the same, but the extraordinary beauty, joined with an understanding yet more extraordinary at her age, which is but few months past sixteen : she is in the post of my chambermaid. I fancy you will tax my discretion for taking a servant thus qualified ; but my woman, who is also my housekeeper, was always

---

* " The Foundling " is, of course, " Tom Jones."

† The girl's name was Francesca, generally called " Chechina " by her mistress. She married in 1750.

teasing me with her having too much work, and complaining of ill-health, which determined me to take her a deputy ; and when I was at Lovere, where I drank the waters, one of the most considerable merchants there pressed me to take this daughter of his : her mother has an uncommon good character, and the girl has had a better education than is usual for those of her rank ; she writes a good hand, and has been brought up to keep accounts, which she does to great perfection ; and had herself such a violent desire to serve me, that I was persuaded to take her : I do not yet repent it from any part of her behaviour. But there has been no peace in the family ever since she came into it ; I might say the parish, all the women in it having declared open war with her, and the men endeavouring at treaties of a different sort : my own woman puts herself at the head of the first party, and her spleen is increased by having no reason for it, the young creature never stirring from my apartment, always at her needle, and never complaining of anything. You will laugh at this tedious account of my domestics (if you have patience to read it over), but I have few other subjects to talk of."

On later occasions she again mentions Fielding, knowing something of his life, from his relationship to her. He had dedicated his first play to her, and submitted his " Modern Husband " for her approval and criticism.

We see her knowledge of his ways in her comments on " Amelia."

" H. Fielding has given a true picture of himself and his first wife, in the characters of Mr. and Mrs. Booth, some compliments to his own figure excepted ; and, I am persuaded, several of the incidents he mentions are real matters of fact. I wonder he does not perceive Tom Jones and Mr. Booth are sorry scoundrels. All these sort of books have the same fault, which I cannot easily pardon, being very mischievous. They place a merit in extravagant passions, and encourage young people to hope for impossible events, to draw them out of the misery they chose to plunge themselves into, expecting legacies from unknown relations, and generous benefactors to distressed virtue, as much out of nature as fairy treasures. Fielding has really a fund of true humour, and was to be pitied at his first entrance into the world, having no choice, as he said himself, but to be a hackney writer, or a hackney coachman. His genius deserved a better fate ; but I cannot help blaming that continued indiscretion, to give it the softest name, that has run through his life, and I am afraid still remains."

It is rather curious to see one who was herself not conspicuous for her respect of conventionality inveighing against the hurtful tendencies of romance. But in criticising literary work her estimate of its artistic merit seems to have been much at the mercy of her opinion as to the moral, social, or political tendency of the book to be considered. Thus she would allow little credit comparatively to Pope, Swift, or Bolingbroke, having a political bias against all three, and a

personal bias against the first and perhaps the second.
Of Fielding she only speaks again on hearing of his
death:

" I am sorry for H. Fielding's death, not only as I
shall read no more of his writings, but I believe he lost
more than others, as no man enjoyed life more than
he did, though few had less reason to do so, the highest
of his preferment being raking in the lowest sinks of
vice and misery. . . . His happy constitution (even
when he had, with great pains, half demolished it)
made him forget everything when he was before a
venison pasty, or over a flask of champagne ; and I am
persuaded he has known more happy moments than
any prince upon earth. His natural spirits gave him
rapture with his cook-maid,* and cheerfulness in a
garret. There was a great similitude between his
character and that of Sir Richard Steele. He had the
advantage both in learning and, in my opinion, genius :
they both agreed in wanting money in spite of all their
friends, and would have wanted it, if their hereditary
lands had been as extensive as their imagination ; yet
each of them [was] so formed for happiness, it is
pity he was not immortal."

Smollett's works, generally mentioned now in the
same breath with Fielding's as typical of the time,
came with them in the boxes of books looked for with
such anxiety at Lovere. Lady Vane's memoirs, in-
serted in " Peregrine Pickle," interested her, as she

---

* Fielding, after the death of his beloved first wife, married her
faithful maid.

knew a good deal of that lady. "Roderick Random" she was inclined to attribute to Fielding on account of its humour; but the "Adventures of Ferdinand, Count Fathom," she at once pronounced not good enough to ascribe to him. Later on she was better informed about the authorship of these novels, and grieves over "my dear Smollett, who, I am sorry, disgraces his talent by writing those stupid romances commonly called history."

With "Peregrine Pickle" came a budget of other novels of the day, which are now completely forgotten. "The History of Charlotte Summers, the Fortunate Parish Girl," is a title that promises little; though "Pompey the Little; or, The Adventures of a Lap-Dog," might perhaps prove entertaining now, if it be so faithful a representation of London manners a century and a half ago as Lady Mary thought it to be.

"The next book I laid my hand on was the Parish Girl, which interested me enough not to be able to quit it till it was read over, though the author has fallen into the common mistake of romance-writers; intending a virtuous character, and not knowing how to draw it; the first step of his heroine (leaving her patroness's house) being altogether absurd and ridiculous, justly entitling her to all the misfortunes she met with. Candles came (and my eyes grown weary), I took up the next book, merely because I supposed from the title it could not engage me long. It was Pompey the Little, which has really diverted me more

14

than any of the others, and it was impossible to go to bed till it was finished. It was a real and exact representation of life, as it is now acted in London, as it was in my time, and as it will be (I do not doubt) a hundred years hence, with some little variation of dress, and perhaps government. I found there many of my acquaintance. Lady T. and Lady O. are so well painted,* I fancied I heard them talk, and have heard them say the very things there repeated. I also saw myself (as I now am) in the character of Mrs. Qualmsick. You will be surprised at this, no Englishwoman being so free from vapours, having never in my life complained of low spirits or weak nerves; but our resemblance is very strong in the fancied loss of appetite, which I have been silly enough to be persuaded into by the physician of this place. He visits me frequently, as being one of the most considerable men in the parish, and is a grave, sober thinking, great fool, whose solemn appearance, and deliberate way of delivering his sentiments, gives them an air of good sense, though they are often the most injudicious that ever were pronounced. By perpetually telling me I eat so little, he is amazed I am able to subsist, he had brought me to be of his opinion; and I began to be seriously uneasy at it. This useful treatise has roused me into a recollection of what I eat yesterday, and do almost every day the same. I wake generally about seven, and drink half a pint of warm asses' milk, after

* In the novel, Lady T. (*Townshend*) is named *Lady Tempest;* Lady O. (*Orford*), *Lady Sophister*.

which I sleep two hours; as soon as I am risen, I constantly take three cups of milk coffee, and two hours after that a large cup of milk chocolate: two hours more brings my dinner, where I never fail swallowing a good dish (I don't mean plate) of gravy soup, with all the bread, roots, etc., belonging to it. I then eat a wing and the whole body of a large fat capon, and a veal sweetbread, concluding with a competent quantity of custard, and some roasted chesnuts. At five in the afternoon I take another dose of asses' milk; and for supper twelve chesnuts (which would weigh twenty-four of those in London), one new laid egg, and a handsome porringer of white bread and milk. With this diet, notwithstanding the menaces of my wise doctor, I am now convinced I am in no danger of starving; and am obliged to Little Pompey for this discovery."

We are also obliged to " Pompey the Little" for this detailed account of Lady Mary's diet, which seems to have been of the substantial nature proper to her nationality. In the long letter of which this is a part, after giving judgment on several novels in which even her tolerance could find no merit, she suddenly breaks off to excuse herself from her daughter's anticipated objection.

" I fancy you are now saying, 'tis a sad thing to grow old; what does my poor mamma mean by troubling me with criticisms on books that nobody but herself will ever read? You must allow something to my solitude. I have a pleasure in writing to my dear child, and not many subjects to write upon. The adventures of people here would not at all amuse you, having no acquaintance with the persons concerned; and an account of myself would hardly gain credit, after having fairly owned to you how deplorably I was misled in regard to my own health; though I have all my life been on my guard against the information by the sense of hearing; it being one of my earliest observations, the universal inclination of human-kind is to be led by the ears; and I am sometimes apt to imagine, that they are given to men, as they are to pitchers, purposely that they may be carried about by them. This consideration should abate my wonder to see (as I do here) the most astonishing legends embraced as the most sacred truths, by those who have always heard them asserted, and never contradicted; they even place a merit in complying in direct opposition to the evidence of all their other senses."

It is amusing to notice her reference to the first appearance of the future " Great Cham " of literature, not yet made known by his Dictionary. Certainly no one could be less of a wanderer than the " Rambler."

" The Rambler is certainly a strong misnomer; he always plods in the beaten road of his predecessors, following the ' Spectator ' (with the same pace a pack-horse would do a hunter) in the style that is proper to lengthen a paper. These writers may, perhaps, be of service to the public, which is saying a great deal in their favour. There are numbers of both sexes who never read anything but such productions, and cannot spare time, from doing nothing, to go through a six-penny pamphlet. Such gentle readers may be improved by a moral hint, which, though repeated over and over from generation to generation, they never heard in their lives. I should be glad to know the name of this laborious author."

Lord Orrery's " Remarks on the Life and Writings of Swift " gave Lady Mary an opportunity of giving her opinion on Pope and Swift, as well as his lordship, whose " family have been smatterers in wit and learning for three generations," his father having been the Boyle of the Phalaris dispute. It is curious to see her attacking the Dean's irreverence and cynicism on the same strictly utilitarian grounds as he himself defended religion—half ironically—against the infidel wits of the time:

" Nobody can deny but religion is a comfort to the distressed, a cordial to the sick, and sometimes a restraint on the wicked ; therefore, whoever would argue or laugh it out of the world, without giving some equivalent for it, ought to be treated as a common enemy : but, when this language comes from a Churchman, who enjoys large benefices and dignities from that very Church he openly despises, it is an object of horror for which I want a name, and can only be excused by madness, which I think the Dean was strongly touched with. His character seems to me a parallel with that of Caligula ; and had he had the same power, would have made the same use of it. That Emperor erected a temple to himself, where he

was his own high priest, preferred his horse to the
highest honours in the state, professed enmity to [the]
human race, and at last lost his life by a nasty jest on
one of his inferiors, which I dare swear Swift would
have made in his place.   There can be no worse
picture made of the Doctor's morals than he has given
us himself in the letters printed by Pope.   We see him
vain, trifling, ungrateful to the memory of his patron,
the E. [Earl] of Oxford, making a servile court where
he had any interested views, and meanly abusive when
they were disappointed, and, as he says (in his own
phrase), flying in the face of mankind, in company with
his adorer Pope.   It is pleasant to consider, that, had
it not been for the good nature of these very mortals
they contemn, these two superior beings were entitled,
by their birth and hereditary fortune, to be only a
couple of link-boys.   I am of opinion their ̄ friendship
would have continued, though they had remained in
the same kingdom : it had a very strong foundation—
the love of flattery on the one side, and the love of
money on the other."

And she goes on to charge Pope with lying in wait
for the inheritances of all his friends.   Deeply as he
had injured her, it is hardly pleasant to find her feeling
against him so strong so many years after his death.

We also find her again referring bitterly to Swift,
contrasting him with her old friend Burnet :

" Doctor Swift, who set at defiance all decency, truth,
or reason, had a crowd of admirers, and at their head
the virtuous and ingenious Earl of Orrery, the polite

and learned Mr. Greville, with a number of ladies of fine taste and unblemished characters; while the Bishop of Salisbury (Burnet, I mean), the most indulgent parent, the most generous Churchman, and the most zealous assertor of the rights and liberties of his country, was all his life defamed and vilified, and after his death most barbarously calumniated, for having had the courage to write a history without flattery. I knew him in my very early youth, and his condescension in directing a girl in her studies is an obligation I can never forget."

Bolingbroke (though his " Idea of a Patriot King" is said to have been the model on which Lord Bute helped to instruct the young Prince of Wales) came in for worse treatment still—though here there was no hint of personal animosity, Lady Mary not having known him, and his later days having been employed in attacking Walpole, much as her own husband had done. Here, again, it is singular to find her including Madame de Sévigné in her condemnation of diffuse writers:

" I shall begin, in respect to his dignity, with Lord B. [Bolingbroke], who is a glaring proof how far vanity may blind a man, and how easy it is to varnish over to one's self the most criminal conduct. He declares he always loved his country, though he confesses he endeavoured to betray her to popery and slavery; and loved his friends, though he abandoned them in distress, with all the blackest circumstances of treachery. His account of the Peace of Utrecht is almost equally unfair or partial:* I shall allow that, perhaps, the

In his "Letters on the Study of History."

views of the Whigs, at that time, were too vast, and
the nation, dazzled by military glory, had hopes too
sanguine; but sure the same terms that the French
consented to, at the treaty of Gertruydenberg, might
have been obtained; or if the displacing of the Duke
of Marlborough raised the spirits of our enemies to a
degree of refusing what they had before offered, how
can he excuse the guilt of removing him from the head
of a victorious army, and exposing us to submit to any
articles of peace, being unable to continue the war?
I agree with him, that the idea of conquering France
is a wild, extravagant notion, and would, if possible, be
impolitic; but she might have been reduced to such a
state as would have rendered her incapable of being
terrible to her neighbours for some ages: nor should we
have been obliged, as we have done almost ever since,
to bribe the French ministers to let us live in quiet.
So much for his political reasonings, which, I confess,
are delivered in a florid, easy style; but I cannot be
of Lord Orrery's opinion, that he is one of the best
English writers. Well-turned periods or smooth lines
are not the perfection either of prose or verse; they
may serve to adorn, but can never stand in the place
of good sense. Copiousness of words, however ranged,
is always false eloquence, though it will ever impose
on some sort of understandings. How many readers
and admirers has Madame de Sévigné, who only gives
us, in a lively manner and fashionable phrases, mean
sentiments, vulgar prejudices, and endless repetitions?
Sometimes the tittle-tattle of a fine lady, sometimes

that of an old nurse, always tittle-tattle ; yet so well gilt over by airy expressions, and a flowing style, she will always please the same people to whom Lord Bolingbroke will shine as a first-rate author. She is so far to be excused, as her letters were not intended for the press; while he labours to display to posterity all the wit and learning he is master of, and sometimes spoils a good argument by a profusion of words, running out into several pages a thought that might have been more clearly expressed in a few lines, and, what is worse, often falls into contradiction and repetitions, which are almost unavoidable to all voluminous writers, and can only be forgiven to those retailers whose necessity compels them to diurnal scribbling, who load their meaning with epithets, and run into digressions, because (in the jockey phrase) it rids the ground, that is, covers a certain quantity of paper, to answer the demand of the day. A great part of Lord B.'s letters are designed to show his reading, which, indeed, appears to have been very extensive ; but I cannot perceive that such a minute account of it can be of any use to the pupil he pretends to instruct ; nor can I help thinking he is far below either Tillotson or Addison, even in style, though the latter was sometimes more diffuse than his judgment approved, to furnish out the length of a daily ' Spectator.' I own I have small regard for Lord B. as an author, and the highest contempt for him as a man. He came into the world greatly favoured both by nature and fortune, blest with a noble birth, heir to a large estate, endowed with a strong constitution, and, as I have heard, a beautiful figure, high spirits, a good memory, and a lively apprehension, which was cultivated by a learned education : all these glorious advantages being left to the direction of a judgment stifled by unbounded vanity, he dishonoured his birth, lost his estate, ruined his reputation, and destroyed his health, by a wild pursuit of eminence even in vice and trifles.

"I am far from making misfortune a matter of reproach. I know there are accidental occurrences not to be foreseen or avoided by human prudence, by which a character may be injured, wealth dissipated, or a constitution impaired : but I think I may reasonably despise the understanding of one who conducts himself in such a manner as naturally produces such lamentable consequences, and continues in the same destructive paths to the end of a long life, ostentatiously boasting of morals and philosophy in print, and with equal ostentation bragging of the scenes of low debauchery in public conversation, though deplorably weak both in mind and body, and his virtue and his vigour in a state of non-existence. His confederacy with Swift and Pope puts me in mind of that of Bessus and his swordmen, in the ' King and no King,' who endeavour to support themselves by giving certificates of each other's merit. Pope has triumphantly declared that they may do and say whatever silly things they please, they will still be the greatest geniuses nature ever exhibited. I am delighted with the comparison given of their benevolence, which is indeed most aptly figured by a circle in the water, which widens till it comes to nothing at all; but I am provoked at Lord B.'s misrepresentation of my favourite Atticus, who seems to have been the only Roman that, from good sense, had a true notion of the times in which he lived, in which the republic was inevitably perishing, and the two factions, who pretended to support it, equally endeavouring to gratify their ambition in its ruin. A wise man, in that case, would certainly declare for neither, and try to save himself and family from the general wreck, which could not be done but by a superiority of understanding acknowledged on both sides. I see no glory in losing life or fortune by being the dupe of either, and very much applaud that conduct which could preserve an universal esteem amidst the fury of opposite parties. We are obliged to act vigorously, where action can do any good; but in a storm, when it is impossible to work with success, the best hands and ablest pilots may laudably gain the shore if they can. Atticus could be a friend to men without engaging in their passions, disapprove their maxims without awaking their resentment, and be satisfied with his own virtue without seeking popular fame: he had the reward of his wisdom in his tranquillity, and will ever stand among the few examples of true philosophy, either ancient or modern."

The mention of Atticus naturally leads to another diatribe against Pope for his virulent attack on Addison under that name.

In a later letter to Lady Bute, Bolingbroke again suffers for his affectation of universal knowledge:

" I am flattered by finding that our sentiments are the same in regard to Lord Bolingbroke's writings, as you will see more clearly, if you ever have the long letter I have wrote to you on that subject. I believe he never read Horace, or any other author, with a design of instructing himself, thinking he was born to give precepts, and not to follow them: at least, if he was not mad enough to have this opinion, he endeavoured to impose it on the rest of the world. All his works, being well considered, are little more than a panegyric on his own universal genius; many of his pretensions as preposterously inconsistent as if Sir Isaac Newton had aimed at being a critic in fashions, and wrote for the information of tailors and mantua-makers. I am of your opinion that he never looked into half the authors he quotes, and am much mistaken if he is not obliged to Mr. Bayle for the generality of his criticisms; for which reason he affects to despise him, that he may steal from him with less suspicion. A diffusive style (though often admired as florid by all half-witted readers) is commonly obscure, and always trifling. Horace has told us, that where words abound, sense is thinly spread: as trees overcharged with leaves bear little fruit."

But the author of whom Lady Mary has most to say is Richardson. She seems to have been in a constant state of uncertainty about him, alternately attracted by his pathos and repelled by his many defects. Especially severe was she on his painting of high life and polite society, of which his knowledge could not but be imperfect; and it is well to note this criticism

when we find authors of to-day, especially (as is
natural) foreigners like M. Taine, taking Richardson's
lapses into vulgarity as typical of the English society
of the time. Perhaps the proverbial New Zealander,
grubbing among the rubbish of some circulating library,
will credit our highly uninteresting and, for the most
part, desperately respectable peerage with the personal
beauty and moral deficiencies of Greek gods.

" Pamela," Richardson's first great success, Lady
Mary had met with abroad, and hence did not desire
to have it sent to her at Lovere. As she writes to her
daughter, who had mentioned a list of novels :

" All the other books would be new to me excepting
' Pamela,' which has met with very extraordinary (and
I think undeserved) success. It has been translated
into French and into Italian ; it was all the fashion at
Paris and Versailles, and is still the joy of the chamber-
maids of all nations."

And her judgment of " Clarissa Harlowe " is the
sharper, one may imagine, from the fact that she had
been unable to resist the pathos of the ending :

" I was such an old fool as to weep over ' Clarissa
Harlowe,' like any milkmaid of sixteen over the ballad
of the Lady's Fall. To say truth, the first volume
softened me by a near resemblance of my maiden days;
but on the whole 'tis most miserable stuff. Miss How,
who is called a young lady of sense and honour, is
not only extreme silly, but a more vicious character
than Sally Martin, whose crimes are owing at first
to seduction, and afterwards to necessity ; while this

virtuous damsel, without any reason, insults her mother at home and ridicules her abroad ; abuses the man she marries ; and is impertinent and impudent with great applause. Even that model of affection, Clarissa, is so faulty in her behaviour as to deserve little compassion. Any girl that runs away with a young fellow, without intending to marry him, should be carried to Bridewell or to Bedlam the next day. Yet the circumstances are so laid, as to inspire tenderness, notwithstanding the low style and absurd incidents ; and I look upon this and ' Pamela ' to be two books that will do more general mischief than the works of Lord Rochester."*

Again, when the ponderous volumes of "Sir Charles Grandison" arrived, the same experience was repeated :

" This Richardson is a strange fellow. I heartily despise him, and eagerly read him, nay, sob over his works in a most scandalous manner. The two first tomes of Clarissa touched me, as being very resembling to my maiden days; and I find in the pictures of Sir Thomas Grandison and his lady, what I have heard of my mother, and seen of my father."

But after the first impression wears off, she falls on him again with even more asperity than before, especially as he had rashly ventured on pictures of Italian life, of which he was more ignorant than of the

---

° Lord Rochester, one of the most dissipated of Charles II.'s courtiers, was notorious for the indecency of his poems.

ways of English "high life," and of which she had enjoyed abundant experience.

"I have now read over Richardson — he sinks horribly in his third volume* (he does so in his story of Clarissa). When he talks of Italy, it is plain he is no better acquainted with it than he is with the kingdom of Mancomugi. He might have made his Sir Charles's amour with Clementina begin in a convent, where the pensioners sometimes take great liberties; but that such familiarity should be permitted in her father's house, is as repugnant to custom, as it would be in London for a young lady of quality to dance on the ropes at Bartholomew fair: neither does his hero behave to her in a manner suitable to his nice notions. It was impossible a discerning man should not see her passion early enough to check it, if he had really designed it. His conduct puts me in mind of some ladies I have known, who could never find out a man to be in love with them, let him do or say what he would, till he made a direct attempt, and then they were so surprised, I warrant you! Nor do I approve Sir Charles's offered compromise (as he calls it). There must be a great indifference as to religion on both sides, to make so strict a union as marriage tolerable between people of such distinct persuasions. He seems to think women have no souls, by agreeing so easily that his daughters should be educated in bigotry and idolatry."

At which point, like a good Protestant, Lady Mary

* " Sir Charles Grandison " is the work referred to.

goes off at a tangent into theological controversy, and
deserts Richardson for several pages. But she has
not done with him yet, and falls on his inaccuracies
with redoubled vigour:

"Richardson is as ignorant in morality as he is in
anatomy, when he declares abusing an obliging husband,
or an indulgent parent, to be an innocent recreation.
His Anna How and Charlotte Grandison are recommended as patterns of charming pleasantry, and applauded by his saint-like dames, who mistake pert
folly for wit and humour, and impudence and ill nature
for spirit and fire. Charlotte behaves like a humor-
some child, and should have been used like one, and
well whipped in the presence of her friendly confidante Harriet. . . . Charlotte acts with an ingratitude
that I think too black for human nature, with such
coarse jokes and low expressions as are only to be
heard among the lowest class of people. . . . I do not
forgive him his disrespect of old china, which is below
nobody's taste, since it has been the D. of Argyll's,
whose understanding has never been doubted either by
his friends or enemies.

"Richardson never had probably money enough to
purchase any, or even a ticket for a masquerade, which
gives him such an aversion to them; though his intended satire against them is very absurd on the
account of his Harriet, since she might have been
carried off in the same manner if she had been going
from supper with her grandmamma. Her whole behaviour, which he designs to be exemplary, is equally

blamable and ridiculous. She follows the maxim of Clarissa, of declaring all she thinks to all the people she sees, without reflecting that in this mortal state of imperfection, fig-leaves are as necessary for our minds as our bodies. He has no idea of the manners of high life: his old Lord M. talks in the style of a country justice, and his virtuous young ladies romp like the wenches round a May-pole."

The general tendency of the novels of the time towards democracy did not go unnoticed, and Lady Mary stated her views on the question with considerable freedom. Whether she was right in attaching so much importance to the evidence of novels may reasonably be doubted.

"The confounding of all ranks, and making a jest of order, has long been growing in England; and I perceive, by the books you sent me, has made a very considerable progress. The heroes and heroines of the age are cobblers and kitchen wenches. Perhaps you will say, I should not take my ideas of the manners of the times from such trifling authors; but it is more truly to be found among them, than from any historian: as they write merely to get money, they always fall into the notions that are most acceptable to the present taste. It has long been the endeavour of our English writers to represent people of quality as the vilest and silliest part of the nation, being (generally) very low-born themselves. I am not surprised at their propagating this doctrine; but I am much mistaken if this levelling principle does not, one day or other, break

15

out in fatal consequences to the public, as it has already done in many private families. You will think I am influenced by living under an aristocratic government, where distinction of rank is carried to a very great height ; but I can assure you my opinion is founded on reflection and experience, and I wish to God I had always thought in the same manner ; though I had ever the utmost contempt for misalliances, yet the silly prejudices of my education had taught me to believe I was to treat nobody as an inferior, and that poverty was a degree of merit : this imaginary humility has made me admit many familiar acquaintances, of which I have heartily repented every one, and the greatest examples I have known of honour and integrity have been among those of the highest birth and fortunes. There are many reasons why it should be so, which I will not trouble you with. If my letter was to be published, I know I should be railed at for pride, and called an enemy of the poor ; but I take a pleasure in telling you my thoughts."

CHAPTER VIII

THOUGHTS ON EDUCATION

Lady Mary's Interest in her Grandchildren—Lady Bute's Happiness —Affectionate Feelings—Education of Girls—Virtues overstrained become Vices—Parents must be prepared for Disappointments—Beauty not to be undervalued—Children never to be deceived—Advantages of Reading—Lady Mary Stuart—Benefits of a Taste for Learning—Girls should read English Poetry—A Plagiarist detected—Ladies must conceal their Learning—True Knowledge begets Modesty—Sewing and Drawing—The Risks of Marriage —Learning a Means of occupying Time—Bad Education usually given to Girls—Ignorance leads to Misconduct—Childhood of Lady Bute—Social Life necessary—Misleading Effects of Books —Richardson again—An Italian Pamela—The Signora Diana The Young Octavia—A Beautiful Servant—Count Sosi's Courtship—Octavia's Return—An Offer of Marriage—Count Sosi marries Octavia—Her Discreet Behaviour—Another Heroine for Richardson—The Marchesa Bentivoglio—Her Pride—She leaves her Husband—Supposed Attempt to poison Her—Her Husband suspected—Sir John Rawdon and his Peerage—His Patience under Insult—Sir Charles Hanbury Williams—Lessons from his Career—Economy advisable in Individuals and Nations—English Public Extravagance—A Policy of Trade the best—Lady Mary's Views on Foreign Policy—War and Progress.

AMONG the subjects which employed the pen of Lady Mary Wortley Montagu in her seclusion at Lovere, none seems to have been nearer to her heart than the

15—2

education of her grandchildren. Though she never saw most of them (her daughter having been married in 1736), she often sent them little presents, inquired after them, and gave Lady Bute advice as to managing them. "I sympathize with you, my dear child," Lady Mary wrote, "in all the concern you express for your family; you may remember, I represented it to you before you were married; but that is one of the sentiments it is impossible to comprehend till it is felt. A mother only knows a mother's fondness. Indeed, the pain so overbalances the pleasure, that I believe, if it could be thoroughly understood, there would be no mothers at all. However, take care that your anxiety for the future does not take from you the comforts you may enjoy in the present hour; it is all that is properly ours; and yet such is the weakness of humanity, we commonly lose what is, either by regretting the past, or by disturbing our minds with the fear of what may be. You have many blessings: a husband you love, and who behaves well to you; agreeable, hopeful children; a handsome, convenient house, with pleasant gardens, in a good air and fine situation; which I place among the most solid satisfactions of life. The truest wisdom is that which diminishes to us what is displeasing, and turns our thoughts to the advantages we possess. I can assure you I give no precepts I do not daily practise. How often do I fancy to myself the pleasure I should take in seeing you in the midst of your little people; and how severe do I then think my destiny, that denies me that happiness. I endeavour to comfort myself by reflecting that we should certainly have perpetual disputes (if not quarrels) concerning the management of them; the affection of a grandmother has generally a tincture of dotage: you would say I spoilt them, and perhaps be not much in the wrong."

This tenderness towards her grandchildren breaks out in a later letter from Venice, in answer to one in which Lady Bute described her family circle:

"I am so highly delighted with this, dated August 4, giving an account of your little colony, I cannot help setting pen to paper, to tell you the melancholy joy I had in reading it. You would have laughed to see the old fool weep over it. I now find that age, when it does not harden the heart and sour the temper, naturally returns to the milky disposition of infancy. Time has the same effect on the mind as on the face. The predominant passion, the strongest feature, become more conspicuous from the others retiring; the various views of life are abandoned, from want of ability to pursue them, as the fine complexion is lost in wrinkles; but, as surely as a large nose grows larger, and a wide mouth wider, the tender child in your nursery will be a tender old woman, though, perhaps, reason may have restrained the appearance of it, till the mind, relaxed, is no longer capable of concealing its weakness; for weakness it is to indulge any attachment at a period of life when we are sure to part with life itself, at a very short warning. According to the good English proverb, young people may die, but old must. You see I am very industrious in finding comfort to myself in my exile, and to guard, as long as I can, against the peevishness which makes age miserable in itself and contemptible to others."

Lady Bute seems to have asked her mother's advice as to how to bring up her rather numerous family; and Lady Mary was ready enough to help. As in other matters, her notions on this subject are full of the clear but cold common sense which is one of her most striking characteristics. Especially noteworthy is the stoical recommendation to repress maternal anxiety and tenderness, and prepare for the inevitable disappointments of a large family. Doubtless she was thinking of the great sorrow of her life—the worthlessness of her son.

" People commonly educate their children as they build their houses, according to some plan they think beautiful, without considering whether it is suited to the purposes for which they are designed. Almost all girls of quality are educated as if they were to be great ladies, which is often as little to be expected, as an immoderate heat of the sun in the north of Scotland. You should teach yours to confine their desires to probabilities, to be as useful as is possible to themselves, and to think privacy (as it is) the happiest state of life. I do not doubt your giving them all the instructions necessary to form them to a virtuous life; but 'tis a fatal mistake to do this without proper restrictions. Vices are often hid under the name of virtues, and the practice of them followed by the worst of consequences. Sincerity, friendship, piety, disinterestedness, and generosity, are all great virtues; but, pursued without discretion, become criminal. I have seen ladies indulge their own ill humour by being very rude and impertinent, and think they deserved approbation by saying ' I love to speak truth.' One of your acquaintance made a ball the next day after her mother died, to show she was sincere. I believe your own reflection will furnish you with but too many examples of the ill effects of the rest of the sentiments I have mentioned, when too warmly embraced. They are generally recommended to young people without limits or distinction, and this prejudice hurries them into great misfortunes, while they are applauding themselves in the noble practice (as they fancy) of very eminent virtues.

" I cannot help adding (out of my real affection to you), I wish you would moderate that fondness you have for your children. I do not mean you should abate any part of your care, or not do your duty to them in its utmost extent : but I would have you early prepare yourself for disappointments, which are heavy in proportion to their being surprising. It is hardly possible, in such a number, that none should be unhappy; prepare yourself against a misfortune of that kind. I confess there is hardly any more difficult to support; yet it is certain imagination has a great share in the pain of it, and it is more in our power than it is commonly believed to soften whatever ills are founded or augmented by fancy. Strictly speaking, there is but one real evil—I mean, acute pain; all other complaints are so considerably diminished by time, that it is plain the grief is owing to our passion, since the sensation of it vanishes when that is over.

"There is another mistake, I forgot to mention, usual in mothers: if any of their daughters are beauties, they take great pains to persuade them that they are ugly, or at least that they think so, which the young woman never fails to believe springs from envy, and is perhaps not much in the wrong. I would, if possible, give them a just notion of their figure, and show them how far it is valuable. Every advantage has its price, and may be either over or undervalued. It is the common doctrine of (what are called) good books, to inspire a contempt of beauty, riches, greatness, etc., which has done as much mischief among the younger of our sex as an over eager desire of them. They should not look on these things as blessings where they are bestowed, though not necessaries that it is impossible to be happy without. I am persuaded the ruin of Lady F. [Frances] M. Meadows]* was in great measure owing to the notions given her by the silly good people that had the care of her. 'Tis true, her circumstances and your daughters' are very different: they should be taught to be content with privacy, and yet not neglect good fortune, if it should be offered them."

It was naturally with the girls that Lady Mary most concerned herself. For the boys of a noble family

---

* Lady Frances Pierrepont, Lady Mary's niece, who eloped with and married a Mr. Meadows in 1734 Her married life seems to have been unhappy.

there was the regular routine of tutors, the public school and the university ; then the "grand tour " with a " governor "; but girls, as Lady Mary knew by bitter experience, were too often left to grow up as they could—abandoned to ignorance, or, at best, taught the superficial accomplishments which might serve to attract suitors. Thus, it is chiefly on their behalf she advises her daughter in the following letter :

" MY DEAR CHILD,—I am extremely concerned to hear you complain of ill health, at a time of life when you ought to be in the flower of your strength. I hope I need not recommend to you the care of it : the tenderness you have for your children is sufficient to enforce you to the utmost regard for the preservation of a life so necessary to their well-being. I do not doubt your prudence in their education : neither can I say anything particular relating to it at this distance, different tempers requiring different management. In general, never attempt to govern them (as most people do) by deceit : if they find themselves cheated, even in trifles, it will so far lessen the authority of their instructor, as to make them neglect all their future admonitions. And, if possible, breed them free from prejudices ; those contracted in the nursery often influence the whole life after, of which I have seen many melancholy examples. I shall say no more of this subject, nor would have said this little if you had not asked my advice : 'tis much easier to give rules than to practise them. I am sensible my own natural temper is too indulgent : I think it the least dangerous error, yet still it is an error. I can only say with truth, that I do not know in my whole life having ever endeavoured to impose on you, or give a false colour to anything that I represented to you. If your daughters are inclined to love reading, do not check their inclination by hindering them of the diverting part of it ; it is as necessary for the amusement of women as the reputation of men ; but teach them not to expect or desire any applause from it. Let their brothers shine, and let them content themselves with making their lives easier by it, which I experimentally know is more effectually done by study than any other way. Ignorance is as much the fountain of vice as idleness, and indeed generally produces it. People that do not read, or work for a livelihood, have many hours they know not how to employ ; especially women, who commonly fall into vapours, or something worse."

When Lady Mary Stuart, her eldest grand-daughter, was growing up, Lady Mary Wortley Montagu developed her ideas on women's education in somewhat more detail, supposing that, with the hereditary good sense of the Pierreponts, the Wortley Montagus, and Lord Bute's family, her grand-children could not fail to have some intellectual capacity.

" I will therefore speak to you as supposing Lady Mary not only capable, but desirous of learning : in that case by all means let her be indulged in it. You will tell me I did not make it a part of your education : your prospect was very different from hers. As you had no defect either in mind or person to hinder, and

much in your circumstances to attract, the highest
offers, it seemed your business to learn how to live in
the world, as it is hers to know how to be easy out of
it. It is the common error of builders and parents to
follow some plan they think beautiful (and perhaps is
so), without considering that nothing is beautiful that
is displaced. Hence we see so many edifices raised
that the raisers can never inhabit, being too large for
their fortunes. Vistas are laid open over barren
heaths, and apartments contrived for a coolness very
agreeable in Italy, but killing in the north of Britain :
thus every woman endeavours to breed her daughter a
fine lady, qualifying her for a station in which she will
never appear, and at the same time incapacitating her
for that retirement to which she is destined. Learning, if she has a real taste for it, will not only make
her contented, but happy in it. No entertainment is
so cheap as reading, nor any pleasure so lasting. She
will not want new fashions, nor regret the loss of expensive diversions, or variety of company, if she can
be amused with an author in her closet. To render
this amusement extensive, she should be permitted to
learn the languages. I have heard it lamented that
boys lose so many years in mere learning of words :
this is no objection to a girl, whose time is not so
precious : she cannot advance herself in any profession,
and has therefore more hours to spare ; and as you
say her memory is good, she will be very agreeably
employed this way. There are two cautions to be
given on this subject : first, not to think herself learned

when she can read Latin, or even Greek. Languages are more properly to be called vehicles of learning than learning itself, as may be observed in many schoolmasters, who, though perhaps critics in grammar, are the most ignorant fellows upon earth. True knowledge consists in knowing things, not words. I would wish her no further a linguist than to enable her to read books in their originals, that are often corrupted, and always injured, by translations. Two hours' application every morning will bring this about much sooner than you can imagine, and she will have leisure enough besides to run over the English poetry, which is a more important part of a woman's education than it is generally supposed. Many a young damsel has been ruined by a fine copy of verses, which she would have laughed at if she had known it had been stolen from Mr. Waller. I remember, when I was a girl, I saved one of my companions from destruction, who communicated to me an epistle she was quite charmed with. As she had a natural good taste, she observed the lines were not so smooth as Prior's or Pope's, but had more thought and spirit than any of theirs. She was wonderfully delighted with such a demonstration of her lover's sense and passion, and not a little pleased with her own charms, that had force enough to inspire such elegancies. In the midst of this triumph I showed her that they were taken from Randolph's poems, and the unfortunate transcriber was dismissed with the scorn he deserved. To say truth, the poor plagiary was very unlucky to fall into my hands ; that author

being no longer in fashion, would have escaped any one
of less universal reading than myself. You should encourage your daughter to talk over with you what she
reads; and, as you are very capable of distinguishing,
take care she does not mistake pert folly for wit and
humour, or rhyme for poetry, which are the common
errors of young people, and have a train of ill consequences. The second caution to be given her (and
which is most absolutely necessary) is to conceal whatever learning she attains, with as much solicitude as
she would hide crookedness or lameness; the parade of
it can only serve to draw on her the envy, and consequently the most inveterate hatred, of all he and she
fools, which will certainly be at least three parts in four
of all her acquaintance. The use of knowledge in our
sex, besides the amusement of solitude, is to moderate
the passions, and learn to be contented with a small
expense, which are the certain effects of a studious
life; and it may be preferable even to that fame which
men have engrossed to themselves, and will not suffer
us to share. You will tell me I have not observed
this rule myself; but you are mistaken: it is only inevitable accident that has given me any reputation
that way. I have always carefully avoided it, and ever
thought it a misfortune. The explanation of this para-
graph would occasion a long digression, which I will
not trouble you with, it being my present design only
to say what I think useful for the instruction of my
grand-daughter, which I have much at heart. If she
has the same inclination (I should say passion) for

learning that I was born with, history, geography, and philosophy will furnish her with materials to pass away cheerfully a longer life than is allotted to mortals. I believe there are few heads capable of making Sir I. Newton's calculations, but the result of them is not difficult to be understood by a moderate capacity. Do not fear this should make her affect the character of Lady ——, or Lady ——, or Mrs. —— ;* those women are ridiculous, not because they have learning, but because they have it not. One thinks herself a complete historian, after reading Echard's Roman History ; another a profound philosopher, having got by heart some of Pope's unintelligible essays ; and a third an able divine, on the strength of Whitefield's sermons : thus you hear them screaming politics and controversy.

" It is a saying of Thucydides, ignorance is bold, and knowledge reserved. Indeed, it is impossible to be far advanced in it without being more humbled by a conviction of human ignorance, than elated by learning. At the same time I recommend books, I neither exclude work nor drawing. I think it as scandalous for a woman not to know how to use a needles, a for a man not to know how to use a sword. I was once extreme fond of my pencil, and it was a great mortification to me when my father turned off my master, having made a considerable progress for the short time I learnt. My over-eagerness in the pursuit of it had brought a weakness on my eyes, that made it necessary to leave it off; and all the advantage I got was the improvement of my

* The blanks are in the original.

hand. I see, by hers, that practice will make her a
ready writer : she may attain it by serving you for a
secretary, when your health or affairs make it troublesome to you to write yourself; and custom will make
it an agreeable amusement to her. She cannot have
too many for that station of life which will probably be
her fate. The ultimate end of your education was to
make you a good wife (and I have the comfort to hear
that you are one) : hers ought to be, to make her happy
in a virgin state. I will not say it is happier ; but it is
undoubtedly safer than any marriage. In a lottery,
where there are (at the lowest computation) ten thousand blanks to a prize, it is the most prudent choice
not to venture. I have always been so thoroughly
persuaded of this truth, that, notwithstanding the
flattering views I had for you (as I never intended you
a sacrifice to my vanity), I thought I owed you the
justice to lay before you all the hazards attending
matrimony : you may recollect I did so in the strongest
manner. Perhaps you may have more success in the
instructing your daughter : she has so much company at home, she will not need seeking it abroad, and
will more readily take the notions you think fit to give
her. As you were alone in my family, it would have
been thought a great cruelty to suffer you no companions of your own age, especially having so many
near relations, and I do not wonder their opinions
influenced yours."

But this plea for a learned education for women was
so contrary to the prejudices and ideas of the time,

that Lady Mary made haste to soften down the impression it might produce on Lord Bute; hence she declared that she merely recommended study as a means of preventing time from hanging heavy on the hands of her grandchildren, especially in case they remained single:

"I cannot help writing a sort of apology for my last letter, foreseeing that you will think it wrong, or at least Lord Bute will be extremely shocked at the proposal of a learned education for daughters, which the generality of men believe as great a profanation as the clergy would do if the laity should presume to exercise the functions of the priesthood. I desire you would take notice, I would not have learning enjoined them as a task, but permitted as a pleasure, if their genius leads them naturally to it. I look upon my granddaughters as a sort of lay nuns: destiny may have laid up other things for them, but they have no reason to expect to pass their time otherwise than their aunts do at present; and I know, by experience, it is in the power of study not only to make solitude tolerable, but agreeable. I have now lived almost seven years in a stricter retirement than yours in the Isle of Bute, and can assure you, I have never had half an hour heavy on my hands, for want of something to do. Whoever will cultivate their own mind, will find full employment. Every virtue does not only require great care in the planting, but as much daily solicitude in cherishing, as exotic fruits and flowers. The vices and passions (which I am afraid are the natural product of the soil) demand perpetual weeding. Add to this the search after knowledge (every branch of which is entertaining), and the longest life is too short for the pursuit of it ; which, though in some regards confined to very strait limits, leaves still a vast variety of amusements to those capable of tasting them, which is utterly impossible for those that are blinded by prejudices which are the certain effect of an ignorant education. My own was one of the worst in the world, being exactly the same as Clarissa Harlowe's ; her pious Mrs. Norton so perfectly resembling my governess, who had been nurse to my mother, I could almost fancy the author was acquainted with her. She took so much pains, from my infancy, to fill my head with superstitious tales and false notions, it was none of her fault I am not at this day afraid of witches and hobgoblins, or turned methodist. Almost all girls are bred after this manner. I believe you are the only woman (perhaps I might say, person) that never was either frighted or cheated into anything by your parents. I can truly affirm, I never deceived anybody in my life, excepting (which I confess has often happened undesignedly) by speaking plainly ; as Earl Stanhope used to say (during his ministry) he always imposed on the foreign ministers by telling them the naked truth, which, as they thought impossible to come from the mouth of a statesman, they never failed to write informations to their respective courts directly contrary to the assurances he gave them : most people confounding the ideas of sense and cunning, though there

16

are really no two things in nature more opposite: it
is, in part, from this false reasoning, the unjust custom
prevails of debarring our sex from the advantages of
learning, the men fancying the improvement of our
understandings would only furnish us with more art
to deceive them, which is directly contrary to the
truth. Fools are always enterprising, not seeing the
difficulties of deceit, or the ill consequences of detec-
tion. I could give many examples of ladies whose il
conduct has been very notorious, which has been owing
to that ignorance which has exposed them to idleness,
which is justly called the mother of mischief. There
is nothing so like the education of a woman of quality
as that of a prince : they are taught to dance, and the
exterior part of what is called good breeding, which,
if they attain, they are extraordinary creatures in their
kind, and have all the accomplishments required by
their directors. The same characters are formed by
the same lessons, which inclines me to think (if I dare
say it) that nature has not placed us in an inferior rank
to men, no more than the females of other animals,
where we see no distinction of capacity; though, I am
persuaded, if there was a commonwealth of rational
horses (as Doctor Swift has supposed), it would be
an established maxim among them, that a mare could
not be taught to pace."

This last little *boutade* indicates with sufficient plainness that the writer, though refraining from affronting
the prejudices of her time, did not share them.

And though Horace Walpole, in one of his letters,

charges her with neglecting her daughter's education, a neglectful mother would hardly have written such a letter as the following :

" For my part, I am so far persuaded of the goodness of your heart, I have often had a mind to write you a consolatory epistle on my own death, which I believe will be some affliction, though my life is wholly useless to you. That part of it which we passed together you have reason to remember with gratitude, though I think you misplace it; you are no more obliged to me for bringing you into the world, than I am to you for coming into it, and I never made use of that common-place (and like most common-place, false) argument, as exacting any return of affection. There was a mutual necessity on us both to part at that time, and no obligation on either side. In the case of your infancy, there was so great a mixture of instinct, I can scarce even put that in the number of the proofs I have given you [of] my love; but I confess I think it a great one, if you compare my after-conduct towards you with that of other mothers, who generally look on their children as devoted to their pleasures, and bound by duty to have no sentiments but what they please to give them ; playthings at first, and afterwards the objects on which they may exercise their spleen, tyranny, or ill humour. I have always thought of you in a different manner. Your happiness was my first wish, and the pursuit of all my actions, divested of all self-interest. So far I think you ought, and believe you do, remember me as your real friend."

While pressing the claims of study for her grand-daughters, Lady Mary did not forget to recommend social life as the only means of obtaining that necessary knowledge of the world which was to correct the false impressions too often gained from books. Through all her letters on the subject of training and educa-tion runs the doctrine that good books are the best guardians against bad books, good society against bad companions, and, in short, that good taste is a far more efficient safeguard than abstinence or prohibition.

" I congratulate my grand-daughters on being born in an age so much enlightened. Sentiments are cer-tainly extreme silly, and only qualify young people to be the bubbles of all their acquaintance. I do not doubt the frequency of assemblies has introduced a more enlarged way of thinking; it is a kind of public education, which I have always thought as necessary for girls as for boys. A woman married at five-and-twenty, from under the eye of a strict parent, is com-monly as ignorant as she was at five; and no more capable of avoiding the snares, and struggling with the difficulties, she will infallibly meet with in the commerce of the world. The knowledge of mankind (the most useful of all knowledge) can only be acquired by conversing with them. Books are so far from giving that instruction, they fill the head with a set of wrong notions, from whence spring the tribes of Clarissas, Harriets, etc. Yet such was the method of education when I was in England, which I had it not in my power to correct; the young will always adopt the opinions of all their companions, rather than the advice of their mothers."

It will be seen from the last extract that Lady Mary had not forgotten her Richardson, and her memory of his novels was quickened by an event which set the little society of Lovere in a turmoil—an Italian servant-girl playing Pamela to the " Mr. B. " of a local count.

" This town is at present in a general stare, or, to use their own expression, *sotto sopra ;* and not only this town, but the capital Bergamo, the whole province, the neighbouring Brescian, and perhaps all the Venetian dominion, occasioned by an adventure exactly resembling, and I believe copied from, Pamela. I know not under what constellation that foolish stuff was wrote, but it has been translated into more languages than any modern performance I ever heard of. No proof of its influence was ever stronger than this story, which, in Richardson's hands, would serve very well to furnish out seven or eight volumes. I shall make it as short as I can.

" Here is a gentleman's family, consisting of an old bachelor and his sister, who have fortune enough to live with great elegance, though without any magnificence, possessed of the esteem of all their acquaintance, he being distinguished by his probity, and she by her virtue. They are not only suffered but sought by all the best company, and indeed are the most conversable, reasonable people in the place. She is an excellent housewife, and particularly remarkable for keeping her pretty house as neat as any in Holland. She appears no longer in public, being past fifty, and passes her time chiefly at home with her work, receiving few visitants. This Signora Diana, about ten years since, saw, at a monastery, a girl about eight years old, who came thither to beg alms for the mother. Her beauty, though covered with rags, was very observable, and gave great compassion to the charitable lady, who thought it meritorious to rescue such a modest sweetness as appeared in her face from the ruin to which her wretched circumstances exposed her. She asked her some questions, to which she answered with a natural civility that seemed surprising; and finding the head of her family (her brother) to be a cobbler, who could hardly live by that trade, and her mother too old to work for her maintenance, she bid the child follow her home; and sending for her parent, proposed to her to breed the little Octavia for her servant. This was joyfully accepted, the old woman dismissed with a piece of money, and the girl remained with the Signora Diana, who bought her decent clothes, and took pleasure in teaching her whatever she was capable of learning. She learned to read, write, and cast accounts, with uncommon facility; and had such a genius for work, that she excelled her mistress in embroidery, point, and every operation of the needle. She grew perfectly skilled in confectionery, had a good insight into cookery, and was a great proficient in distillery. To these accomplishments she was so handy, well bred, humble and modest, that not only her master and mistress, but everybody that frequented the house, took notice of her. She lived thus nine years, never going out but to church. However, beauty is as difficult to conceal as light; hers began to make a great noise. Signora Diana told me she observed an unusual concourse of peddling women that came on pretext to sell penn'orths of lace, china, etc., and several young gentlemen, very well powdered, that were perpetually walking before her door, and looking up at the windows. These prognostics alarmed her prudence, and she listened very willingly to some honourable proposals that were made by many honest, thriving tradesmen. She communicated them to Octavia, and told her, that though she was sorry to lose so good a servant, yet she thought it right to advise her to choose a husband. The girl answered modestly, that it was her duty to obey all her commands, but she found no inclination to marriage; and if she would permit her to live single, she should think it a greater obligation than any other she could bestow. Signora Diana was too conscientious to force her into a state from which she could not free her, and left her to her own disposal. However, they parted soon after: whether (as the neighbours say) Signor Aurelio Ardinghi, her brother, looked with too much attention on the young woman, or that she herself (as Diana says) desired to seek a place of more profit, she removed to Bergamo, where she soon found preferment, being strongly recommended by the Ardinghi family. She was advanced to be first

waiting-woman to an old Countess, who was so well
pleased with her service, she desired, on her death-bed,
Count Jeronimo Sosi, her son, to be kind to her. He
found no repugnance to this act of obedience, having
distinguished the beautiful Octavia from his first sight
of her ; and, during the six months that she had served
in the house, had tried every art of a fine gentleman,
accustomed to victories of that sort, to vanquish the
virtue of this fair virgin. He has a handsome figure,
and has had an education uncommon in this country,
having made the tour of Europe, and brought from
Paris all the improvements that are to be picked up
there, being celebrated for his grace in dancing, and
skill in fencing and riding, by which he is a favourite
among the ladies, and respected by the men. Thus
qualified for conquest, you may judge of his surprise
at the firm yet modest resistance of this country girl,
who was neither to be moved by address, nor gained
by liberality, nor on any terms would be prevailed on
to stay as his housekeeper, after the death of his mother.
She took that post in the house of an old judge, where
she continued to be solicited by the emissaries of the
Count's passion, and found a new persecutor in her
master, who after three months offered her marriage.
She chose to return to her former obscurity, and
escaped from his pursuit, without asking any wages,
and privately returned to the Signora Diana. She
threw herself at her feet, and, kissing her hands, begged
her, with tears, to conceal her at least some time, if
she would not accept of her service. She protested she

had never been happy since she left it. While she was making these submissions, Signor Aurelio entered. She entreated his intercession on her knees, who was easily persuaded to consent she should stay with them, though his sister blamed her highly for her precipitate flight, having no reason, from the age and character of her master, to fear any violence, and wondered at her declining the honour he offered her. Octavia confessed that perhaps she had been too rash in her proceedings, but said, that he seemed to resent her refusal in such a manner as frighted her; she hoped that after a few days' search he would think no more of her; and that she scrupled entering into the holy bands of matrimony, where her heart did not sincerely accompany all the words of the ceremony. Signora Diana had nothing to say in contradiction to this pious sentiment; and her brother applauded the honesty which could not be perverted by any interest whatever. She remained concealed in their house, where she helped in the kitchen, cleaned the rooms, and redoubled her usual diligence and officiousness. Her old master came to Lovere on pretence of adjusting a lawsuit, three days after, and made private inquiry after her; but hearing from her mother and brother (who knew nothing of her being here) that they had never heard of her, he concluded she had taken another route, and returned to Bergamo; and she continued in this retirement near a fortnight.

"Last Sunday, as soon as the day was closed, arrived at Signor Aurelio's door a handsome equipage

in a large bark, attended by four well-armed servants
on horseback. An old priest stepped out of it, and
desiring to speak with Signora Diana, informed her
he came from the Count Jeronimo Sosi to demand
Octavia; that the Count waited for her at a village
four miles from hence, where he intended to marry
her; and had sent him, who was engaged to perform
the divine rite, that Signora Diana might resign her
to his care without any difficulty. The young damsel
was called for, who entreated she might be permitted
the company of another priest with whom she was
acquainted: this was readily granted; and she sent
for a young man that visits me very often, being
remarkable for his sobriety and learning. Meanwhile,
a valet-de-chambre presented her with a box, in which
was a complete genteel undress for a lady. Her laced
linen and fine nightgown were soon put on, and away
they marched, leaving the family in a surprise not to
be described.

"Signor Aurelio came to drink coffee with me next
morning: his first words were, he had brought me the
history of Pamela. I said, laughing, I had been tired
with it long since. He explained himself by relating
this story, mixed with great resentment for Octavia's
conduct. Count Jeronimo's father had been his
ancient friend and patron; and this escape from his
house (he said) would lay him under a suspicion of
having abetted the young man's folly, and perhaps
expose him to the anger of all his relations, for contriving an action he would rather have died than

suffered, if he had known how to prevent it. I easily believed him, there appearing a latent jealousy under his affliction, that showed me he envied the bridegroom's happiness, at the same time he condemned his extravagance.

"Yesterday noon, being Saturday, Don Joseph returned, who has got the name of Parson Williams by this expedition: he relates, that when the bark which carried the coach and train arrived, they found the amorous Count waiting for his bride on the bank of the lake: he would have proceeded immediately to the church; but she utterly refused it, till they had each of them been at confession; after which the happy knot was tied by the parish priest. They continued their journey, and came to their palace at Bergamo in a few hours, where everything was prepared for their reception. They received the communion next morning, and the Count declares that the lovely Octavia has brought him an inestimable portion, since he owes to her the salvation of his soul. He has renounced play, at which he had lost a great deal of time and money. She has already retrenched several superfluous servants, and put his family into an exact method of economy, preserving all the splendour necessary to his rank. He has sent a letter in his own hand to her mother, inviting her to reside with them, and subscribing himself her dutiful son: but the Countess has sent another privately by Don Joseph, in which she advises the old woman to stay at Lovere, promising to take care she shall want nothing, accompanied with a token of twenty sequins,* which is at least nineteen more than ever she saw in her life.

"I forgot to tell you that from Octavia's first serving the old lady, there came frequent charities in her name to her poor parent, which nobody was surprised at, the lady being celebrated for pious works, and Octavia known to be a great favourite with her. It is now discovered that they were all sent by the generous lover, who has presented Don Joseph very handsomely, but he has brought neither letter nor message to the house of Ardinghi, which affords much speculation."

Another Italian lady of the time, though conforming less closely to Richardson's pattern, was regarded by Lady Mary as deserving the honour — not of the greatest, in her estimation — of being celebrated by him: the Marchesa Licinia Bentivoglio.

"A late adventure here makes a great noise from the rank of the people concerned: the Marchioness Lyscinnia† Bentivoglio, who was heiress of one branch of the Martinenghi, and brought forty thousand gold sequins to her husband, and the expectation of her father's estate, three thousand pounds per annum, the most magnificent palace at Brescia (finer than any in London), another in the country, and many other advantages of woods, plate, jewels, etc. The Cardinal Bentivoglio, his uncle, thought he could not choose better, though his nephew might certainly have chose

---

* About ten guineas English
† Lady Mary probably spelt phonetically.

among all the Italian ladies, being descended from the
sovereigns of Bologna,* actually a grandee of Spain, a
noble Venetian, and in possession of twenty-five thousand
pounds sterling per annum, with immense wealth in
palaces, furniture, and absolute dominion in some of his
lands. The girl was pretty, and the match was with
the satisfaction of both families; but she brought with
her such a diabolical temper, and such *Luciferan* pride,
that neither husband, relations, nor servants, had ever
a moment's peace with her. After about eight years'
warfare, she eloped one fair morning and took refuge
in Venice, leaving her two daughters, the eldest scarce
six years old, to the care of the exasperated Marquis.
Her father was so angry at her extravagant conduct,
he would not, for some time, receive her into his house;
but, after some months, and much solicitation, parental
fondness prevailed, and she remained with him ever
since, notwithstanding all the efforts of her husband,
who tried kindness, submission, and threats, to no purpose. The Cardinal came twice to Brescia, her own
father joined his entreaties, nay, *his Holiness* wrote a
letter with his own hand, and made use of the Church
authority, but he found it harder to reduce one woman
than ten heretics. She was inflexible, and lived ten
years in this state of reprobation. Her father died last
winter, and left her his whole estate for her life, and
afterwards to her children. Her eldest was now mar-
riageable, and disposed of to the nephew of Cardinal

---

* The Bentivogli had been Lords of Bologna. They claimed
descent from Enzio, son of the Emperor Frederick II.

Valentino Gonzagua, first minister at Rome. She would neither appear at the wedding, nor take the least notice of a dutiful letter sent by the bride. The old Cardinal (who was passionately fond of his illustrious name) was so much touched with the apparent extinction of it, that it was thought to have hastened his death. She continued in the enjoyment of her ill-humour, living in great splendour, though almost solitary, having, by some impertinence or other, disgusted all her acquaintance, till about a month ago, when her woman brought her a basin of broth, which she usually drank in her bed. She took a few spoonfuls of it, and then cried out it was so bad it was impossible to endure it. Her chambermaids were so used to hear her exclamations they had not the worse opinion of it, and eat it up very comfortably; they were both seized with the same pangs, and died the next day. She sent for physicians, who judged her poisoned; but, as she had taken a small quantity, by the help of antidotes she recovered, yet is still in a languishing condition. Her cook was examined, and racked, always protesting entire innocence, and swearing he had made the soup in the same manner he was accustomed. You may imagine the noise of this affair. She loudly accused her husband, it being the interest of no other person to wish her out of the world. He resides at Ferrara (about which the greatest part of his lands lie), and was soon informed of this accident. He sent doctors to her, whom she would not see, sent vast alms to all the convents to pray for her health, and ordered a number of masses

to be said in every church of Brescia and Ferrara. He
sent letters to the Senate at Venice, and published
manifestoes in all the capital cities, in which he professes his affection to her, and abhorrence of any
attempt against her, and has a cloud of witnesses
that he never gave her the least reason of complaint,
and even since her leaving him has always spoke of her
with kindness, and courted her return. He is said to
be remarkably sweet tempered, and has the best character of any man of quality in this country. If the
death of her women did not seem to confirm it, her
accusation would gain credit with nobody. She is
certainly very sincere in it herself, being so persuaded
he has resolved her death, that she dare not take the
air, apprehending to be assassinated, and has imprisoned herself in her chamber, where she will neither
eat nor drink anything that she does not see tasted by
all her servants. The physicians now say that perhaps
the poison might fall into the broth accidentally; I confess I do not perceive the possibility of it. As to the
cook suffering the rack, that is a mere jest where people
have money enough to bribe the executioner. I decide
nothing; but such is the present destiny of a lady, who
would have been one of Richardson's heroines, having
never been suspected of the least gallantry; hating,
and being hated universally; of a most noble spirit,
it being proverbial, 'As proud as the Marchioness Lys-
cinnia.' "

As a contrast to this instance of Italian pride may
be appended here an equally sublime specimen of Eng-

lish humility of which Lady Mary was reminded by an
item of news in one of her daughter's letters. It appears
that an acquaintance of hers in Italy, Sir John Rawdon,
was raised to the Irish peerage; and her comments on
the transaction are more pithy than complimentary :

" I cannot believe Sir John's advancement is owing
to his merit, though he certainly deserves such a distinction; but I am persuaded the present disposers of
such dignities are neither more clear-sighted nor more
disinterested than their predecessors.   Ever since I
knew the world, Irish patents have been hung out to
sale, like the laced and embroidered coats in Monmouth-
street, and bought up by the same sort of people; I
mean those who had rather wear shabby finery than no
finery at all; though I do not suppose this was Sir
John's case. That good creature (as the country saying
is) has not a bit of pride in him.   I dare swear he purchased his title for the same reason he used to purchase
pictures in Italy; not because he wanted to buy, but
because somebody or other wanted to sell.   He hardly
ever opened his mouth but to say ' What you please,
sir;'—' At your service;'—' Your humble servant;' or
some gentle expression to the same effect.   It is scarce
credible that with this unlimited complaisance he should
draw a blow upon himself; yet it so happened that one
of his own countrymen was brute enough to strike him.
As it was done before many witnesses, Lord Mansel
heard of it; and thinking that if poor Sir John took no
notice of it, he would suffer daily insults of the same
kind, out of pure good nature resolved to spirit him up

at least to some show of resentment, intending to make up their matter afterwards in as honourable a manner as he could for the poor patient. He represented to him very warmly that no gentleman could take a box on the ear. Sir John answered with great calmness, ' I know that, but this was not a box on the ear; it was only a slap of the face.' "

Of another English acquaintance of hers Lady Mary heard casually—the former Sir Charles Hanbury Williams, whose lively verses had been sometimes attributed to herself. He had for some time been English Ambassador at St. Petersburg; and his foolish extravagance at home and abroad gave her an opportunity for moralizing on the benefits of economy—a virtue which she was generally credited with carrying to excess. As she writes to Lady Bute:

" I inquired after my old acquaintance Sir Charles Williams, who I hear is much broken, both in spirits and constitution. How happy that man might have been if there had been added to his natural and acquired endowments a dash of morality! If he had known how to distinguish between false and true felicity; and instead of seeking to increase an estate already too large, and hunting after pleasures that have made him ridiculous, he had bounded his desires of wealth, and followed the dictates of his conscience. His servile ambition has gained him two yards of red ribbon, and an exile into a miserable country, where there is no society and so little taste, that I believe he suffers under a dearth of flatterers. This is said for the

17

use of your growing sons, whom I hope no golden
temptations will induce to marry women they cannot
love, or comply with measures they do not approve.
All the happiness this world can afford is more within
reach than is generally supposed. Whoever seeks
pleasure will undoubtedly find pain ; whoever will
pursue ease will as certainly find pleasures. The
world's esteem is the highest gratification of human
vanity; and that is more easily obtained in a moderate
fortune than an overgrown one, which is seldom
possessed, never gained, without envy. I say esteem ;
for, as to applause, it is a youthful pursuit, never to
be forgiven after twenty, and naturally succeeds the
childish desire of catching the setting sun, which I can
remember running very hard to do : a fine thing truly
if it could be caught ; but experience soon shows it to
be impossible. A wise and honest man lives to his own
heart, without that silly splendour that makes him a
prey to knaves, and which commonly ends in his
becoming one of the fraternity. I am very glad to hear
Lord Bute's decent economy sets him above anything
of that kind. I wish it may become national. A col-
lective body of men differs very little from a single man;
frugality is the foundation of generosity. I have often
been complimented on the English heroism, who have
thrown away so many millions, without any prospect
of advantage to themselves, purely to succour a distressed princess.* I never could hear these praises

* Alluding to the large subsidies given by England to Maria
Theresa during the War of the Austrian Succession.

without some impatience; they sounded to me like panegyrics made by the dependents on the D. [Duke] of N. [Newcastle] and poor Lord Oxford, bubbled when they were commended, and laughed at when undone. Some late events will, I hope, open our eyes: we shall see we are an island, and endeavour to extend our commerce, rather than the Quixote reputation of redressing wrongs and placing diadems on heads that should be equally indifferent to us. When time has ripened mankind into common sense, the name of conqueror will be an odious title. I could easily prove that, had the Spaniards established a trade with the Americans, they would have enriched their country more than by the addition of twenty-two kingdoms, and all the mines they now work—I do not say possess, since, though they are the proprietors, others enjoy the profits."

This last passage is interesting, as setting forth Lady Mary's own views on English policy—a view closely agreeing with the notions ascribed to the Manchester School of later times. It is curious, however, to notice how she condemned Bolingbroke for his unpatriotic haste in concluding the Treaty of Utrecht, when her own son-in-law, Lord Bute, had already, before her death, begun to carry out a pacification, which in its abandonment of allies and surrender of advantages was quite as scandalous as Bolingbroke's. Again, it was precisely that English trade which she desired to see extended that had caused the wars which she condemned. Apparently she expected to see war abolished by the progress of mankind, which, to her idea, had barely emerged from childhood :

" When I reflect on the vast increase of useful, as well as speculative, knowledge the last three hundred years has produced, and that the peasants of this age have more conveniences than the first emperors of Rome had any notion of, I imagine that we are now arrived at that period which answers to fifteen. I cannot think we are older, when I recollect the many palpable follies which are still (almost) universally persisted in : I place that of war amongst the most glaring, being fully as senseless as the boxing of schoolboys, and whenever we come to man's estate (perhaps a thousand years hence), I do not doubt it will appear as ridiculous as the pranks of unlucky lads. Several discoveries will then be made, and several truths made clear, of which we have now no more idea than the ancients had of the circulation of the blood, or the optics of Sir I. Newton."

CHAPTER IX

LAST YEARS AND DEATH

THE last few years of Lady Mary Wortley Montagu's life were spent in much the same occupations as she

had previously described in her letters to her daughter
—residing at one or other of the towns of the Venetian
territory, at first generally near Brescia, but afterwards
alternating between Padua and Venice.   Her life was
uneventful, marked only by the approach of old age
and the growth of infirmities.   Yet she had a wonderful
power of rallying from illness, as was shown by the
description she gives of her recovery from a fever—a
result which may fairly be ascribed as much to the
goodness of her constitution as to the "miraculous"
doctor who attended her.   Her return to Lovere at
his orders led her to take another residence there.
Probably the "dairy-house" and gardens had been
given up.

> "Lovere, June 23, N.S. [1754].

"Soon after I wrote my last letter to my dear
child, I was seized with so violent a fever, accompanied
with so many bad symptoms, my life was despaired
of by the physician of Gottolengo, and I prepared
myself for death with as much resignation as that
circumstance admits : some of my neighbours, without my knowledge, sent express for the doctor of this
place, whom I have mentioned to you formerly as
having uncommon secrets.   I was surprised to see
him at my bedside.   He declared me in great danger,
but did not doubt my recovery, if I was wholly under
his care ; and his first prescription was transporting
me hither ; the other physician asserted positively I
should die on the road.   It has always been my
opinion that it is a matter of the utmost indifference

where we expire, and I consented to be removed. My
bed was placed on a brancard ; my servants followed
in chaises ; and in this equipage I set out. I bore the
first day's journey of fifteen miles without any visible
alteration. The doctor said, as I was not worse, I
was certainly better ; and the next day proceeded
twenty miles to Iseo, which is at the head of this lake.
I lay each night at noblemen's houses, which were
empty. My cook, with my physician, always preceded
two or three hours, and I found my chamber, and all
necessaries, ready prepared with the exactest attention.
I was put into a bark in my litter bed, and in three
hours arrived here. My spirits were not at all wasted
(I think rather raised) by the fatigue of my journey. I
drank the water next morning, and, with a few doses
of my physician's prescription, in three days found
myself in perfect health, which appeared almost a
miracle to all that saw me. You may imagine I am
willing to submit to the orders of one that I must
acknowledge the instrument of saving my life, though
they are not entirely conformable to my will and
pleasure. He has sentenced me to a long continuance
here, which, he says, is absolutely necessary to the
confirmation of my health, and would persuade me
that my illness has been wholly owing to my omission
of drinking the waters these two years past. I dare
not contradict him, and must own he deserves (from
the various surprising cures I have seen) the name
given to him in this country of the miraculous man.
Both his character and practice are so singular, I

cannot forbear giving you some account of them. He will not permit his patients to have either surgeon or apothecary : he performs all the operations of the first with great dexterity ; and whatever compounds he gives, he makes in his own house : those are very few ; the juice of herbs, and these waters, being commonly his sole prescriptions. He has very little learning, and professes drawing all his knowledge from experience, which he possesses, perhaps, in a greater degree than any other mortal, being the seventh doctor of his family in a direct line. His forefathers have all of them left journals and registers solely for the use of their posterity, none of them having published anything; and he has recourse to these manuscripts on every difficult case, the veracity of which, at least, is unquestionable. His vivacity is prodigious, and he is indefatigable in his industry : but what most distinguishes him is a disinterestedness I never saw in any other : he is as regular in his attendance on the poorest peasant, from whom he never can receive one farthing, as on the richest of the nobility ; and, whenever he is wanted, will climb three or four miles in the mountains, in the hottest sun, or heaviest rain, where a horse cannot go, to arrive at a cottage, where, if their condition requires it, he does not only give them advice and medicines gratis, but bread, wine, and whatever is needful. There never passes a week without one or more of these expeditions. His last visit is generally to me. I often see him as dirty and tired as a foot post, having eat nothing all day but a roll or two that he carries in his pocket, yet blest with such a perpetual flow of spirits, he is always gay to a degree above cheerfulness. There is a peculiarity in his character that I hope will incline you to forgive my drawing it.

" I have already described to you this extraordinary spot of earth, which is almost unknown to the rest of the world, and indeed does not seem to be destined by nature to be inhabited by human creatures, and I believe would never have been so, without the cruel civil war between the Guelphs and Ghibelines. Before that time here were only the huts of a few fishermen, who came at certain seasons on account of the fine fish with which this lake abounds, particularly trouts, as large and red as salmon. The lake itself is different from any other I ever saw or read of, being the colour of the sea, rather deeper tinged with green, which convinces me that the surrounding mountains are full of minerals, and it may be rich in mines yet undiscovered, as well as quarries of marble, from whence the churches and houses are ornamented, and even the streets paved, which, if polished and laid with art, would look like the finest mosaic work, being a variety of beautiful colours. I ought to retract the honourable title of street, none of them being broader than an alley, and impassable for any wheel-carriage, except a wheel-barrow. This town (which is the largest of twenty-five that are built on the banks of the lake) is near two miles long, and the figure of a semicircle. If it was a regular range of building, it would appear magnificent ; but, being founded accidentally by those who sought a refuge from the violences of those bloody times, it is a mixture of shops and palaces, gardens and houses, which ascend a mile high, in a confusion which is not disagreeable. After this salutary water was found, and the purity of the air experienced, many people of quality chose it for their summer residence, and embellished it with several fine edifices. It was populous and flourishing, till that fatal plague which overran all Europe in the year 1626. It made a terrible ravage in this place : the poor were almost destroyed, and the rich deserted it. Since that time it has never recovered its former splendour ; few of the nobility returned ; it is now only frequented during the water-drinking season. Several of the ancient palaces [are] degraded into lodging-houses and others stand empty in a ruinous condition : one of these I have bought. I see you lift up your eyes in wonder at my indiscretion. I beg you to hear my reasons before you condemn me. In my infirm state of health the unavoidable noise of a public lodging is very dis-agreeable ; and here is no private one : secondly, and chiefly, the whole purchase is but one hundred pounds, with a very pretty garden in terraces down to the water, and a court behind the house. It is founded on a rock, and the walls so thick, they will probably remain as long as the earth. It is true, the apartments are in most tattered circumstances, without doors or windows. The beauty of the great saloon gained my affection : it is forty-two feet in length by twenty-five,

proportionably high, opening into a balcony of the
same length, with marble balusters : the ceiling and
flooring are in good repair, but I have been forced to
the expense of covering the wall with new stucco ; and
the carpenter is at this minute taking measure of the
windows, in order to make frames for sashes. The
great stairs are in such a declining way, it would be a
very hazardous exploit to mount them : I never intend
to attempt it. The state bedchamber shall also remain
for the sole use of the spiders that have taken possession of it, along with the grand cabinet, and some other
pieces of magnificence, quite useless to me, and which
would cost a great deal to make habitable. I have
fitted up six rooms, with lodgings for five servants,
which are all I ever will have in this place ; and I am
persuaded that I could make a profit if I would part
with my purchase, having been very much befriended
in the sale, which was by auction, the owner having
died without children, and I believe he had never seen
this mansion in his life, it having stood empty from
the death of his grandfather. The Governor bid for
me, and nobody would bid against him. Thus I am
become a citizen of Lovere, to the great joy of the
inhabitants, not (as they would pretend) from their
respect for my person, but I perceive they fancy I
shall attract all the travelling English ; and, to say the
truth, the singularity of the place is well worth their
curiosity ; but, as I have no correspondents, I may be
buried here fifty years, and nobody know anything of
the matter."

It was this hope of profit from English visitors that induced the people of Lovere to offer the honour of a statue to Lady Mary ; but they must have been also actuated by more local considerations.   The Doge of Venice, Grimani, was her old friend, and when he died she had still the favour of the Archbishop of Brescia, Cardinal Querini, an ecclesiastic of some learning and great pretensions :

" I have not yet lost all my interest in this country by the death of the Doge, having another very con-siderable friend, though I cannot expect to keep him long, he being near fourscore.   I mean the Cardinal Querini, who is Archbishop of this diocese, and con-sequently of great power, there being not one family, high or low, in this province, that has not some ecclesiastic in it, and therefore all of them have some dependence on him.   He is of one of the first families of Venice, vastly rich of himself, and has many great benefices beside his archbishopric ; but these advantages are little in his eyes, in comparison of being the first author (as he fancies) at this day in Christendom ; and indeed, if the merit of the books consisted in bulk and number, he might very justly claim that character.   I believe he has published, yearly, several volumes for above fifty years, beside corresponding with all the literati of Europe, and, among these, several of the senior fellows at Oxford, and some members of the Royal Society, that neither you nor I ever heard of, who he is persuaded are the most eminent men in England.   He is at present employed in writing his

own life, of which he has already printed the first
tome; and if he goes on in the same style, it will be a
most voluminous performance. He begins from the
moment of his birth, and tells us that, in that day, he
made such extraordinary faces, the midwife, chambermaids, and nurses all agreed, that there was born a
shining light in church and state. You'll think me
very merry with the failings of my friend. I confess I
ought to forgive a vanity to which I am obliged for
many good offices, since I do not doubt it is owing to
that, that he professes himself so highly attached to
my service, having an opinion that my suffrage is of
great weight in the learned world, and that I shall not
fail to spread his fame, at least, all over Great Britain.
He sent me a present last week of a very uncommon
kind, even his own picture, extremely well done, but
so flattering, it is a young old man, with a most
pompous inscription under it. I suppose he intended
it for the ornament of my library, not knowing it is
only a closet: however, these distinctions he shows
me, give me a figure in this town, where everybody
has something to hope from him; and it was certainly
in a view to that they would have complimented me
with a statue, for I would not have you mistake so far
as to imagine there is any set of people more grateful
or generous than another. Mankind is everywhere the
same: like cherries or apples, they may differ in size,
shape, or colour, from different soils, climate, or
culture, but are still essentially the same species; and
the little black wood cherry is not nearer akin to the

[may-]dukes that are served at great tables, than the wild, naked negro to the fine figures adorned with coronets and ribands. This observation might be carried yet further : all animals are stimulated by the same passions, and act very near alike, as far as we are capable of observing them."

Unfortunately this friendship was troubled for a time by that which caused most of Lady Mary's troubles--her literary tastes. Formerly she had been assailed by Pope for writing libels which she very probably had nothing to do with ; now she was threatened with losing Querini's favour for want of producing her works in numerous volumes.

She writes plaintively to her daughter : " This letter will be very dull or very peevish (perhaps both). I am at present much out of humour, being on the edge of a quarrel with my friend and patron, the C. [Cardinal]. He is really a good-natured and generous man, and spends his vast revenue in (what he thinks) the service of his country, besides contributing largely to the building of a new cathedral, which, when finished, will stand in the rank of fine churches (where he has already the comfort of seeing his own busto), finely done both within and without. He has founded a magnificent college for one hundred scholars, which I don't doubt he will endow very nobly, and greatly enlarged and embellished his episcopal palace. He has joined to it a public library, which, when I saw it, was a very beautiful room : it is now finished and furnished, and open twice in a week with proper attendance. Yesterday here arrived one of his chief chaplains, with a long compliment, which concluded with desiring I would send him my works; having dedicated one of his cases to English books, he intended my labours should appear in the most conspicuous place. I was struck dumb for some time with this astonishing request; when I recovered my vexatious surprise (foreseeing the consequence), I made answer, I was highly sensible of the honour designed me, but, upon my word, I had never printed a single line in my life. I was answered in a cold tone, his eminence could send for them to England, but they would be a long time coming, and with some hazard; and that he had flattered himself I would not refuse him such a favour, and I need not be ashamed of seeing my name in a collection where he admitted none but the most eminent authors. It was to no purpose to endeavour to convince him. He would not stay dinner, though earnestly invited; and went away with the air of one that thought he had reason to be offended. I know his master will have the same sentiments, and I shall pass in his opinion for a monster of ingratitude, while it is the blackest of vices in my opinion, and of which I am utterly incapable—I really could cry for vexation.

"Sure nobody ever had such various provocations to print as myself. I have seen things I have wrote, so mangled and falsified, I have scarce known them. I have seen poems I never read, published with my name at length; and others, that were truly and singly wrote by me, printed under the names of others. I have made myself easy under all these mortifications, by the reflection I did not deserve them, having never aimed at the vanity of popular applause; but I own my philosophy is not proof against losing a friend, and it may be making an enemy of one to whom I am obliged."

In 1755, the year after the preceding letter was written, the Cardinal died:

" My old friend the Cardinal [Querini] is dead of an apoplectic fit, which I am sorry for, notwithstanding the disgust that happened between us, on the ridiculous account of which I gave you the history a year ago. His memory will, probably, last as long as this province, having embellished it with so many noble structures, particularly a public library well furnished, richly adorned, and a college built for poor scholars, with salaries for masters, and plentifully endowed; many charitable foundations, and so large a part of the new cathedral (which will be one of the finest churches in Lombardy) has been built at his expense, he may be almost called the founder of it. He has left a consider-able annuity to continue it, and deserves an eminent place among the few prelates that have devoted what they received from the Church to the use of the public, which is not here (as in some countries) so ungrateful to overlook benefits. Many statues have been erected, and medals cast to his honour, one of which has the figures of Piety, Learning, and Munificence, on the reverse, in the attitude of the three Graces. His funeral has been celebrated by the city with all the splendour it was capable of bestowing, and waited on by all ranks of the inhabitants."

His death was followed by that of a more eminent virtuoso:

"This year has been fatal to the literati of Italy. The Marquis Maffei soon followed Cardinal Querini. He was in England when you were married. Perhaps you may remember his coming to see your father's Greek inscription;* he was then an old man, and consequently now a great age; but preserved his memory and senses in their first vigour. After having made the tour of Europe in the search of antiquities, he fixed his residence in his native town of Verona, where he erected himself a little empire, from the general esteem, and a conversation (so they call an assembly) which he established in his palace, which is one of the largest in that place, and so luckily situated, that it is between the theatre and the ancient amphitheatre. He made piazzas leading to each of them, filled with shops, where were sold coffee, tea, chocolate, all sort of cool [drinks?] and sweetmeats, and in the midst, a court well kept, and sanded, for the use of those young gentlemen who would exercise their managed horses, or show their mistresses their skill in riding. His gallery was open every evening at five o'clock, where he had a fine collection of antiquities, and two large cabinets of medals, intaglios, and

---

* The inscription from the Troas, already mentioned, which was given by Mr. Wortley Montagu to Trinity College, Cambridge.

cameos, ranged in exact order. His library joined to
it ; and on the other side a suite of five rooms, the first
of which was destined to dancing, the second to cards
(but all games of hazard excluded), and the others
(where he himself presided in an easy-chair) sacred to
conversation, which always turned upon some point
of learning, either historical or poetical. Controversy
and politics being utterly prohibited, he generally
proposed the subject, and took great delight in
instructing the young people, who were obliged to
seek the medal, or explain the inscription, that illus-
trated any fact they discoursed of. Those who chose
the diversion of the public walks, or theatre, went
thither, but never failed returning to give an account
of the drama, which produced a critical dissertation
on that subject, the Marquis having given shining
proofs of his skill in that art. His tragedy of Merope,
which is much injured by Voltaire's translation, being
esteemed a masterpiece ; and his comedy of the
Ceremonies, being so just a ridicule of those formal
fopperies, it has gone a great way in helping to banish
them out of Italy."

Pietro Grimani, the Doge of Venice, Lady Mary's
old friend, had died in 1752, much to her grief :

" He is lamented here by all ranks of people, as their
common parent. He really answered the idea of Lord
Bolingbroke's imaginary Patriot Prince, and was the
only example I ever knew of having passed through the
greatest employments, and most important negotiations,
without ever making an enemy. When I was at Venice,

which was some months before his election, he was the
leading voice in the senate, and possessed of so strong
a popularity as would have been dangerous in the hands
of a bad man : yet he had the art to silence envy ; and
I never once heard an objection to his character, or
even an insinuation to his disadvantage. I attribute
this peculiar happiness to be owing to the sincere
benevolence of his heart, joined with an easy cheerfulness of temper, which made him agreeable to all companies, and a blessing to all his dependents. Authority
appeared so *aimable* in him, no one wished it less, except
himself, who would sometimes lament the weight of it,
as robbing him too much of the conversation of his
friends, in which he placed his chief delight, being so
little ambitious, that (to my certain knowledge), far
from caballing to gain that elevation to which he was
raised, he would have refused it, if he had not looked
upon the acceptance of it as a duty due to his country.
This is only speaking of him in the public light. As
to myself, he always professed, and gave me every
demonstration of, the most cordial friendship. Indeed,
I received every good office from him I could have
expected from a tender father, or a kind brother :
and though I have not seen him since my last return to Italy, he never omitted an opportunity of
expressing the greatest regard for me, both in his
discourse to others, and upon all occasions where he
thought he could be useful to me. I do not doubt I
shall very sensibly miss the influence of his good intentions."

But, as before, Lady Mary was not dependent on her Italian friends for occupying her time. She probably read as much as ever, though there are fewer allusions to books in the published letters; and she wrote letters so voluminous as to excite political suspicion.

"An old priest made me a visit as I was folding my last packet to my daughter. Observing it to be large, he told me I had done a great deal of business that morning. I made answer, I had done no business at all; I had only wrote to my daughter on family affairs, or such trifles as make up women's conversation. He said gravely, People like your excellenza do not use to write long letters upon trifles. I assured him, that if he understood English, I would let him read my letter. He replied, with a mysterious smile, If I did understand English, I should not understand what you have written, except you would give me the key, which I durst not presume to ask. What key? (said I, staring) there is not one cypher besides the date. He answered, cyphers were only used by novices in politics, and it was very easy to write intelligibly, under feigned names of persons and places, to a correspondent, in such a manner as should be almost impossible to be understood by anybody else.

"Thus I suppose my innocent epistles are severely scrutinised: and when I talk of my grandchildren, they are fancied to represent all the potentates of Europe. This is very provoking. I confess there are good reasons for extraordinary caution at this juncture;

but 'tis very hard I cannot pass for being as insignificant as I really am."

Not only did she go on with her correspondence, but amused herself with writing memoirs—though unfortunately they have not, like those of her friend Lord Hervey, been allowed to come down to us by the author. Perhaps, however, in destroying her work, she only anticipated the action of her daughter.

" You will confess my employment much more trifling than yours, when I own to you (between you and I) that my chief amusement is writing the history of my own time. It has been my fortune to have a more exact knowledge both of the persons and facts that have made the greatest figure in England in this age, than is common ; and I take pleasure in putting together what I know, with an impartiality that is altogether unusual. Distance of time and place has totally blotted from my mind all traces either of resentment or prejudice ; and I speak with the same indifference of the court of G. B. [Great Britain] as I should do of that of Augustus Cæsar. I hope you have not so ill an opinion of me to think I am turning author in my old age. I can assure you I regularly burn every quire as soon as it is finished ; and mean nothing more than to divert my solitary hours. I know mankind too well to think they are capable of receiving the truth, much less of applauding it : or, were it otherwise, applause to me is as insignificant as garlands on the dead."

Lady Mary seems to have seen a good deal of the

priests of the country. We have seen that she invited them in to play whist; and they, or some of them, were anxious to repay her hospitality by converting her from her heresy. However, she was a stanch Protestant, and well grounded in the reasons for her religion; and when it came to controversy, according to her own account, she carried too many guns for her clerical assailants.

"I have never been attacked a second time in any of the towns where I have resided, and perhaps shall never be so again after my last battle, which was with an old priest, a learned man, particularly esteemed as a mathematician, and who has a head and heart as warm as poor Whiston's. When I first came hither, he visited me every day, and talked of me everywhere with such violent praise, that, had we been young people, God knows what would have been said. I have always the advantage of being quite calm on a subject which they cannot talk of without heat. He desired I would put on paper what I had said. I immediately wrote one side of a sheet, leaving the other for his answer. He carried it with him, promising to bring it the next day, since which time I have never seen it, though I have often demanded it, being ashamed of my defective Italian. I fancy he sent it to his friend the Archbishop of Milan. I have given over asking for it, as a desperate debt. He still visits me, but seldom, and in a cold sort of a way. When I have found disputants I less respected, I have sometimes taken pleasure in raising their hopes by my concessions: they are charmed when I agree with them in the number of the sacraments; but are horribly disappointed when I explain myself by saying the word sacrament is not to be found either in Old or New Testament; and one must be very ignorant not to know it is taken from the listing oath of the Roman soldiers, and means nothing more than a solemn, irrevocable engagement. Parents vow, in infant baptism, to educate their children in the Christian religion, which they take upon themselves by confirmation; the Lord's Supper is frequently renewing the same oath. Ordination and matrimony are solemn vows of a different kind: confession includes a vow of revealing all we know, and reforming what is amiss: extreme unction, the last vow, that we have lived in the faith we were baptised: in this sense they are all sacraments. As to the mysteries preached since, they are all invented long after, and some of them repugnant to the primitive institution."

Whether, however, Lady Mary's doctrine concerning the sacraments would be thought that of a good Churchwoman may reasonably be doubted. She certainly had an instinctive repulsion from mysticism of all kinds, and from asceticism; and while she regarded monasteries in general as pernicious institutions, she reserved her approval for a decidedly worldly sort of convent:

"I have little to say from this solitude, having already sent you a description of my garden, which, with my books, takes up all my time. I made a small excursion last week to visit a nunnery twelve miles

from hence, which is the only institution of the kind
in all Italy. It is in a town in the state of Mantua,
founded by a princess of the house of Gonzaga, one of
whom (now very old) is the present abbess: they are
dressed in black, and wear a thin cypress veil at the
back of their heads, excepting which, they have no
mark of a religious habit, being set out in their hair,
and having no guimpe, but wearing *des collets montés*,
for which I have no name in English, but you may
have seen them in very old pictures, being in fashion
both before and after ruffs. Their house is a very large
handsome building, though not regular, every sister
having liberty to build her own apartment to her taste,
which consists of as many rooms as she pleases; they
have each a separate kitchen, and keep cooks and what
other servants they think proper, though there is a
very fine public refectory: they are permitted to dine
in private whenever they please. Their garden is very
large, and the most adorned of any in these parts.
They have no grates, and make what visits they will,
always two together, and receive those of the men as
well as ladies. I was accompanied when I went with
all the nobility of the town, and they showed me all
the house, without excluding the gentlemen; but what
I think the most remarkable privilege is a country
house, which belongs to them, three miles from the
town, where they pass every vintage, and at any time
any four of them may take their pleasure there, for as
many days as they choose. They seem to differ from
the *chanoinesses* of Flanders only in their vow of

celibacy. They take pensioners, but only those of quality. I saw here a niece of General Brown.* Those that profess, are obliged to prove a descent as noble as the knights of Malta. Upon the whole, I think it the most agreeable community I have seen, and their behaviour more decent than that of the cloistered nuns, who I have heard say themselves, that the grate permits all liberty of speech since it leaves them no other, and indeed they generally talk according to that maxim. My house at Avignon joined to a monastery, which gave me occasion to know a great deal of their conduct, which (though the convent of the best reputation in that town, where there is fourteen) was such, as I would as soon put a girl into the playhouse for education as send her among them."

Probably these quiet years were among the happiest of Lady Mary's life, before the infirmities of age became burdensome to her, and after she had given up her former ambitions. It was the Indian summer of her life. She writes to her daughter :

" I no more expect to arrive at the age of the Duchess of Marlborough than to that of Methusalem ; neither do I desire it. I have long thought myself useless to the world. I have seen one generation pass away ; and it is gone ; for I think there are very few of those left that flourished in my youth. You will

---

* There were several Browns and Brownes who distinguished themselves in war about this time ; but Lady Mary probably meant Count Browne, in the Austrian service, the brave General who was mortally wounded at the battle of Prague, 1757.

perhaps call these melancholy reflections: they are not so. There is a quiet after the abandoning of pursuits, something like the rest that follows a laborious day. I tell you this for your comfort. It was formerly a terrifying view to me, that I should one day be an old woman. I now find that Nature has provided pleasures for every state. Those are only unhappy who will not be contented with what she gives, but strive to break through her laws, by affecting a perpetuity of youth, which appears to me as little desirable at present as the babies* do to you, that were the delight of your infancy."

But this somewhat stoical mood of tranquillity was broken up when Lady Mary moved from the country to Venice, where (and at Padua) the remaining years of her stay abroad were spent. The post of British Resident at Venice had recently been given to a Mr. Murray, his predecessor Sir James Gray having gone to Naples. She evidently had no good opinion of him before she met him; and, indeed, he seems to have been a man with whom it was hard not to quarrel. Lady Mary's letters are full of complaints of his persecutions, which fell not only on her, but on her friends, Sir James and Lady Steuart, of Colthurst, who, as exiled Jacobites, were the objects of Murray's jealous suspicion.

"I am surprised," Lady Mary writes, "I am not oftener low-spirited, considering the vexations I am exposed to by the folly of Murray; I suppose he

---

* That is, the dolls.

attributes to me some of the marks of contempt he
is treated with ; without remembering that he was
in no higher esteem before I came. I confess I have
received great civilities from some friends that I made
here so long ago as the year '40, but upon my honour
have never named his name, or heard him mentioned
by any noble Venetian whatever; nor have in any
shape given him the least provocation to all the low
malice he has shown me, which I have overlooked as
below my notice, and would not trouble you with any
part of it at present if he had not invented a new
persecution, which may be productive of ill consequences. Here arrived, a few days ago, Sir James
Steuart with his lady ;* that name was sufficient to
make me fly to wait on her. I was charmed to find a
man of uncommon sense and learning, and a lady that
without beauty is more amiable than the fairest of her
sex. I offered them all the little good offices in my
power, and invited them to supper; upon which our wise
minister has discovered that I am in the interest of
popery and slavery. As he has often said the same
thing of Mr. Pitt, it would give me no mortification, if
I did not apprehend that his fertile imagination may
support this wise idea by such circumstances as may

---

* According to Murray's own account, Sir James asked to be
received by him, but was refused. It is possible, therefore, that
Lady Mary was obnoxious as consorting with rebels. She herself
protested against it being thought that any conduct of hers could
have given the pretext for his action ; but remembering how
she had incurred resentment at home, we may perhaps surmise
that she had not been quite so prudent as she thought.

influence those that do not know me. It is very remarkable that after having suffered all the rage of that
party at Avignon for my attachment to the present
reigning family, I should be accused here of favouring
rebellion, when I hoped all our odious divisions were
forgotten."

She writes to her daughter :

" I am afraid you may think some imprudent behaviour of mine has occasioned all this ridiculous persecution ; I can assure you I have always treated him
and his family with the utmost civility, and am now
retired to Padua, to avoid the comments that will certainly be made on his extraordinary conduct towards
me. I only desire privacy and quiet, and am very well
contented to be without visits, which oftener disturb
than amuse me. My single concern is the design he
has formed of securing (as he calls it) my effects immediately on my decease; if they ever fall into his
hands, I am persuaded they will never arrive entire
into yours, which is a very uneasy thought."

This fear of having her possessions appropriated if
she should die in Venice seems to have persistently
beset Lady Mary. She refers to it again :

" I own I could wish that we had a minister here
who I had not reason to suspect would plunder my
house if I die while he is in authority. General
Graham is exceedingly infirm, and also so easily imposed on, that whatever his intentions may be, he is
incapable of protecting anybody. You will (perhaps)
laugh at these apprehensions, since whatever happens

in this world after our death is certainly nothing to us.
It may be thought a fantastic satisfaction, but I confess
I cannot help being earnestly desirous that what I
leave may fall into your hands. Do not so far mistake
me as to imagine I would have the present M.
[minister] removed by advancement, which would have
the sure consequence of my suffering, if possible, more
impertinence from his successor."

Venetian friends to a certain extent made up for the
coldness of English visitors; and some of them showed
her much kindness.

"I lose very little," she writes, "in not being visited
by the English; boys and governors being commonly
(not always) the worst company in the world. I am no
other ways affected by it, than as it has an ill appearance
in a strange country, though hitherto I have not found
any bad effect from it among my Venetian acquaintance.
I was visited, two days ago, by my good friend Cavalier
Antonio Mocenigo, who came from Venice to present to
me the elected husband of his brother's great grand-
daughter, who is a noble Venetian (Signor Zeno), just
of age, heir to a large fortune, and is one of the most
agreeable figures I ever saw; not beautiful, but has an
air of so much modesty and good sense, I could easily
believe all the good Signor Antonio said of him. They
came to invite me to the wedding. I could not refuse
such a distinction, but hope to find some excuse before
the solemnity, being unwilling to throw away money on
fine clothes, which are as improper for me as an embroidered pall for a coffin. But I durst not mention

age before my friend, who told me he is eighty-six. I
thought him four years younger; he has all his senses
perfect, and is as lively as a man of thirty. It was very
pleasing to see the affectionate respect of the young
man, and the fond joy that the old one took in praising
him. They would have persuaded me to return with
them to Venice; I objected that my house was not
ready to receive me; Signor Antonio laughed, and
asked me, if I did not think he could give me an
apartment (in truth it was very easy, having five
palaces in a row, on the great canal, his own being the
centre, and the others inhabited by his relations). I
was reduced to tell a fib (God forgive me!), and pretend
a pain in my head; promising to come to Venice before
the marriage, which I really intend. They dined here;
your health was the first drunk; you may imagine I did
not fail to toast the bride. She is yet in a convent, but
is to be immediately released, and receive visits of con-
gratulation on the contract, till the celebration of the
church ceremony, which perhaps may not be this two
months; during which time the lover makes a daily
visit, and never comes without a present, which custom
(at least sometimes) adds to the impatience of the bridegroom, and very much qualifies that of the lady. You
would find it hard to believe a relation of the magnificence, not to say extravagance, on these occasions;
indeed, it is the only one they are guilty of, their lives in
general being spent in a regular handsome economy;
the weddings and the creation of a procurator being the
only occasions they have of displaying their wealth,

which is very great in many houses, particularly this of
Mocenigo, of which my friend is the present head. I
may justly call him so, giving me proofs of an attachment quite uncommon at London, and certainly disinterested, since I can no way possibly be of use to him.
I could tell you some strong instances of it, if I did
not remember you have not time to listen to my
stories."

The annoyances of Murray, however petty, seem to
have joined with growing infirmities to cloud over the
good spirits which had hitherto seldom failed Lady
Mary. She become anxious about her daughter when
the post failed; and Mr. Murray apparently would not
lend her the English newspapers:

"If half of the letters I have sent to you have reached
you, I believe you think I have always a pen in my hand;
but, I am really so uneasy by your long silence, I cannot
forbear inquiring the reason of it, by all the methods I
can imagine. My time of life is naturally inclined to fear;
and though I resist (as well as I can) all the infirmities
incident to age, I feel but too sensibly the impressions
of melancholy, when I have any doubt of your welfare.
You fancy, perhaps, that the public papers give me information enough; and that when I do not see in them
any misfortune of yours, I ought to conclude you have
none. I can assure you I never see any, excepting by
accident. Our resident has not the good breeding to
send them to me; and after having asked for them once
or twice, and being told they were engaged, I am unwilling to demand a trifle at the expense of thanking a

man who does not desire to oblige me; indeed, since the ministry of Mr. Pitt, he is so desirous to signalize his zeal for the contrary faction, he is perpetually saying ridiculous things, to manifest his attachment; and, as he looks upon me (nobody knows why) to be the friend of a man I never saw, he has not visited me once this winter. The misfortune is not great. I cannot help laughing at my being mistaken for a politician. I have often been so, though I ever thought politics so far removed from my sphere. I cannot accuse myself of dabbling in them, even when I heard them talked over in all companies; but, as the old song says,

> " Tho' through the wide world we should range,
> 'Tis in vain from our fortune to fly."

Again her passion for reading made her fear for her eyesight, and began to tell on her general health. She confesses as much in a letter of 1759 to Lady Bute:

' I own I have too much indulged a sedentary humour, and have been a rake in reading. You will laugh at the expression, but I think the literal meaning of the ugly word rake is one that follows his pleasures in contradiction to his reason. I thought mine so innocent I might pursue them with impunity. I now find that I was mistaken, and that all excesses are (though not equally) blamable. My spirits in company are false fire: I have a damp within; from marshy grounds frequently arises an appearance of light. I grow splenetic, and consequently ought to stop my pen, for fear of conveying the infection."

Even the liberty for which she had given up so much seemed a deception, like all else. She writes to her daughter:

"I believe, like all others of your age, you have long been convinced there is no real happiness to be found or expected in this world. You have seen a court near enough to know neither riches nor power can secure it; and all human endeavours after felicity are as childish as running after sparrows to lay salt on their tails; but I ought to give you another information, which can only be learned by experience, that liberty is an idea equally chimerical, and has no real existence in this life. I can truly assure you I have never been so little mistress of my own time and actions, as since I have lived alone. Mankind is placed in a state of dependency, not only on one another (which all are in some degree), but so many inevitable accidents thwart our designs, and limit our best laid projects. The poor efforts of our utmost prudence and political schemes, appear, I fancy, in the eyes of some superior beings, like the pecking of a young linnet to break a wire cage, or the climbing of a squirrel in a hoop; the moral needs no explanation: let us sing as cheerfully as we can in our impenetrable confinement, and crack our nuts with pleasure from the little store that is allowed us."

And, again, in another letter to the same:

"I am now grown timorous, and inclined to low spirits, whatever you may hear to the contrary. My cheerfulness is like the fire kindled in brushwood, which makes a show, but is soon turned to cold

19

ashes. I do not, like Madame Maintenon, grieve at the decay which is allotted to all mortals, but would willingly excuse to you the heat that was in my last. I would by no means have you give the least uneasiness to your father. At his time of life the mind should be vacant and quiet. As for the rest, let Providence as it will dispose of your most affectionate mother."

Possibly there was an epidemic of low spirits at Venice, or Lady Mary had infected others with her own gloom ; for she chronicles the sudden prevalence of a practice generally supposed to be peculiarly English :

" Here is a fashion sprung up entirely new in this part of the world ; I mean suicide : a rich parish priest and a young Celestine monk have disposed of themselves last week in that manner without any visible reason for their precipitation. The priest, indeed, left a paper in his hat to signify his desire of imitating the indifference of Socrates and magnanimity of Cato : the friar swung out of the world without giving any account of his design. You see it is not in Britain alone that the spleen spreads his dominion. I look on all excursions of this kind to be owing to that distemper, which shows the necessity of seeking employment for the mind, and exercise for the body ; the spirits and the blood stagnate without motion."

To this length Lady Mary had no intention of going; little as she now clung to life, she had no idea of quitting it before necessary. She continued to enjoy her life at Venice; and though she declined her daughter's offers of sending anything she might want, had no objection to receiving some china to enable her to make a figure there:

" My dear child, do not think of reversing nature by making me presents. I would send you all my jewels and my toilet, if I knew how to convey them, though they are in some measure necessary in this country, where it would be, perhaps, reported I had pawned them, if they did not sometimes make their appearance. I know not how to send commissions for things I never saw; nothing of price I would have, as I would not new furnish an inn I was on the point of leaving; such is this world to me. Though china is in such estimation here, I have sometimes an inclination to desire your father to send me the two large jars that stood in the windows in Cavendish Square. I am sure he don't value them, and believe they would be of no use to you. I bought them at an auction, for two guineas, before the D. of Argyll's example had made all china, more or less, fashionable."

English wares seem to have been in vogue at Venice at the time:

" In general, all the shops are full of English merchandise, and they boast [of] everything as coming from London, in the same style as they used to do from Paris. I was showed (of their own invention) a set of furniture, in a taste entirely new: it consists of eight large armed-chairs, the same number of sconces, a table, and prodigious looking-glass, all of glass. It is impossible to imagine their beauty; they deserve being placed in a prince's dressing-room, or grand cabinet; the price demanded is £400. They would be a very proper decoration for the apartment of a prince so young and beautiful as ours."

Lady Mary asked for Horace Walpole's " Royal and Noble Authors," remembering her meeting with him at Florence. Walpole, in his letters, alludes several times to a copy of this book as to be sent to her; though it was eventually despatched after she had left Venice on her way home.

It is curious to note the kindliness of her references to him, as compared with his uniform spitefulness in speaking of her :

" I was well acquainted with Mr. Walpole at Florence, and indeed he was particularly civil to me. I have great encouragement to ask a favour of him, if I did not know that few people have so good memories to remember so many years backwards as have passed since I have seen him. If he has treated the character of Queen Elizabeth with disrespect, all the women should tear him to pieces, for abusing the glory of their sex.* Neither is it just to put her in the list of authors, having never published anything, though we have Mr. Camden's authority that she wrote many valuable pieces, chiefly Greek translations. I wish all monarchs would bestow their leisure hours on such studies: perhaps they would not be very useful to

* Alluding to the character of Queen Elizabeth, in his " Royal and Noble Authors."

mankind ; but it may be asserted, for a certain truth,
their own minds would be more improved than by the
amusements of Quadrille or Cavagnole.

" I desire you would thank your father for the china
jars ; if they arrive safe, they will do me great honour
in this country. The Patriarch died here a few days
ago. He had a large temporal estate ; and, by long
life and extreme parsimony, has left four hundred
thousand sequins in his coffers, which is inherited by
two nephews ; and I suppose will be dissipated as
scandalously as it has been accumulated. The town
is at present full of factions, for the election of his
successor : the ladies are always very active on these
occasions. I have observed that they ever have more
influence in republics than [in a] monarchy. In
commonwealths, votes are easily acquired by the fair ;
and she, who has most beauty or art, has a great sway
in the senate."

To guard against overtaxing her eyes, Lady Mary
tried dictating to a secretary ; but she soon dropped
this, as appears from an entertaining letter to Sir James
Steuart, which also gives us a glimpse (apparently) of
one of Murray's receptions :

" I am extremely obliged for the valuable present
you intend me.* I believe you criticise yourself too
severely on your style : I do not think that very smooth
harmony is necessary in a work which has a merit of
a nobler kind ; I think it rather a defect, as when a

---

* Sir James Steuart's " Political Economy," of which he afterwards sent her a copy in manuscript.

Roman emperor (as we see him sometimes represented on a French stage) is dressed like a petit maître. I confess the crowd of readers look no further; the tittle-tattle of Madame de Sévigné, and the *clinquant* of Telemachus, have found admirers from that very reason. Whatever is clearly expressed, is well wrote in a book of reasoning. However, I shall obey your commands in telling you my opinion with the greatest sincerity.

" Thus far I have dictated for the first time of my life, and perhaps it will be the last, for my amanuensis is not to be hired, and I despair of ever meeting with another. He is the first that could write as fast as I talk, and yet you see there are so many mistakes, it wants a comment longer than my letter to explain my insignificant meaning, and I have fatigued my poor eyes more with correcting it than I should have done in scribbling two sheets of paper. You will think, perhaps, from this idle attempt, that I have some fluxion on my sight; no such matter; I have suffered myself to be persuaded by such sort of arguments as those by which people are induced to strict abstinence, or to take physic. Fear, paltry fear, founded on vapours rising from the heat, which is now excessive, and has so far debilitated my miserable nerves that I submit to a present displeasure, by way of precaution against a future evil, that possibly may never happen. I have this to say in my excuse, that the evil is of so horrid a nature, I own I feel no philosophy that could support me under it, and no mountain girl ever trembled more at one of Whitfield's pathetic lectures than I do at the word blindness, though I know all the fine things that may be said for consolation in such a case : but I know, also, they would not operate on my constitution. 'Why, then' (say my wise monitors), 'will you persist in reading or writing seven hours in a day?' 'I am happy while I read and write.' 'Indeed, one would suffer a great deal to be happy,' say the men, sneering ; and the ladies wink at each other, and hold up their fans. A fine lady of three score had the goodness to add, 'At least, madam, you should use spectacles ; I have used them myself these twenty years ; I was advised to it by a famous oculist when I was fifteen. I am really of opinion that they have preserved my sight, notwithstanding the passion I always had both for reading and drawing.' This good woman, you must know, is half blind, and never read a larger volume than a newspaper. I will not trouble you with the whole conversation, though it would make an excellent scene in a farce ; but after they had in the best bred way in the world convinced me that they thought I lied when I talked of reading without glasses, the foresaid matron obligingly said she should be very proud to see the writing I talked of, having heard me say formerly I had no correspondents but my daughter and Mr. Wortley. She was inter-rupted by her sister, who said, simpering, 'You forgot Sir J. S.' I took her up something short, I confess, and said in a dry stern tone, 'Madam, I do write to Sir J. S., and will do it as long as he will permit that

honour.'   This rudeness of mine occasioned a profound
silence for some minutes, and they fell into a good-
natured discourse of the ill consequences of too much
application, and remembered how many apoplexies,
gouts, and dropsies had happened amongst the hard
students of their acquaintance.   As I never studied
anything in my life, and have always (at least from
fifteen) thought the reputation of learning a misfortune
to a woman, I was resolved to believe these stories
were not meant at me : I grew silent in my turn, and
took up a card that lay on a table, and amused myself
with smoking it over a candle.   In the mean time (as
the song says) :

> " ' Their tattles all run, as swift as the sun,
>   Of who had won, and who was undone
>   By their gaming and sitting up late.'

When it was observed I entered into none of these
topics, I was addressed by an obliging lady, who pitied
my stupidity.   ' Indeed, madam, you should buy
horses to that fine machine you have at Padua; of
what use is it standing in the portico ?'   ' Perhaps,'
said another, wittily, ' of as much use as a standing
dish.'   A gaping schoolboy added with still more wit,
' I have seen at a country gentleman's table a venison-
pasty made of wood.'   I was not at all vexed by said
schoolboy, not because he was (in more senses than
one) the highest of the company, but knowing he did
not mean to offend me.   I confess (to my shame be it
spoken) I was grieved at the triumph that appeared in
the eyes of the king and queen of the company, the

court being tolerably full.* His majesty walked off early with the air befitting his dignity, followed by his train of courtiers, who, like courtiers, were laughing amongst themselves as they followed him: and I was left with the two queens, one of whom was making ruffles for the man she loved, and the other slopping tea for the good of her country. They renewed their generous endeavours to set me right, and I (graceless beast that I am) take up the smoked card which lay before me, and with the corner of another wrote—

> "'If ever I one thought bestow
>   On what such fools advise,
> May I be dull enough to grow
>   Most miserably wise,'

and flung down the card on the table, and myself out of the room, in the most indecent fury."

Such conduct was hardly, perhaps, calculated to disarm the hostility of Murray and his circle; and so disagreeable did they become that Lady Mary had thoughts of leaving Venice and joining her friends the Steuarts, with whom she now corresponded regularly, at Tübingen; but age and infirmity forbade the journey.

"I have indulged myself some time with day-dreams of the happiness I hoped to enjoy this summer in the conversation of Lady Fanny and Sir James S.; but I hear such frightful stories of precipices and hovels

---

* The "king" was probably Murray, and "the two queens" his wife and sister—the latter married to Mr. Smith, the English Consul.

during the whole journey, I begin to fear there is no
such pleasure allotted me in the book of fate : the Alps
were once molehills in my sight when they interposed
between me and the slightest inclination; now age
begins to freeze, and brings with it the usual train of
melancholy apprehensions.   Poor humankind! We
always march blindly on ; the fire of youth represents
to us all our wishes possible ; and, that over, we fall
into despondency that prevents even easy enterprises :
a stove in winter, a garden in summer, bounds all our
desires, or at least our undertakings.   If Mr. Steuart*
would disclose all his imaginations, I dare swear he has
some thoughts of emulating Alexander or Demosthenes,
perhaps both : nothing seems difficult at his time of
life, everything at mine.   I am very unwilling, but am
afraid I must submit to the confinement of my boat
and my easy-chair, and go no farther than they can
carry me.   Why are our views so extensive and our
power so miserably limited ?   This is among the
mysteries which (as you justly say) will remain ever
unfolded to our shallow capacities.   I am much
inclined to think we are no more free agents than the
queen of clubs when she victoriously takes prisoner
the knave of hearts ; and all our efforts (when we rebel
against destiny) as weak as a card that sticks to a glove
when the gamester is determined to throw it on the
table.   Let us then (which is the only true philosophy)
be contented with our chance, and make the best of
that very bad bargain of being born in this vile planet ;

* Afterwards General Steuart, Sir James's son.

where we may find, however (God be thanked), much to laugh at, though little to approve.

" I confess I delight extremely in looking on men in that light. How many thousands trample under foot honour, ease, and pleasure, in pursuit of ribands of certain colours, dabs of embroidery on their clothes, and gilt wood carved behind their coaches in a particular figure! Others breaking their hearts till they are distinguished by the shape and colour of their hats; and, in general, all people earnestly seeking what they do not want, while they neglect the real blessings in their possession—I mean, the innocent gratification of their senses, which is all we can properly call our own."

And this somewhat epicurean philosophy is developed further in another letter to Sir James Steuart:

" My chief study all my life has been to lighten misfortunes, and multiply pleasures, as far as human nature can : when I have nothing to find in myself from which I can extract any kind of delight, I think on the happiness of my friends, and rejoice in the joy with which you converse together, and look on the beautiful young plant* from which you may so reasonably expect honour and felicity. In other days I think over the comic scenes that are daily exhibited on the great stage of the world for my entertainment. I am charmed with the account of the Moravians, who certainly exceed all mankind in absurdity of principles and madness of practice; yet these people walk erect, and are numbered amongst rational beings. I imagined after three

* The youthful son of Sir James.

thousand years' working at creeds and theological whimsies, there remained nothing new to be invented; I see the fund is inexhaustible, and we may say of folly what Horace has said of vice:

> " Ætas parentum pejor avis tulit
> Nos nequiores, mox daturos
> Progeniem vitiosiorem."

"I will not ask pardon for this quotation; it is God's mercy I did not put it into English: when one is haunted (as I am) by the Demon of Poesie, it must come out in one shape or another, and you will own that nobody shows it to more advantage than the author I have mentioned."

The promised "Political Economy" came, as a slight consolation to Lady Mary for being unable to rejoin her friends; and she wrote most warmly about it to Sir James:

"I have now with great pleasure, and I flatter myself with some improvement, read over again your delightful and instructive treatise; you have opened to me several truths of which I had before only a confused idea. I confess I cannot help being a little vain of comprehending a system that is calculated only for a thinking mind, and cannot be tasted without a willingness to lay aside many prejudices which arise from education and the conversation of people no wiser than ourselves. I do not only mean my own sex when I speak of our confined way of reasoning; there are many of yours as incapable of judging otherwise than they have been early taught, as the most ignorant milkmaid : nay, I believe a girl out of a village or a nursery more capable of receiving instruction than a lad just set free from the university. It is not difficult to write on blank paper, but 'tis a tedious if not an impossible task to scrape out nonsense already written, and put better sense in the place of it.''

The long life of travel and independence was now drawing to a close. In 1761 came the news of Mr. Wortley Montagu's death, at the age of eighty-three, and although no allusions to it are mentioned in the few letters of a later date published, there is no doubt that Lady Mary felt the loss of one whom (as far as we can tell) she had always respected and loved. Some pleasure was caused her by the rapid rise of the Earl of Bute after the accession of George III. ; yet she did not desire to leave Venice, as is clear from her letter to Sir James Steuart :

" The happiness of domestic life seems the most laudable as it is certainly the most delightful of our prospects, yet even that is denied, or at least so mixed, ' we think it not sincere, or fear it cannot last.' A long series of disappointments have perhaps worn out my natural spirits, and given a melancholy cast to my way of thinking. I would not communicate this weakness to any but yourself, who can have compassion even where your superior understanding condemns. I confess that though I am (it may be) beyond the strict bounds of reason pleased with my Lord Bute's and my daughter's prosperity, I am doubtful whether I will attempt to be a spectator of it. I have so many years indulged my natural inclinations to solitude and reading, I am unwilling to return to crowds and bustle, which would be unavoidable in London. The few friends I esteemed are now no more : the new set of people who fill the stage at present are too indifferent to me even to raise my curiosity. I now begin to feel (very late, you'll say) the worst effects of age, blindness excepted ; I am grown timorous and suspicious ; I fear the inconstancy of that goddess so publicly adored in ancient Rome, and so heartily inwardly worshipped in the modern. I retain, however, such a degree of that uncommon thing called common sense, not to trouble the felicity of my children with my foreboding dreams, which I hope will prove as idle as the croaking of ravens, or the noise of that harmless animal distinguished by the odious name of screech-owl."

However, at the request of her daughter, who wished her to help in settling her husband's affairs, Lady Mary resolved to set out for England, the more readily, perhaps, because she probably knew that she was smitten with an incurable disease, and had but a short time to live. She set out in the winter—a far different winter journey from that which had begun her travels, and led her into the magnificent East. Though passing near her friends the Steuarts, she was unable to meet them ; finally she reached Rotterdam, and there was delayed by storms. From thence she wrote to Sir James :

" I tried in vain to find you at Amsterdam ; I began to think we resembled two parallel lines, destined to be always near and never to meet. You know there is no

fighting (at least no overcoming) destiny. So far I am
a confirmed Calvinist, according to the notions of the
country where I now exist. I am dragging my ragged
remnant of life to England. The wind and tide are
against me; how far I have strength to struggle against
both I know not; that I am arrived here is as much a
miracle as any in the golden legend; and if I had foreseen half the difficulties I have met with, I should not
certainly have had the courage to undertake it."

She did not forget her friends when at last she
reached England; constantly she pressed on Lord
Bute the claims of Sir James Steuart to a pardon.
This she never saw granted, though it was conceded
at last. She was now dying of cancer, and her letters
must have been few; but she found time and strength
to reassure Lady Frances Steuart of her zeal in the
service of her friends. Her very last published letter
relates to this :

" I have been ill a long time, and am now so bad I
am little capable of writing, but I would not pass in
your opinion as either stupid or ungrateful. My heart
is always warm in your service, and I am always told
your affairs shall be taken care of. You may depend,
dear madam, nothing shall be wanting on the part of
    " Your ladyship's faithful humble servant."

This was written in July, 1762; and on August 21,
Lady Mary died at a little house she had taken in
George Street, Hanover Square.

Her personal appearance was evidently capable of

giving very different impressions to different observers. She was tall, with black hair and eyes—the latter appearing prominent from the loss of her eyelashes through the small-pox.

In the published correspondence between Lady Pomfret and Lady Hertford—both friends of Lady Mary's —there is one passage which would seem to imply that the disfigurement suffered at that time was much greater than this. Lady Hertford, commenting on that one of Lady Mary's "Court Eclogues" entitled "Flavia; or, The Small-pox," and supposed to reflect the author's own feelings while recovering from that illness, says:

"Nothing can be more natural than the complaint for the loss of her beauty; but as that was only one of her various powers to charm, I should have imagined she would have only felt a very small part of the regret that many other people have suffered on a like misfortune, who have had nothing but the loveliness of their persons to claim admiration; and consequently, by the loss of that [beauty], have found all their hopes of it [admiration] vanish much earlier in life than Lady Mary;—for, if I do not mistake, she was near thirty before she had to deplore the loss of beauty greater than I ever saw in any face besides her own."

Lady Hertford does mistake, for Lady Mary could not have been more than twenty-six when she had the small-pox; the loss of beauty is also probably exaggerated, for after her return from Turkey her charms were still the theme for admiration. It is probable,

however, that even in the days when she was a recog-
nised beauty, her charm was rather in expression and
sprightliness than in symmetry of feature; and as
she grew older, " Wortley's eyes " were no longer be-
rhymed, but called " wild and staring " by hostile
critics.

In dress, too, she seems to have grown slovenly;
perhaps the impossibility of keeping neat during a
journey in those days gradually destroyed even the
desire to appear neat, or perhaps her eccentricity was
merely the deliberate defiance of that most irrational of
conventionalities, fashion.

INDEX

www.ingramcontent.com/pod-product-compliance
Lightning Source LLC
Chambersburg PA
CBHW021123270326
41929CB00009B/1019